RESEARCHING RESILIENCE

Edited by Linda Liebenberg and Michael Ungar

Researching Resilience brings together an international group of experts to examine approaches to research with youth living in adversity. Aimed at graduate students, frontline workers, and professional researchers, the volume presents a variety of successful research methods and strategies, and suggests how these can be adapted to create effective interventions with at-risk youth.

The chapters discuss methods that are applicable in a variety of personal circumstances and international contexts; they focus not only on the individual, but also the broader contexts in which youth find themselves, reflecting a more inclusive, less Eurocentric approach to researching mental health and resilience in youth. The authors address questions of ethics in regard to engaging with youth participating in resilience research, scientific rigour in quantitative methods, qualitative research such as image-based methods, use of mixed methods, program evaluation, and the linking of research to effective interventions. A comprehensive review of the literature shows continuity in the development of these ideas across disciplines and cultures. The first book in the field to address the topic of resilience specifically from the point of view of research methods and challenges, *Researching Resilience* demonstrates how cultural sensitivity and heterogeneity can be strategically balanced with sound and valid research.

LINDA LIEBENBERG is an adjunct professor in the Department of Social Work and the Director of Research of the Pathways to Resilience Research Program at Dalhousie University.

MICHAEL UNGAR is a professor in the Department of Social Work at Dalhousie University.

EDITED BY
LINDA LIEBENBERG AND MICHAEL UNGAR

Researching Resilience

UNIVERSITY OF TORONTO PRESS
Toronto Buffalo London

© University of Toronto Press Incorporated 2009
Toronto Buffalo London
www.utppublishing.com
Printed in Canada

ISBN 978-0-8020-9268-7 (cloth)
ISBN 978-0-8020-9470-4 (paper)

Printed on acid-free paper

Library and Archives Canada Cataloguing in Publication

Researching resilience / edited by Linda Liebenberg and Michael Ungar.

Includes bibliographical references.
ISBN 978-0-8020-9268-7 (bound). ISBN 978-0-8020-9470-4 (pbk.)

1. Resilience (Personality trait) in adolescence – Research.   2. Resilience
(Personality trait) in children – Research.   3. Resilience (Personality trait)
in adolescence – Cross-cultural studies.   4. Resilience (Personality trait)
in children – Cross-cultural studies.   I. Ungar, Michael, 1963–
II. Liebenberg, Linda

BF724.3.R47R45 2009   155.2′4072   C2009-903261-9

This book has been published with the help of a grant from the Canadian
Federation for the Humanities and Social Sciences, through the Aid to
Scholarly Publications Programme, using funds provided by the Social
Sciences and Humanities Research Council of Canada.

University of Toronto Press acknowledges the financial assistance to its
publishing program of the Canada Council for the Arts and the Ontario
Arts Council.

University of Toronto Press acknowledges the financial support for its
publishing activities of the Government of Canada through the
Book Publishing Industry Development Program (BPIDP).

Contents

Acknowledgments

As with *Resilience in Action* (2008), this book stems from the inspiration of youth around the world, who not only survive but thrive amidst adversity. Beyond these youth, we also owe a debt to the groundbreaking work of researchers like Ruth Smith, Emmy Werner, and Michael Rutter whose efforts contributed to the shift in research from which we benefit today.

We would also like to acknowledge those who contributed to the realization of this work and to the 2005 International Pathways to Resilience conference in Halifax, Canada, from which this book stems. Special thanks are extended to Nora Didkowsky, conference organizer, and Amy Hum for her assistance in preparing the manuscript. We are also indebted to the editorial staff at the University of Toronto Press for their invaluable assistance, most notably senior editor Virgil Duff and managing editor Anne Laughlin, who have both worked so patiently with us on this project.

And we would like to acknowledge our families for their enduring support and encouragement.

Lastly, we appreciate greatly the assistance of the various granting agencies, whose financial support contributed not only to this publication but to the research upon which it is based. Specifically, we would like to thank the Canadian Federation for the Humanities and Social Sciences for funding the publication of this book, as well as the Social Sciences and Humanities Research Council of Canada and the Nova Scotia Health Research Foundation for their support.

Author Biographies

Katherine Ann Best, PhD, LCSW, MSW, MPH, an adjunct professor in the School of Social Work and College of Public Health at the University of South Florida, is currently working on a national project addressing child abuse and family interventions. Other areas of her research have included the cumulative impact of adverse exposures to trauma and violence on the rate of change in psychological distress; emotional reactions to research participation; and the impact of maternal substance use on birth outcomes. In addition, Dr Best maintains a small group practice in Sarasota/Bradenton, Florida. Her clinical expertise includes phobias and anxiety, post-traumatic stress disorder, marriage and family therapy, substance abuse, and domestic violence. She also brings thirty years of experience as a teacher-coach across various international settings.

Roger A. Boothroyd, PhD, is a professor and associate chair of the Department of Mental Health Law and Policy at Louis de la Parte Florida Mental Health Institute at the University of South Florida, where he has worked for the past eleven years. Dr Boothroyd received his PhD in educational psychology from the State University of New York at Albany, specializing in measurement, evaluation, and research design. He is principal investigator on a contract with Florida's Agency for Health Care Administration designed to evaluate Florida Medicaid–managed care programs. He is also co-principal investigator on a National Science Foundation Research Experience for Undergraduates and co-principal investigator on an NIH-funded grant focused on research ethics. Dr Boothroyd was formerly a research scientist with the New York State Office of Mental Health. He has taught courses on social issues in testing, provides intensive workshops on research ethics, and is an alternate member of the social-behavioural IRB for USF.

Catherine Ann Cameron, PhD, is Honorary Professor of Psychology at the University of British Columbia, Emerita and Honorary Research Professor at the University of New Brunswick, and an adjunct professor at the University of Victoria, Canada. A developmental psychologist, she studies the cognitive and emotional development of children and adolescents focusing on the acquisition of thoughts, emotions, and communication skills. Specifically, Dr Cameron explores contextual factors in the development of resilience, cross-cultural differences in truth telling and verbal deception, early telephone communications and their relationship to emergent written expression, gender-differentiated responses to school-based violence-prevention interventions, and adolescent physiological responses to psychosocial stress. Her work has appeared in *Developmental Psychology, Child Development, Discourse Processes, Applied Psycholinguistics, Educational Psychology Review,* and the *British Journal of Developmental Psychology.* She recently co-edited *Understanding Abuse: Partnering for Change* (University of Toronto Press). She earned her PhD at Bedford College, University of London.

Anita DeLongis, PhD, is an associate professor in the Department of Psychology at the University of British Columbia. She has published numerous journal articles and book chapters on stress, coping, and social support. Her work examines individual differences in the effects of stress on health and well-being, with a focus on the role of social relationships in adjustment to stress. Her current work includes studies of stepfamilies, as well as those of couples in which one or both members are facing a chronic health challenge. Ongoing research includes multifaceted studies of coping with rheumatoid arthritis, spinal cord injury, and the threat of infectious diseases such as SARS, West Nile virus, avian flu, and HIV.

Dave Este, PhD, is a professor and associate dean (Research and Partnerships) in the Faculty of Social Work, University of Calgary. He completed his MSW at the University of Toronto and his PhD at Wilfrid Laurier University. During the past decade most of his research has focused on the acculturation experiences of immigrants and refugees. He is involved in a number of multisite research projects, including the

New Canadian Children and Youth Study; Experiences of Russian and Sudanese Men as Fathers in the Canadian Context; the Racism, Violence, and Health Study; and Experiences of Visible Minority Social Workers in British Columbia, Alberta, and Ontario. He is co-editor of three books and has published several journal articles and book chapters focused on issues related to diversity.

Linda Liebenberg, PhD, director of research for the Resilience Research Centre at Dalhousie University, is a methodologist with an interest in both image-based methods and mixed-methods designs. Her research examines the use of visual methods and mixed-method research designs and how these facilitate an understanding of women and children in developing contexts, in particular South Africa. She has previously managed a number of programs pertaining to these interests, including the International Resilience Project, Dalhousie University. Other projects she has coordinated relate to out-of-school youth in informal settlements surrounding Cape Town (Department of Educational Psychology and Specialised Education, Stellenbosch University, South Africa) and research with women on farms in the Winelands region of South Africa (Department of Psychology, Stellenbosch University).

Bruce MacLaurin, doctoral candidate, MSW, is an assistant professor at the Faculty of Social Work, University of Calgary. His research and publishing has focused on child maltreatment, child welfare service delivery, foster care outcomes, and street youth in Canada. Bruce also has more than fifteen years' experience in non-profit children's services in Alberta and Ontario, as well as extensive research experience. He was a co-investigator on both cycles of the Canadian Incidence Study of Reported Child Abuse and Neglect (CIS-1998 and CIS-2003); principal investigator on the first Alberta Incidence Study of Reported Child Abuse and Neglect (AIS-2003); and co-principal investigator on a CIHR street youth study examining health and HIV.

Donna M. Mertens, PhD, professor, Department of Educational Foundations and Research at Gallaudet University in Washington, DC, teaches research methods and program evaluation to graduate-level deaf and hearing students. A past president (1998) of the American Evaluation Association, she provided leadership for AEA's Diversity Initiative and its resulting Graduate Internship for Evaluators of Color, as well as for the establishment of the International Organization for Cooperation in Evaluation. She has authored or edited several books, including *Transformative Research and Evaluation* (Guilford Press, 2009), *Handbook of Social Research Ethics* (with Pauline Ginsberg, co-editor; Sage, 2009), *Research and Evaluation in Education and Psychology: Integrating Diversity* (Sage, 2005), *Research and Evaluation Methods in Special Education* (with John McLaughlin, co-author; Corwin, 2004), *Parents and Their Deaf Children: The Early Years* (with Kay Meadow Orlans and Marilyn Sass Lehrer, co-authors; Gallaudet Press, 2003), and *Research and Inequality* (with Carole Truman and Beth Humphries, co-editors; Taylor & Francis, 2000), as well as published in such journals as the *American Journal of Evaluation, American Annals of the Deaf*, and *Educational Evaluation and Policy Analysis*.

Johann Mouton, PhD, is professor in sociology and social anthropology at Stellenbosch University, South Africa. He also runs Evaluation Research Agency, a company that conducts program evaluations in South Africa and various other African countries. His main research interests are social science research methodology, program evaluation studies, and science and technology policy studies. He has published a number of textbooks in research methods, including *The Practice of Social Research* (with Earl Babbie; Oxford University Press, 2001) and *How to Succeed in Your Masters and Doctoral Studies* (JL van Schaik, 2000). He is currently a member of four international editorial boards, including the *International Journal of Social Research Methodology*.

Robyn Munford, PhD, is a professor of social work, Massey University, Palmerston North, New Zealand. She has qualifications in social work, sociology, and disability studies. She lectures in social and community work, disability studies, and research methods. A key focus of her academic work is the supervision of master's and doctoral theses and research projects. Of particular interest is the mentoring of emerging researchers in social science and in social work practice research. Robyn has extensive experience in disability and family research and has worked for the past decade on family well-being research, including research on young people. This program utilizes participatory and action research methodologies. She has published widely on social work theory and practice, community development, bicultural frameworks for social and community work practice, social service interventions, and family well-being.

Jackie Sanders, PhD, is a senior researcher and the director of the Children, Youth and Families Research Project, School of Sociology, Social Policy and Social Work, Massey University, Palmerston North, New Zealand. This research program focuses on identifying changing patterns of family life and the different ways in which parents and children/young people respond to change. Jackie has twenty years of experience in health and social service planning and management. Her interests are the study of children and families, evaluation and planning for social service delivery, and the development of new models of practice. She maintains an active research practice program through ongoing relationships with a number of key social service providers in New Zealand and is a member of the International Association for Outcome-Based Evaluation and Research in Child and Family Services. She is an editor and reviewer for a number of key social work journals.

Kathleen Sitter, MCS, is currently a Master of Social Work student at the University of Calgary. She received her Master of Communication Studies from the University of Calgary (2002) and her Bachelor of Public Relations (BPR) from Mount Saint Vincent University of Halifax, Nova Scotia (1997). Kathleen has over twelve years of research experience in both corporate and academic settings, and has taught a number of business courses at Mount Royal College in Calgary, Alberta. Her research interests include organizational communications, social marketing, corporate integrity, and how participatory video can be used as a tool to facilitate social change.

Alexa Smith-Osborne, PhD, is an assistant professor in the School of Social Work at the University of Texas at Arlington, and earned her MSW and PhD from the School of Social Work of the University of Maryland at Baltimore. She has been a social work practitioner for over thirty years, specializing in child and adolescent developmental issues, maternal and child health, women's issues, rural mental health and community mental health programs, children with chronic illnesses and who are differently abled, learning differences and educational attainment, and early-onset mental disorders. Research interests include intervention and resiliency research in child and adolescent mental health, women's issues, military families, military members' life trajectories, and persons with disabilities; outcomes evaluation of social programs and social work education; mixed methods research designs and methodologies; and systematic reviews.

Paul G. Stiles, JD, PhD, is an associate professor in the Department of Mental Health Law & Policy at the Louis de la Parte Florida Mental Health Institute, University of South Florida (USF). He received his PhD in clinical psychology from Hahnemann University and JD from Villanova University Law School. Dr Stiles' clinical experience includes providing psychological and neuropsychological services in both private and public psychiatric facilities as well as nursing homes. In addition to a substantive focus on geriatric mental health services and policy, his research has involved the compilation, integration, analysis, and dissemination of relatively large administrative data sets (e.g., Medicaid/Medicare eligibility and claims files) and the application of findings to public mental health systems and the mental health of older persons. He teaches courses on legal and ethical issues in aging, provides intensive workshops on research ethics, and chairs the social-behavioural IRB for USF.

Eli Teram, PhD, was born in India and grew up in Israel, where he worked with street gangs and as a community organizer in Tel Aviv. He received his BA (Social Work) and MSc (Management) from Tel Aviv University and his PhD from McGill University. Since 1987 he has been teaching policy, research and organization, and management courses in the MSW and doctoral programs at Wilfrid Laurier University. His research interests relate to the organizational context of social work practice, including professional power and the processing of clients, teamwork, inter-organizational relations, and organizational control. Eli is currently writing a case-based study of a merger between four agencies working with youth-in-trouble. His other research projects include an action-oriented study of ethical issues in social work practice (with Marshall Fine) and an exploration of the experience of childhood sexual abuse survivors working with health professionals (with Candice Schachter and Carol Stalker). He is also a member of the International Resilience Project team.

Roger G. Tweed, PhD, teaches at Kwantlen Polytechnic University in Surrey, British Columbia. He received his PhD in psychology from the University of British Columbia. Roger has examined cultural differences and similarities in coping strategies, and has also developed a Confucian-versus-Socratic framework to summarize some culturally influenced differences in learning style. Most of his cross-cultural work has focused on comparisons of East Asian and North American cultures, but more recently he has initiated projects including Eastern European cultures. Currently he is conducting a longitudinal study of factors that help people escape homelessness.

Michael Ungar, PhD, is the author of eight books including *Strengths-Based Counseling with At-Risk Youth* and *Handbook for Working with Children and Youth: Pathways to Resilience across Cultures and Contexts.* He has worked for over twenty years as a social worker and marriage and family therapist with children and families in child welfare, mental health, educational, and correctional settings. He is now a professor at the School of Social Work, Dalhousie University, Halifax, where he leads the Resilience Research Centre, a collaboration between researchers in eleven countries on five continents. In addition to his research and writing interests, Dr Ungar maintains a small family therapy practice for troubled youth and their families.

Lauren Wildschut, MPhil, is a researcher at the Centre for Science and Technology (CREST), Stellenbosch University, South Africa. Lauren has extensive experience in the education and training sector. She has been involved in curriculum and materials development for both the school and the teacher education sector, and has acted as research coordinator in a non-governmental organization, designing instruments, conducting fieldwork, and engaging in capture of data, analysis, and report writing. She has also delivered training workshops on educational management and leadership development as well as program evaluation in the education and training sector, with a specific focus on fieldwork methods. Her MPhil in social science methods was titled 'The Role of Qualitative Data in a Mixed-Method Evaluation Design.' Lauren also lectures in the Social Science Methods and Postgraduate Diploma in Monitoring and Evaluation Methods degree programs at CREST.

OVERVIEW

1 Introduction:
The Challenges in Researching Resilience

LINDA LIEBENBERG AND MICHAEL UNGAR

A survey of what we know about the experiences of children growing up under stress would quickly reveal an abundant literature that details disease, disorder, and dysfunction. What we know far less about is the ways in which large numbers of young people not only survive stressful environments but thrive in spite of the risks to which they are exposed. The experience of health under stress, and the dynamic processes that contribute to positive development, have come to be known as resilience (Masten, 2001; Ungar, 2005). Researchers concerned with the study of resilience have had to be innovative in their methods. Studying young people's problems is not necessarily the same as studying the solutions to those problems. In this volume we have brought together researchers curious about how to study young people's developmental pathways to well-being. Though in many ways this work shares similarities with that of researchers concerned with vulnerability, researching resilience has become common enough to merit a discussion of its own.

Ironically, we can't study resilience without studying risk. Resilience is the positive end of the developmental continuum that occurs for children who experience both acute and chronic exposure to stressors like poverty, abuse, war, violence, neglect, drug addictions, mental illness, disability, marginalization, racism, and a myriad of other ways their well-being is threatened. Studying resilience requires that we assess the level of risk posed to children, which means we must get close enough to vulnerable individuals to understand their lives within the culture and context in which they live. It is little wonder, then, that research with vulnerable populations has proven difficult. As Hutz and Koller (1999), commenting on their work with homeless youth on the streets of Brazil, tell us, 'The study of street children presents researchers with challenges and difficulties that can hardly be overstated' (p. 59). These same challenges appear in work with any number of diverse populations of youth, such as those facing the effects of gang violence, family disintegration in the face of epidemics such as HIV/AIDs, or the disintegration of their communities and culture through war or diminishing job opportunities resulting from globalization and the southerly flow of production. Each of these threats affects children differently, with the impact of risk mitigated by the quality and quantity of exposure and the meaning individuals and their families attribute to their experience. Just how at risk a child really is can never be easily discerned without understanding the child in context.

Examining the capacities of young people to cope with adversity and the responsiveness of their environments to provide them with the resources they need to thrive, researchers enter the murky waters of having to account for a large number of confounding variables. Studying resilience means understanding not only the threats facing young people, but also the interactions between their risk exposure and the solutions they find to cope with personal and environmental challenges. Those of us studying children's pathways to healthy functioning believe young people are motivated to seek well-being (Dallape, 1996). Their success depends on factors generic across populations, such as a meaningful role in one's community, self-efficacy, self-esteem, secure attachments, safety, and optimism (see Kirby & Fraser, 1997). Children's thriving also has more culturally embedded expressions, with aspects of their lives such as patterns of interaction with parents, feelings of responsibility for others, rites of passage, religious affiliations, a sense of humour, and gender-based expectations all combining to shape how young people achieve a sense of well-being when risk is present in one particular environment (McCubbin et al., 1998; Ungar, 2005).

At the intersection of individual motivation and the resources an environment has to offer to mitigate risk exposure lies young people's hidden resilience (Ungar, 2004), patterns of coping that allow youth to subjectively experience their lives as successful whether others outside their culture and context see them that way or not. As Luthar (1999) explains, there are 'innumerable ways in which potentially powerful risk and protective factors do not operate in directions that may be intuitively anticipated, but often can reflect complicated, conditional and even counterintuitive trends' (p. 3). Two companion volumes to this one, *Resilience in Action* (Liebenberg & Ungar, 2008) and *The Handbook for Working with Children and Youth: Pathways to Resilience across Cultures and Contexts* (Ungar, 2005), have explored the practicalities of nurturing resilience in populations of youth around the world. While we know anecdotally that efforts by our many colleagues are proving successful, there remains a need for research that can validate the advantages of initiatives that build capacity rather than those that alleviate disorder. To accomplish this we need to find ways to accurately document the person–environment interaction that determines whether a particular capacity, of the individual or his or her community, is the one most likely to produce positive growth and development. In this volume, we have brought together authors concerned with the shift in focus from problems to solutions and the research methods required to document the complexity of resilience as both outcome and process.

The bulk of the chapters that follow were initially presented as papers at the June 2005 Pathways to Resilience conference in Halifax, Canada. Many of the 320 delegates from twenty-two countries who attended identified both difficulties and shortcomings in their work researching resilience among children and youth. There was consensus at that meeting that studying well-being in relation to adversity demands research methods that are better tailored to the needs of resilience researchers.

The Complexity of Resilience

The complexity of researching resilience is not only the result of ours being a relatively young field of research, nor of the number of variables that must be accounted for whether one is working qualitatively or quantitatively. Resilience as a construct has remained conceptually fuzzy with little consistency in how the term is operationalized (Lerner, 2006; Luthar, Cicchetti, & Becker, 2000). Sometimes considered a process, just as often understood as an outcome, resilience as a concept has been used to describe both aspects of positive development, or thriving, under stress. Of course, what we define as positive development and what we experience as stress must be negotiated. As Glantz and Sloboda (1999) observed, 'the concept of resilience is heavily laden with subjective, often unarticulated assumptions and it is fraught with major logical, measurement and pragmatic problems'

(p. 110). This can be tricky terrain to navigate, even more so when we appreciate the culturally diverse manifestations of well-being found globally among young people (Johnson-Powell & Yamamoto, 1997; Ungar, 2006, 2008; Wong & Wong, 2006). The result is a field building from the bottom up.

Researchers since the 1950s have focused attention first on outcomes (young people who beat the odds and survive poverty or the mental illness of a parent) and the presence or absence of intrinsic qualities like temperament that interact with a young person's social environment (Anthony, 1987). A second wave of researchers investigated protective mechanisms and processes, arguing that resilience was to be understood as the dynamic interaction between person and environment (Rutter, 1987). More recently, researchers have focused on assets of child and youth populations, arguing that positive development, coping, and resilience are present among those who have both internal and external resources (Lerner & Benson, 2003). A fourth wave, represented by this work and others like it, is broadening the discussion further, arguing that how we understand resilience is negotiated discursively and influenced by the culture and context in which it is found (Boyden & Mann, 2005; Ungar, 2004).

Of course, each wave remains part of a larger body of thought that is focused on people's successful growth rather than breakdown. But the complexity each group of researchers has introduced to our understanding of resilience has resulted in an array of possible research methods but no clear consensus on what resilience is, if it can be defined objectively at all. Despite these inconsistencies, and following on the findings of researchers such as Werner and Smith (1992), Rutter (1985), Garmezy, Masten, and Tellegen (1984) and Benson (1997), substantial development in the theory of resilience continues to occur.

Recently, in an effort to reconcile the disparate definitions of resilience as both outcome and process, individual and environmental, Ungar (2008) suggested resilience be defined as follows:

> In the context of exposure to significant adversity, whether psychological, environmental, or both, resilience is both the capacity of individuals to navigate their way to health-sustaining resources, including opportunities to experience feelings of well-being, and a condition of the individual's family, community and culture to provide these health resources and experiences in culturally meaningful ways. (p. 225)

The problem posed by such a definition is that we must as researchers seek to understand not just individuals, but also the capacity of their environments to deliver resources. Thus, resilience is no longer just the everyday magic that Masten (2001) eloquently speaks of, but also the very gritty reality of families, communities, and governments changing the opportunity structures around children in order to make successful development more likely. The provision of resources and expressions of well-being that follow are necessarily culturally determined.

Researchers seeking to understand the phenomenon of well-being might best take a postmodern approach to their work and embrace the notion that experience is socially constructed (Berger & Luckmann, 1966). For researchers, this means a greater likelihood of mixed-method designs and the inclusion on ethical grounds of marginalized voices in research in order to create findings that are valid, reliable, and trustworthy. We understand 'trustworthy' in a qualitative sense: that our report of a participant's experience is an authentic account representing his or her life as lived (Lincoln & Guba, 1985). This is the research frontier that this volume seeks to explore. We proceed, however, cautiously.

Measuring and understanding resilience in order to develop meaningful theories regarding youth thriving are never unbiased efforts. They encounter the inherent pitfalls of research disciplines firmly routed in the white, Western ideologies that dominate research in human development. Most of what we know about resilience is based on quantitative studies that have employed standardized measures that were not intended to measure health, but were screens for mental illness. Health is implied by the absence of disorder rather than theorized for its own dimensions. Other efforts at developing resilience measures have tended to survey the literature and then be developed based on the consensus of experts, with post hoc validation following. The inherent selection bias of such designs leaves out alternative explanations for health that might have been found if a more iterative, contextualized instrument development process had taken place. After all, mightn't children's culturally embedded well-being have unique dimensions of which adults (and especially adult researchers) remain unaware?

Our historical penchant for objectivity has produced research methods that are quickly showing their wear in a post-colonial world of competing health discourses. More nuanced efforts to examine findings, aided by advances in computer technology, are highlighting the very same complexity in how we understand resilience that individuals have complained were absent from the theories that were being published. For example, in a recent effort by Thoeokas and Lerner (2006), clear distinctions between internal and external health resources were found to be inconsistent, with some internal factors appearing to cluster with external variables and vice versa. Another study by the same research group found that a hypothesized relationship between more assets and better well-being breaks down when environments change (Phelps et al., 2007). A child entering junior high, for example, may actually show a decrease in well-being even when assets increase. Such anomalies are to be embraced for the chaotic, contextual specificity they suggest. These findings, however, should not surprise us. As Luthar, Cicchetti, and Becker (2000) have shown, there are multiple models to account for the variability in the relationship between the factors that affect resilience and the processes of growth vulnerable individuals engage in. Those models explain processes related to resilience that are protective, stabilizing, or reactive. Each is reflective of the interaction between individual and environmental factors. Future research is going to have to account for the uniqueness of the pathways children follow as they cope with risk.

Sometimes rising above the fray, other times actually showing a decline in functioning (but not as much decline as might be expected), are among the many paths forming the ups and downs of development that complicate the work of resilience researchers. Sadly, for proponents of causal models, human growth is not linear and predictable. The factors that associate with outcomes are not always generic and measurable across all populations. If this, then, is the case, how are we to argue convincingly that resilience is a construct worthy of study? Why focus on researching something that appears to be so indeterminate?

There are no quick answers to these questions, but the chapters that follow do explore some tentative methodological solutions to studying a concept like resilience that varies across contexts. What all these authors share is a tolerance for diversity, both in operationalization of the resilience construct and in methods for its study. In particular, we will need to diversify with whom we generate theory. Although several researchers have made meaningful inroads into this discussion around research with marginalized communities (see, for example, Boyden & Mann, 2005; McCubbin et al., 1998), there is a need not only to continue addressing these questions and concerns, but also to bring more focus to working with specific groups in contexts other than Western democracies, or mainstream populations therein. Greater complexity, not less, is needed in order to research resilience, even if there is the potential for the construct to remain ambiguous in how it is theorized. As van de Vijver and Leung (1997) argue, although cross-cultural research can highlight the global relevance of theories and findings, this should not be at the expense of our understanding of the unique qualities of diverse populations.

An Evolving Research Paradigm for Resilience

In order to research well-being among youth, our own experience and that of our colleagues tells us that a more participatory, contextually attuned approach is needed whether one is working within a qualitative or quantitative research paradigm. The very nature of the gap between adult researcher and youth participant is accentuated when issues of diversity (class, ability, gender, sexual orientation, race, etc.) are added. If we are to accurately *re-present* the experiences of young people who thrive despite adversity, we will need to reach across this us-them divide. This makes research messy. The criteria for quality can no longer be just objectivity, but must also consider authenticity. How well, we need to ask, does our theory account for the experiences of those we study? This problem has always plagued the psychological sciences, and investigations of resilience are no different. However, ours being an emerging field, with an emerging body of truth claims, it presents an opportunity for more contextually fluid definitions grounded in novel research paradigms. If the tendency in the study of disorder has been to objectively assess problems, we are seeing less tolerance for absolutes among those tackling positive aspects of development. Occurring at the same time as a number of trends in research design, the study of resilience has the potential to do things differently. It is these innovations that have much to offer the study of resilience. Below, and throughout this volume, we review several of these advances, including power relations, ways to address the oppressiveness of methods, cultural sensitivity, and participation.

Power Relations

More often than not, researchers find themselves crossing boundaries of age, culture, language, economics, race, sex, and experience.

Perhaps the most obvious challenge stemming from the multiple boundaries between researchers and participants in the study of resilience is the unequal power relations characterizing these relationships (see, for example, Erben, 2000; Finch, 1984; Fine et al., 2000; Oakley, 1994; Pole, Mizen, & Bolton, 1999). Researchers who deconstruct the potential for bias resulting from one's chronological standpoint emphasize that it is incumbent upon researchers to acknowledge such imbalance and to account for it in their research (Bemak, 1996; Dallape, 1996; Kefyalew, 1996; Morris, Woodward, & Peters, 1998; Oakley, 1981; Volpi, 2002; West, 1996; Whitmore & McKee, 2001). This entails a consideration of researcher role in the field, field relations, and how youth participants are incorporated into research, including methods chosen. Many authors emphasize the importance of youth perspectives in guiding research questions. In order to achieve this, more participatory methods are required that will draw youth voices into the research process. Researchers such as Morrow (1999) and Whitmore and McKee (2001) suggest the use of creative yet age-appropriate activities.

When understanding something as ambiguous as well-being, it seems naive to assume that researchers who are living lives different from a study's participants should be able to decide the criteria for successful adaptation. Blindsided by age and other dimensions of their social identity, adult researchers need to exercise caution when engaging young people in research (Greene & Hill, 2005).

Oppressive Methods

Oppressive methods dislocate trust. Laird (2003), Nsamenang (2002), Oakley (1994), and Whitmore and McKee (2001) all criticize research that treats participants as subordinates, questioning the possibility of honest, open, and revealing responses by people who are subjected to the same disdain and exercise of hierarchical power as is practised by their oppressors. The youth who, for example, drops out of school as a way to cope with a sense of failure may be protecting his or her self-concept from further assault (see Dei et al., Massuca, McIsaac & Zine, 1997). However, how are we to measure such a unique pathway to resilience when it is goes counter to what we believe instills well-being, that being to stay in school? Not surprisingly, such nuanced constructions of health, when at odds with the dominant discourse of a community, are seldom well expressed by participants, if there is room for them to be heard at all. Instead, in our experience, participants with marginalized points of view are more likely to decline to participate in research, more comfortable with their marginalization than the not-so-subtle exclusion they may experience as a subject.

Boundaries between researchers and researched are further entrenched when researchers fail to acknowledge the positioning of their own experiences and education as the 'biologically situated researcher' (Denzin & Lincoln, 1998, p. 23). Denzin and Lincoln explain that many researchers approach research from their own contextually bound academic positioning. Researchers impose these perspectives on the 'other' who is then studied within a research context heavily influenced by the politics and the ethics that surround what we accept as science (Denzin, 2007; Kotze & Kotze, 1996). Discourses of what counts as a healthy, well-adjusted child have deep roots in each culture. Unfortunately, researchers who have been educated in the dominant Western models of thought very often attempt to enforce their 'best fit' practices within contexts that they believe they understand. Thus, we may overlook a child's own positive interpretation of being employed, a street youth, or a child soldier or of caring for younger siblings. While we might wish that such paths to a positive self-concept were different, for example less parentifying, the study of resilience and its complex interplay of risk with opportunity attunes us to the myriad of potential ways children beat the odds against them. Studying these pathways as viable alternatives requires a humility on the part of researchers, a capacity to admit we don't know as much as we think about these 'others.'

Concerns regarding the contextual positioning of resilience researchers are clearly articulated in the work of authors such as Glantz and Sloboda (1999) who caution against the selection of outcome variables based on value judgments stemming from the researcher's own cultural background. And as Cavin (1994) and Karlsson (2001) argue in their studies of child and youth perspectives, outsider (adult) perspectives can be and often are profoundly different from how youth see and interpret their world. Such experiences are echoed by Dallape (1996), who, commenting on his work with youth living on the street, says, 'we were amazed by the precision with which they [the youth in the study] stated the socioeconomic and political nature of the problems they identified, showing where the locus of responsibility for change lay' (p. 291).

When discursive space is opened for children's own accounts of their well-being, resilience researchers are finding a large number of unique accounts of health. The child who feels oppressed by the research process, however, is more likely to resist, a strategy that is protective and adaptive when one is under threat. As Oakley (1981) suggests, researchers are highly dependent on participants' willingness to be researched. Not surprisingly, without a relationship of mutual trust being established between researcher and participant, young people are likely to experience the process of research as oppressive. The work of researchers such as Whitemore and McKee (2001) and Sanders and Munford (2005) has clearly demonstrated how more equitable relationships enhance a sense of ownership and accountability amongst youth participants. These efforts, though, are more typically qualitative. There remains a need to discover more participatory forms of research that are quantitative in their design.

Cultural Sensitivity

The combination of constructed meanings, complex communication processes, and trust undermined by power imbalances can perpetuate discriminatory and oppressive practices during research (Kotze & Kotze, 1996). In her critique of methodologies, Smith (1999) accuses social researchers of voyeuristically studying indigenous societies, not fully understanding individual communities, yet holding the 'power to define' (p. 58). Arguably, youth, especially youth from diverse cultures and contexts, can suffer the same objectification. Smith points to the 'cultural system of classification and representation' (p. 44) that underlies research findings and that is based on views regarding human nature, morality, and virtue, and conceptions of space and time and of gender, age, and race. Dominant ideas about these constructs determine what counts as real. Thus health, development, even resilience, are not independent terms but concepts crafted over time by those whose voices are loudest in the scientific discourse.

When objectification, or the 'othering' of youth as research participants, goes unchecked, research findings are most likely to be incorporated into existing systems of power and domination. Services to youth may calcify around simplistic solutions such as 'stay-in-school' and 'abstinence' programs that promote a singular definition of resilience as adaptation as defined by middle-class white Western elites. The diversity and alternate discourses of those being studied can in this process become silenced, and cultural heterogeneity masked under the guise of the generalizability of results across all populations and expectations that the same outcomes be associated with resilience for all youth globally.

If we sound somewhat hyperbolic on this point it is because there is little in mainstream academic journals to challenge how research is done. Indeed, in this volume we accept these same conventions. Not every author reflects so radical a perspective, though all would argue for the need for some degree of participation by youth to validate findings and for cultural issues to be taken into consideration. Without this vigorous debate, however, youths' pathways to resilience across contexts and cultures will evade study, continuing to be made invisible by the homogenizing discourse of researchers.

More recently, resilience researchers, like other social scientists, are attempting to work reflexively, soliciting a 'multi-voiced text that is grounded in the experiences of oppressed peoples' (Denzin & Lincoln, 1998, p. 28). This shift correlates with a call for a critical method that treats people as active subjects in the construction of their worlds and experiences, a method based on dialogue across cultures (Grover, 2004; Hill, 2006; Smith, 1999). Individuals' preferred realities are situated within their own communities' systems of knowledge, culture, and power (Smith, 1999). Traditional research processes, however, exclude participants from the decision-making process, alienating the participant from the inquiry and from the knowledge that is subsequently generated, thereby 'invalidating any claim the methods have to the science of persons' (Reason, 1994, p. 325). Voices of research participants must therefore be included in the research process in such a manner that the impact of historically located contexts is brought to the fore. Doing so highlights participants' insight into their own lives and contexts (Luthar, 1999; Narayan, 1992). Such insights are particularly relevant when speaking about marginalized youth who exist in culturally diverse situations. Stanley and Wise (1993), like Smith (1999), correctly point to the value of personal experience that undergirds research that speaks to the experiences of those marginalized. If we are to understand youth pathways to resilience, we will need to find methods of inquiry that open space for the perspectives of individuals from diverse backgrounds.

Participation

In recent years there has been a growing emphasis on including youth in the processes that generate policies and practices aimed at bolstering their well-being (Connolly & Ennew, 1996; Dallape, 1996; James & Prout, 1990; Lee, 2001; Morrow & Richards, 1996; Oakley, 1994). Luthar (1999) argues that it is only by centring youth voices in research that we can truly explore and understand the myriad of ways in which youth manage to support their lives in complex environments. She writes, 'it is critical to consider not only mainstream views on salient risk and protective factors, but also the *people's own perceptions* of positive and negative ramifications of particular behaviours or outcomes' (p. 78). Many would argue that this is especially true in the case of girls whose voices are silenced by the intersecting oppressions of gender, age and, when relevant, culture and race (Brown & Gilligan, 1992; Hill-Collins, 1990; hooks, 1981; Leadbeater & Way, 1996; McAdam-Crisp, Aptekar, & Kironyo, 2005; Pipher, 1994; Spivak, 1993).

The critical question, then, is not '*whether* to do research, but rather *what kind* of research to carry out? Which research questions should receive priority? What kinds of epidemiological, ethnographic, clinical science, and health services data are needed as a first step?' (Desjarlais et al., 1995, p. 279). Such questions do not necessarily preclude the use of particular research tools, but rather challenge researchers to reconsider *how* and *when* available methods are used. Thus, in a study of the impact of a violence prevention program on children in Medellin, Colombia, a purely quantitative approach to evaluating the program's effectiveness longitudinally was supplemented with reports back to the families and policy makers in the communities from which participants were drawn (Duque et al., 2005). While not entirely participatory, the emphasis on dialogue was a step in the right direction even within a research paradigm that was epidemiological and quantitative. The more that research methods are inclusive of youth and treat them as more than just subjects of study, the greater the likelihood that participants will be able to define the constructs to be studied. The more the research is tailored to their needs, the better it will be in informing programs to help young people build and sustain resilience.

Thus, we believe that centring youth voices in research is critical. Designing research to have permeable boundaries between researchers and participants, considering carefully our choice of methods, and making efforts to include youth perspectives in all phases of the work where realistically possible are research imperatives.

Many of the chapters in this volume suggest that successful research is community based and sensitive to local institutions, traditions, and values. It may also profit from community members having substantial control over the research process. Such an approach provides a space for youth to actively contribute to generating ideas, designing and managing the project, and drawing conclusions from the experience. Research based on more equitable and democratic criteria becomes empowering by turning a potentially oppressive situation into an opportunity for growth and learning, providing participants a forum to reflect on their lives. Through this reflection and participation, the goal is to generate new knowledge that is meaningful and relevant to young people's lives. This is what Harper (2002) regards as 'postmodern dialogue based on the authority of the subject rather than the researcher' (p. 15). There is arguably something synchronic in this approach to the study of resilience. The very process of the research contributes to the honouring of the capacities it seeks to document.

Guidelines to implementing such research are to be gleaned from a number of sources, but are found most often in descriptions of action research (Bradbury & Reason, 2003; Elabor-Idemudia, 2002; Gustavsen, 2003; Ospina et al., 2004). Action researchers seek to resolve possible contradictions between the demands for participation, the need for practical outcomes to derive from research, and requirements to demonstrate methodological and theoretical rigour. By allowing participating communities and young people to guide the research process, positioning participants as experts on the research topic, one intentionally places the 'interviewee more center stage and to some extent reflects the concerns of postmodernists and new ethnographers to give "voice" to those we study' (Prosser, 2002, p.1).

Approaches to Resilience Research

The challenge facing resilience researchers is to engage in the use of research methods that take many of the realities of conducing research with marginalized groups into account. As Rogoff (1998) says:

> To be able to assemble a group of materials and a variety of methodological analyses around an issue that is determined out of cultural and political realities rather than out of traditions of learned arguments, seems an important step forward in the project of reformulating knowledge to deal responsibly with the lived conditions of highly contested realities, such as we face at the turn of this century. (p. 23)

Within the field of resilience research specifically, these concerns are echoed by authors such as Ungar (2003) as well as Tweed and DeLongis (2006), who raise concerns about methodological approaches to the study of resilience and coping. Both qualitative (Ungar, 2003) and quantitative (Tweed & DeLongis, 2006) approaches to research can be used when pursing an understanding of resilience. In fact, as the diversity of the chapters that follow shows, if we are to understand resilience as a concept of process and outcome (Glantz & Sloboda, 1999), from an eco-systems point of view (Garmezy, 1985; Masten, Best, & Garmezy, 1990; Rutter, 1990), we need to find ways to take all methodological approaches into account when designing our research. In particular, resilience research needs to reflect the best of what we know about social sciences investigations. There are several challenges to achieving this goal.

How, for instance, do we establish the bigger picture? How do we effectively and sensitively make use of quantitative methods? Specifically, how do we balance the ideographic with the generic: distinguishing what is unique from that which is common across populations? This challenge is of increasing importance to researchers operating within a climate of rapid globalization (Sanchez, Spector, & Cooper, 2006). Of fundamental importance is how instruments are established, as well as how we use these instruments across a multitude of cultures and research sites (Sanchez, Spector, & Cooper, 2006; Ungar et al., 2005). Efforts in this regard have shown the need to use qualitative methods to inform both the development of quantitative measures and the interpretation of results. We will also have to break ground conceptually in order to better understand how to conduct the meta-analysis of findings from diverse sources of research in order to discover within a quantitative paradigm the commonalities in how resilience is to be understood. This issue of meta-analysis is investigated further in chapter 7 by Alexa Smith-Osborne.

As the arguments stack up, it is difficult to not become biased towards mixed-method designs for the study of resilience. This both-and approach to research offers a great deal of flexibility and honours the advances achieved among researchers from both methodological paradigms. Finding ways, then, to create dialogue between research paradigms to better account for how resilience is understood by populations of children at risk is one of the not-so-subtle goals of this volume.

Arguably, the process of discovering an accurate account of resilience that transcends temporal, geographic, and cultural boundaries requires back–and-forth movement between qualitative and quantitative methods within the same study. This point is developed in chapter 8 by Este, Sitter, and MacLaurin, and in chapter 12 by Donna Mertens. In this regard, we follow the advice of researchers like Glantz and Sloboda (1999), who say that resilience research and theory development should stem from multiple perspectives, methods, and voices. Luthar (1999), too, tells us that research designs incorporating qualitative and qualitative methods can substantially enhance the veracity of findings, teasing apart the complexity of resilience. Drawing on the work of Cohler, Stott, and Musick (1995), Luthar writes that to substantiate research findings from studies of resilience, 'We must understand how persons within a culture or ethnic group symbolically construct concepts such as self and others before we can understand factors attributed to vulnerability and resilience' (p. 781). Similarly, Todd, Nerlich, and McKeown (2004) show that a combination of methods can heighten explorations of the same phenomenon at different levels, resulting in improvements in theory. The practical relevance of a mixed-methods approach to research is further supported by Earls and Carlson (1999), who argue that in order to progress in the delivery of effective health and education of youth across cultures and contexts, we require more meaningful indicators of well-being. Specifically, 'it is essential that this be done with a degree of conceptual and methodological uniformity to permit comparisons and contrasts across cultural and national groups. Ethnographic and descriptive approaches present an important step toward this goal, but they should be combined with larger-scale surveys that document the growth parameters, health status, and psychological development of these children' (p. 80). All these authors seem to agree. The study of resilience is still too unwieldy and the conceptual terrain too unexplored to proceed with quantitative methods alone.

The Need for Careful Study of Resilience

Resilience research has the potential to add substantially to our knowledge of applied research methods in the social sciences. The shift from the study of disorder to the study of health requires an equally profound shift in methods and theory. We need to be congruent, however, investigating solutions in ways that honour strengths. This approach to our work is not just theoretically sound, but also ethical. As under-standings of the terms 'child,' 'childhood,' and 'adolescence' come under increasing scrutiny in the wake of the UN Convention on the Rights of the Child, how we engage with youth, particularly those living at the margins of society, raises many ethical challenges. While these concerns are addressed at length in chapter 2 by Boothroyd, Stiles, and Best, the discussion of exemplary research methods throughout this volume is never put forth without some attention to the ethics of inclusion when studying resilience among those at risk. Critically, as Jansson et al. (2006) point out, 'the literature [on research with youth] places less emphasis on the ethical issues that may arise and how they may be resolved' (p. 59) than on findings and theory.

A critical component of the ethical conduct of researchers must therefore be the translation of findings into programs and policies when appropriate. The study of resilience is particularly well suited to this translation. Resilience research is about identifying the strengths of individuals and communities in order to replicate what is working in the lives of those who cope successfully, helping others who are equally vulnerable to change the odds stacked against them.

Increasingly, the study of resilience is moving beyond the study of individuals to consider individuals in interaction with their environ-ments and the adaptive qualities of both. From this perspective, research frequently has as its goal both the exploration of the factors that predict resilience and to the use of findings to inform policy and program initiatives to put knowledge into practice. The study of resilience has a unique advantage in this regard over studies of the eti-ology of disorder. The successful adaptation of children tells us which individual and collective factors are most likely to contribute to suc-cessful development. Thus, children who explain their success based on access to mentors, consistent parenting, or culturally appropriate education are our best experts on the most effective ways to intervene in the lives of other youth who have less access to these same health resources. In this regard, researchers like Bemak (1996) emphasize the importance of evaluating programs aimed at youth on the margins of society, not only to assess the effectiveness of interventions but also to better align them with what we understand contributes to their resilience.

Though this is the direction we propose, we are aware of the chal-lenges. Rosenblatt and Woodbridge (2003) point out the complexities in designing evaluation research that will establish effectiveness in terms of youth outcomes, program outcomes, and influence on policy. Farmer (2000) suggests that such difficulties stem from the complexity of the target population of such services, complexity of the actual services provided, and challenges in defining expected outcomes for youth. The solutions, it seems, are to be found in our previous points: including participant voices to ensure the trustworthiness of findings; decentring the researcher as the sole arbiter of knowledge; using quantitative data carefully; and encouraging the use of mixed-method designs in order to break ground theoretically.

Our work around the globe has convinced us that communities and their youth want greater reciprocity in research design. They want accountability from researchers. They want their rights respected, which means threats to the objectivity that comes with science-as-usual. This is uncharted terrain in a post-colonial world of competing discourses regarding health. The resolution is to be found, we believe, in seeking innovation in methodology and creating dialogue across research paradigms in order to find new ways of answering difficult questions. In the process we will transform what we define as ethical research when studying resilience. We will find a way to understand youth pathways to health without prejudicing our findings.

References

Anthony, E.J. (1987). Children at high risk for psychosis growing up successfully. In E.J. Anthony & B.J. Cohler (Eds.), *The invulnerable child* (pp. 147–84). New York: Guilford.

Bemak, F. (1996). Street researchers: A new paradigm redefining future research with street children. *Childhood, 3,* 147–56.

Benson, P.L. (1997). *All kids are our kids.* Minneapolis: Search Institute.

Berger, P.L., & Luckmann, T. (1966). *The social construction of reality: A treatise in the sociology of knowledge.* Garden City, NY: Anchor.

Boyden, J., & Mann, G. (2005). Children's risk, resilience, and coping in extreme situations. In M. Ungar (Ed.), *Handbook for working with children and youth: Pathways to resilience across cultures and contexts* (pp. 3–26). Thousand Oaks, CA: Sage.

Bradbury, H., & Reason, P. (2003). Action research: An opportunity for revitalizing research purpose and practices. *Qualitative Social Work, 2*(2), 155–75.

Brown, L.M., & Gilligan, C. (1992). *Meeting at the crossroads.* New York: Ballantine.

Cavin, E. (1994). In search of the viewfinder: A study of child's perspective. *Visual Sociology, 9*(1), 27–42.

Cohler, B.J., Stott, F.M., & Musick, J.S. (1995). Adversity, vulnerability and resilience: Cultural and developmental perspectives. In D. Cicchetti & D. J. Cohen (Eds.), *Developmental psychopathology,* Vol.2: *Risk, disorder and adaptation* (pp. 753–800). New York: Wiley.

Connolly, M., & Ennew, J. (1996). Introduction: Children out of place. *Childhood, 3,* 131–45.

Dallape, F. (1996). Urban children: A challenge and an opportunity. *Childhood, 3,* 283–94.

Dei, G.J.S., Massuca, J., McIsaac, E., & Zine, J. (1997). *Reconstructing 'drop-out': A critical ethnography of the dynamics of black students' disengagement from school.* Toronto: University of Toronto Press.

Denzin, N.K. (2007). The international congress of qualitative inquiry. *Qualitative research in organisations and management, 1*(2), 130–4.

Denzin, N.K., & Lincoln, Y.S. (1998). Introduction: Entering the field of qualitative research. In N.K. Denzin & Y.S. Lincoln (Eds.), *Collecting and interpreting qualitative materials* (pp. 1–34). London: Sage.

Desjarlais, R., Eisenberg, L., Good, B., & Kleinman, A. (1995). *World mental health: Problems and priorities in low-income countries.* New York: Oxford University Press.

Duque, L.F., Klevens, J., Ungar, M., & Lee, A.W. (2005). Violence prevention programming in Colombia: Challenges in project design and fidelity. In M. Ungar (Ed.), *Handbook for working with children and youth: Pathways to resilience across cultures and contexts* (pp. 455–71). Thousand Oaks, CA: Sage.

Earls, F., & Carlson, M. (1999). Children at the margins of society: Research and practice. *New Directions for Child and Adolescent Development, 85,* 71–82.

Elabor-Idemudia, P. (2002). Participatory research: A tool in the production of knowledge in development discourse. In K. Saunders (Ed.), *Feminist post-development thought: Rethinking modernity, post-colonialism and representation* (pp. 227–42). London: Zed.

Erben, M. (2000). Ethics, education, narrative communication and biography. *Educational Studies, 26*(3), 379–90.

Farmer, E.M.Z. (2000). Issues confronting effective services in systems of care. *Children and Youth Services Review, 22*(8), 627–50.

Finch, J. (1984). 'It's great to have someone to talk to': The ethics and politics of interviewing women. In C. Bell & H. Roberts (Eds.), *Social researching: Politics, problems, practice* (pp. 70–87). London: Routledge and Kegan Paul.

Fine, M., Weis, L., Weseen, S., & Wong, L. (2000). For whom? Qualitative research, representations and social responsibilities. In N.K. Denzin & Y.S.

Lincoln (Eds.), *Handbook of qualitative research* (2nd ed., pp. 107–31). Thousand Oaks, CA: Sage.

Garmezy, N. (1985). Broadening research on developmental risk. In W. Frankenburg, R. Emde, & J. Sullivan (Eds.), *Early identification of children at risk: An international perspective* (pp. 289–303). New York: Plenum.

Garmezy, N., Masten, A.S., & Tellegen, A. (1984). The study of stress and competence in children: A building block for developmental psychopathology. *Child Development, 55,* 97–111.

Glantz, M.D., & Sloboda, Z. (1999). Analysis and reconceptualisation resilience. In M.D. Glantz & J.L. Johnson (Eds.), *Resilience and development: Positive life adaptations* (pp. 109–26). New York: Kluwer Academic/Plenum.

Greene, S., & Hill, M. (2005). Researching children's experience: Methods and methodological issues. In S. Greene & D. Hogan (Eds.), *Researching children's experience: Methods and approaches* (pp. 1–21). Thousand Oaks, CA: Sage.

Grover, S. (2004). Why won't they listen to us? On giving power and voice to children participating in research. *Childhood, 11*(1), 81–93.

Gustavsen, B. (2003). New forms of knowledge production and the role of action research. *Action Research, 1*(2), 153–64.

Harper, D. (2002). Talking about pictures: A case for photo elicitation. *Visual Studies, 17*(1), 13–26.

Hill, M. (2006). Children's voices on ways of having a voice: Children's and young people's perspectives on methods used in research and consultation. *Childhood, 13*(1), 69–89.

Hill-Collins, P. (1990). *Black feminist thought: Knowledge, consciousness and the politics of empowerment.* Boston: Unwin Hyman.

hooks, b. (1981). *Ain't I a woman: Black women and feminism.* Boston: South End.

Hutz, C.S., & Koller, S.H. (1999). Methodological and ethical issues in research with street children. *New Directions for Child and Adolescent Development, 85,* 59–70.

James, A., & Prout, A. (Eds.) (1990). *Constructing and reconstructing childhood: Contemporary issues in the sociological study of childhood.* Basingstoke: Falmer.

Jansson, M., Mitic, W., Hultun, T., & Dhami, M. (2006). A youth population health survey. In B. Leadbeater, E. Banister, C. Benoit, M. Jansson, A. Marshall, & T. Riecken (Eds.), *Ethical issues in community-based research with children and youth* (pp. 59–69). Toronto: University of Toronto Press.

Johnson-Powell, G., & Yamamoto, J. (Eds.). (1997). *Transcultural child development: Psychological assessment and treatment.* New York: John Wiley & Sons.

Karlsson, J. (2001). Doing visual research with school learners in South Africa. *Visual Sociology, 16*(2), 23–37.

Kefyalew, F. (1996). The reality of child participation in research: Experience from a capacity-building programme. *Childhood, 3*, 203–13.

Kirby, L.D., & Fraser, M.W. (1997). Risk and resilience in childhood. In M. Fraser (Ed.), *Risk and resilience in childhood: An ecological perspective* (pp. 10–33). Washington, DC: NASW Press.

Kotze, D.A., & Kotze, P.M.J. (1996). What is wrong in development? *Focus,* May/June, 4–8.

Laird, S.E. (2003). Evaluating social work outcomes in Sub-Saharan Africa. *Qualitative Social Work, 2*(3), 251–70.

Leadbeater, B., & Way, N. (Eds.). (1996). *Urban girls: Resisting stereotypes, creating identities.* New York; New York University Press.

Lee, N. (2001). *Childhood and society: Growing up in an age of uncertainty.* Maidenhead: Open University Press.

Lerner, R.M. (2006). Resilience as an attribute of the developmental system. In B.M. Lester, A. Masters, & B. McEwan (Eds.), *Resilience in children: Annals of the New York Academy of Sciences.* New York: New York Academy of Sciences.

Lerner, R.M., & Benson, P.L. (Eds.). (2003). *Developmental assets and asset-building communities: Implications for research, policy, and practice.* New York: Kluwer Academic/Plenum.

Liebenberg, L., & Ungar, M. (Eds.). (2008). *Resilience in action.* Toronto: University of Toronto Press.

Lincoln, Y., & Guba, E. (1985). *Naturalistic inquiry.* New York: Sage.

Luthar, S.S. (1999). *Poverty and children's adjustment.* Thousand Oaks, CA: Sage.

Luthar, S.S., Cicchetti, D., & Becker, B. (2000). The construct of resilience: A critical evaluation and guidelines for future work. *Child Development, 71*(3), 543–62.

Masten, A. (2001). Ordinary magic: Resilience processes in development. *American Psychologist, 56*(3), 227–38.

Masten, A., Best K., & Garmezy, N. (1990). Resilience and development: Contributions from the study of children who overcame adversity. *Development and Psychopathology, 5,* 703–17.

McAdam-Crisp, J. Aptekar, L., & Kironyo, W. (2005). The theory of resilience and its application to street children in the minority and majority worlds. In M. Ungar (Ed.), *Handbook for working with children and youth: Pathways to resilience across cultures and contexts* (pp. 455–71). Thousand Oaks, CA: Sage.

McCubbin, H.I., Fleming, W.M., Thompson, A.I., Neitman, P., Elver, K.M., & Savas, S.A. (1998). Resiliency and coping in 'at risk' African-American youth and their families. In H.I. McCubbin, E.A. Thompson, A.I. Thompson, & J.A. Futrell (Eds.), *Resiliency in African-American families* (pp. 287–328). Thousand Oaks, CA: Sage.

Morris, K., Woodward, D., & Peters, E. (1998). 'Whose side are you on?': Dilemmas in conducting feminist ethnographic research with young women. *International Journal of Social Research Methodology, 1*(3), 217–30.

Morrow, V. (1999). If you were a teacher, it would be harder to talk to you: Reflections on qualitative research with children in school. *International Journal of Social Research Methodology, 1*(4), 297–313.

Morrow, V., & Richards, M.P.M. (1996). The ethics of social research with children: An overview. *Children and Society, 10*(2), 90–105.

Narayan, U. (1992). The project of feminist epistemology: Perspectives from a nonwestern feminist. In A.M. Jaggar & S.R. Bordo (Eds.), *Gender/body/knowledge: Feminist reconstructions of being and knowing* (pp. 256–69). New Brunswick, NJ: Rutgers University Press.

Nsamenang, A.B. (2002). Adolescence in Sub-Saharan Africa: An image constructed from Africa's triple inheritance. In B. Bradford Brown, R.W. Larson, & T.S. Saraswathi (Eds.), *The world's youth: Adolescence in eight regions of the globe* (pp. 61–104). Cambridge: Cambridge University Press.

Oakley, A. (1981). Interviewing women: A contradiction in terms. In H. Roberts (Ed.), *Doing feminist research* (pp. 30–61). London: Routledge.

Oakley, A. (1994). Women and children first and last: Parallels and differences between children and women's studies. In B. Mayal (Ed.), *Children's childhoods observed and experienced* (pp. 13–32). Thousand Oaks, CA: Sage.

Ospina, S., Dodge, J., Godsoe, B., Minieri, J., Reza, S., & Schall, E. (2004). From consent to mutual inquiry: Balancing democracy and authority in action research. *Action Research, 2*(1), 47–69.

Phelps, E., Balsano, A.B., Fay, K., Peltz, J.S., Zimmerman, S.M., Lerner, R.M., & Lerner, J.V. (2007). Nuances in early adolescent developmental trajectories of positive and of problematic/risk behaviors: Findings from the 4-H study of positive youth development. *North American Clinics of Child and Adolescent Psychiatry, 16*(2), 473–96.

Pipher, M. (1994). *Reviving Ophelia: Saving the selves of adolescent girls.* New York: Ballentine.

Pole, C., Mizen, P., & Bolton, A. (1999). Realising children's agency in research: Partners and participants? *International Journal of Social Research Methodology, 2*(1), 39–54.

Prosser, J. (2002). Editorial. *Visual Studies, 17*(1), 1–2.

Reason, P. (1994). Three approaches to participative inquiry. In N.K. Denzin & Y.S. Lincoln (Eds.), *Handbook of qualitative research* (pp. 324–39). London: Sage.

Rogoff, I. (1998). Studying visual culture. In N. Mirzoeff (Ed.), *The visual culture reader* (pp. 14–26). London: Routledge.

Rosenblatt, A., & Woodbridge, M.W. (2003). Deconstructing research in systems of care for youth with EBD. *Journal of Emotional and Behavioural Disorders, 11*(1), 27–37.

Rutter, M. (1985). Resilience in the face of adversity: Protective factors and resistance to psychiatric disorder. *British Journal of Psychiatry, 147,* 598–611.

Rutter, M. (1987). Psychosocial resilience and protective mechanisms. *American Journal of Orthopsychiatry, 57,* 316–31.

Rutter, M. (1990). Psychosocial resilience and protective mechanisms. In J. Rolf, A. Masten, D. Cicchetti, K. Nuechterlein, & S. Weintraub (Eds.), *Risk and protective factors in the development of psychopathology* (pp. 181–214). Cambridge: Cambridge University Press.

Sanchez, J.I., Spector, P.E., & Cooper, C.L. (2006). Frequently ignored methodological issues in cross-cultural stress research. In P.T.P. Wong & L.C.J. Wong (Eds.), *Handbook of multicultural perspectives on stress and coping* (pp. 187–201). New York: Springer.

Sanders, J., & Munford, R. (2005). Activity and reflection: Research and change with diverse groups of young people. *Qualitative Social Work, 4*(2), 197–209.

Smith, L.T. (1999). *Decolonising methodologies: Research and indigenous peoples.* London: Zed.

Spivak, G. (1993). Can the subaltern speak? In P. Williams & L. Chrisman (Eds.), *Colonial discourse and post-colonial theory* (pp. 66–111). New York: Harvester Wheatsheaf.

Stanley, L., & Wise, S. (1993). *Breaking out again: Feminist ontology and epistemology.* New York: Routledge.

Thoeokas, C., & Lerner, R.M. (2006). Observed ecological assets in families, schools, and neighbourhoods: Conceptualization, measurement, and relations with positive and negative developmental outcomes. *Applied Developmental Science, 10*(2), 61–74.

Todd, Z., Nerlich, B., & McKeown, S. (2004). Introduction. In Z. Todd, B. Nerlich, S. McKeown, & D.D. Clarke (Eds.), *Mixing methods in psychology: The integration of qualitative and quantitative methods in theory and practice* (pp. 3–16). New York: Psychology Press, Taylor and Francis Group.

Tweed, R.G., & DeLongis, A. (2006). Problems and strategies when using rating scales in cross-cultural coping research. In P.T.P. Wong & L.C.J. Wong (Eds.), *Handbook of multicultural perspectives on stress and coping* (pp. 203–21). New York: Springer.

Ungar, M. (2003). Qualitative contributions to resilience research. *Qualitative Social Work, 2*(1), 85–102.

Ungar, M. (2004). A constructionist discourse on resilience: Multiple contexts, multiple realities among at-risk children and youth. *Youth and Society, 35*(3), 341–65.

Ungar, M. (Ed). (2005). *Handbook for working with children and youth: Pathways to resilience across cultures and contexts.* Thousand Oaks, CA: Sage.

Ungar, M. (2006). *Strengths-based counseling with at-risk youth.* Thousand Oaks, CA: Corwin.

Ungar, M. (2008). Resilience across cultures. *British Journal of Social Work, 38*(2), 218–35.

Ungar, M., Clark, S., Kwong, W.M., Cameron, A., & Makhnach, A. (2005). Researching resilience across cultures. *Journal of Cultural and Ethnic Social Work, 14*(3/4), 1–20.

van de Vijver, F., & Leung, K. (1997). *Methods and data analysis for cross-cultural research.* Thousand Oaks, CA: Sage.

Volpi, E. (2002). *Street children: Promising practices and approaches.* Washington, DC: World Bank Institute.

Werner, E., & Smith, R. (1992). *Overcoming the odds: High risk children from birth to adulthood.* Ithaca, NY: Cornell University Press.

West, A. (1996). Children's own research: Street children and care in Britain and Bangladesh. *Childhood, 6*(1), 145–55.

Whitmore, E., & McKee, C. (2001). Six street youth who could .... In P. Reason & H. Bradbury (Eds.), *Handbook of action research: Participative inquiry and practice* (pp. 396–402). London: Sage.

Wong, P.T.P., & Wong, L.C.J. (Eds.). (2006). *Handbook of multicultural perspectives on stress and coping.* New York: Springer.

2 The Ethical Conduct of Research Involving Children in International Settings

ROGER A. BOOTHROYD, PAUL G. STILES, AND
KATHERINE A. BEST

Conducting international research on resilience and well-being in youth poses several unique challenges for researchers. First, many countries have specialized regulations and/or guidelines governing research involving youth. These regulations and guidelines generally provide protections to youth involved in research beyond those required in research with adults, and also frequently include additional requirements for researchers regarding procedures for obtaining informed consent. The rationale for affording youth involved in research additional protections relative to adults is well supported by the differences noted between adults and youth that have been extensively described in the literature. Morrow and Richards (1999) and Glantz (1996), for example, highlight the power differential, general competencies, and experiential differences that exist between adults and youth. Punch (2002) notes many of the same issues but also cautions against 'bracketing all children together as a group in opposition to adults, and overlooking diversity among children' (p. 338).

The second challenge for investigators conducting international research involving youth is that regulations and guidelines governing ethical conduct of research with youth can differ significantly across countries, and thus require investigators to be familiar with and responsive to the requirements contained within these various ethical research codes. In fact, these requirements can even differ within a country (e.g., by state in the United States). Given this, researchers may need to tailor their research protocols to comply with the specific regulations and guidelines for the countries in which they are conducting research. This having been said, Hyder and colleagues (2004) noted that one in four health-related studies conducted in so-called developing, or majority world, countries were not reviewed by an international, national, or governmental ethics board. A survey of countries in the World Health Organization (WHO) African Region revealed that one third of the countries responding had no mechanism in place for conducting research ethics reviews (Kirigia, Wambebe, & Baba-Moussa, 2005). These authors suggested improving international research reviews by using technologies of teleconferencing, video conferencing, or emailing to have protocols reviewed in a timely fashion, saving time and money on face-to-face meetings. They also suggested regional committees as well as intercountry mechanisms to monitor health research. The critical issue that international researchers are contending with may simply be inadequate scientific and ethics infrastructures for reviewing processes (Benatar, 2002).

A third issue involves the very nature of research on resilience. As noted by Luthar, Cicchetti, and Becker (2000), by definition resilience research requires that youth of interest have been exposed to 'a significant threat or severe adversity' (p. 543), which potentially renders them some of the most vulnerable individuals investigators can study. The specific adversity youth experience will vary depending on whether it arises out of abuse, abject poverty, war, or personal victimization. However, the fact that these youth have experienced some form of trauma places additional challenges on researchers to ensure the research process itself does not serve to revictimize them.

In this chapter, we provide a brief summary of the ethical codes for conducting research within various international contexts. This summary is not intended to be a comprehensive analysis of each code included, but rather is meant to highlight some of the similarities and differences that investigators conducting resilience research with youth in international settings might encounter. Throughout this chapter we employ a framework we believe is useful to researchers in analysing their obligations regarding research ethics. Simply stated, the framework asks researchers to assess, given the existing ethical guidelines, whether they must, may, or should act or respond in a specific manner. Answers to these questions can be helpful in guiding researchers' behaviours. If ethical codes require researchers to take certain actions or steps, then they *must* comply with these requirements. However, codes governing the ethical conduct of research often provide exceptions to certain requirements, meaning the researcher *may* use procedures that differ from stated guidelines. Although these exceptions allow researchers to employ research strategies that differ from those stated in the guidelines, they need to ask themselves if they *should* deviate. As a general rule, a strategy's being more convenient, cheaper, or easier is typically not a good enough reason to deviate from the recommended guidelines. In contrast, adapting procedures to better conform to local cultural norms or to minimize participant burden provides a more compelling rationale for departing from preferred standards.

The next section of this chapter provides a discussion of research ethics with youth in the international context, including international codes and some specific country examples. As Ungar and Liebenberg (2005) have noted in their work with the International Resilience Project, 'decontextualized findings that are generalized across populations of differing cultures are problematic in terms of construct validity' (p. 212); so it is with decontextualized regulations and codes of conduct. Considerations of context are the underpinnings of moral and ethical reasoning (Benatar & Singer, 2000); therefore, it is important for us as authors to note our context and circumstances of residing in the United States as researchers employed by a state university system. While we have framed our discussion using the United States federal regulations (45 CFR 46), we have also included some of the key differences found in the Canadian Tri-Council policy statement (Canadian Tri-Council Working Group, 2005). We attempt to highlight situations or contexts that might be more often encountered by investigators conducting research on resilience. This is followed by a summary and discussion of various ethical issues involving research with youth. These include: (1) inclusion and exclusionary criteria, (2) risks and benefits, (3) informed consent/assent, (4) privacy/confidentiality, and (5) differences between therapeutic versus non-therapeutic research. We conclude the chapter by highlighting some 'universal principles' that investigators believe are useful when conducting international research involving young people.

We want to emphasize from the start that although this book is focused primarily on the study of resilience, hardiness, and well-being in youth, the ethical considerations for researchers do not vary based on the substantive focus of the research. Investigators studying any topic have a professional responsibility and ethical obligation to treat participants respectfully, to minimize their exposure to risk, and to be fair in the distributions of risks and benefits across subgroups of individuals. This having been said, we acknowledge that the practices and procedures implemented by investigators to meet these responsibilities necessarily will be altered to fit the specific context and situation in which the research is being conducted. Hopefully, this will be driven by universal principles and the ethical obligations of international researchers to understand the host country's social, cultural, economic, and political milieux before embarking upon a study.

Development of an International Code of Research Ethics Involving Human Subjects

Over the years there have been various efforts to develop and codify a universal set of ethical principles governing the conduct of research with human subjects. The proposed guidelines often differ by the type of research being conducted (e.g., therapeutic versus non-therapeutic), the population involved (e.g., youth versus adults), and the locations in which studies are conducted (e.g., 'developing' versus 'developed' countries). A list of some of the more prominent efforts to develop universal standards for the ethical conduct of research is summarized in Table 2.1 along with the codes of selected countries. These are described briefly below.

The first internationally accepted codification concerning the ethical conduct of research emerged in 1947 following the Nuremberg Military Tribunal's verdict in the case *United States v. Karl Brandt et al.* Several of the German doctors accused of inhumane experimentation conducted during the war argued in their own defense that their experiments differed little from pre-war research conducted by American and German physicians and that no international laws or guidelines differentiating between legal and illegal experiments existed. This defense concerned Dr Andrew Ivy and Dr Leo Alexander, who were working with the U.S. counsel, and prompted them to develop six principles outlining legitimate research. According to their guidelines, humane experimentation is justified only if its results benefit society and it is conducted in accordance with basic principles that 'satisfy moral, ethical, and legal concepts.' Their original six points were revised into ten and contained in the verdict of the trail. These points became known as the 'Nuremberg Code' (1949) and were accepted worldwide, although the legal force of the document was never established. Among the ten points, the code required that human experimentation include voluntary informed consent and respect the right of the individual to control his/her own body. It also recognized that risk must be weighed against expected benefit, and

Table 2.1: International Guidelines for the Ethical Conduct of Research

Code	Author	Original Date of Issue	Dates of Revision/ Follow-up Reports
Nuremberg Code http://ohsr.od.nih.gov/guidelines/nuremberg.html	Nuremberg Military Tribunal	1947	NA
Declaration of Helsinki http://www.wma.net/e/policy/b3.htm	World Medical Association	1964	October 1975 October 1983 September 1989 October 1996 October 2000 2002 2004 October 2008
International Ethical Guidelines for Biomedical Research Involving Human Subjects http://www.cioms.ch/frame_guidelines_nov_2002.htm	Council for International Organizations of Medical Sciences (CIOMS)	1982	1993 2002
The Ethics of Research Related to Healthcare in Developing Countries http://www.nuffieldbioethics.org/go/ourwork/developingcountries/ publication_309.html	Nuffield Council on Bioethics	1999	2002 2005
International Compilation of Human Subject Research Protections www.hhs.gov/ohrp/international/HSPCompilation.pdf	Office for Human Research Protections, U.S. Dept. of Health and Human Services	2007	

that unnecessary pain and suffering must be avoided. Like many codes, Nuremberg did not provide specific procedures or processes to guide researchers in the implementation of these principles.

The Nuremberg Code has been largely superseded by the *Declaration of Helsinki* published by the World Medical Association (WMA, 1964) as the international guideline governing human subject research. The WMA believed that there was a need to provide physicians all over the world with guidelines for conducting biomedical research involving human subjects. The declaration is important in that it represented the first significant effort of the medical community to regulate itself. It also differed from the Nuremberg Code in that it drew an important distinction between therapeutic and non-therapeutic research. Like the Nuremburg Code, the declaration highlighted informed consent as the central requirement for ethical research while allowing for surrogate consent when the research participant is incompetent, physically or mentally incapable of giving consent, or a minor. The declaration also stated that research with the latter groups should be conducted only when that research is necessary to promote the health of the population represented and cannot be performed on legally competent persons. It further states that when the participant is legally incompetent but able to give consent to decisions about participation in research, assent must be obtained from the subject in addition to the consent of the legally authorized representative.

In 1993, following the *Declaration of Helsinki*, the Council for International Organizations of Medical Sciences (CIOMS), published the *International Ethical Guidelines for Biomedical Research Involving Human Subjects* indicating how the principles contained in the declaration could be effectively applied to research conducted in majority world countries. The CIOMS guidelines acknowledged the challenges associated with applying universal ethical principles in a complex world with vastly different resources. In 2002 the CIOMS revised, updated, and expanded these guidelines. The current document consists of twenty-one guidelines that address, among other issues:

• ethical justification and scientific validity of research
• ethical review
• informed consent
• vulnerability of individuals, groups, communities, and populations
• women as research subjects
• equity regarding burdens and benefits

- choice of control in clinical trials
- confidentiality
- compensation for injury
- strengthening of national or local capacity for ethical review
- obligations of sponsors to provide health care services

Each guideline is followed by interpretative commentaries. The guidelines are intended for use by countries in defining national policies on the ethics of biomedical research involving human participants, applying ethical standards in local circumstances, and establishing or improving ethical review mechanisms. The revised guidelines were updated to incorporate changes, advances, and controversies that have occurred in biomedical research ethics during preceding decades.

More recently, the Nuffield Council on Bioethics was established in 1991 to examine ethical issues raised by new developments in biology and medicine. The council is an independent body that includes clinicians, educators, lawyers, nurses, philosophers, scientists, and theologians. It is jointly funded by the Nuffield Foundation, the Medical Research Council of England, and the Wellcome Trust of England. It has achieved an international reputation, providing advice that assists policymaking, addresses public concerns, and stimulates debate in bioethics. The council issued a paper entitled *The Ethics of Research Related to Healthcare in Developing Countries* (2005) that provides an introductory exploration of key ethical issues related to conducting research in these countries. This document examined issues such as what treatment should be provided to participants after the research is completed and what constitutes 'standard care.' Although these issues are not confined to research in majority world countries, they tend to be exacerbated when limited resources are available, in countries where basic health care is not widely available, and where research ethics committees are often underdeveloped or absent.

The U.S. Department of Health and Human Services (DHHS), Office for Human Research Protections (2007) has published a useful compilation of human subjects research legislation, regulations, and/or guidelines for seventy-nine countries, two confederations (the European Union and the Commonwealth of Independent States), and several international organizations. The information was obtained from numerous published documents. Data were then verified using Internet searches. This compilation was created for ethics review boards, researchers, funding agencies, and others who are involved in international research, with the intent of familiarizing groups with laws, regulations, and guidelines relevant to research contexts, to ensure that those standards are followed appropriately.

Despite these efforts, the development of universal codes governing ethical conduct of research involving human participants remains difficult. Benatar (2002) notes that ethical requirements for conducting research in majority world countries have undergone considerable debate in recent years. Palys (1997), in his comments on Canada's Tri-Council Working Group's Code of Ethical Conduct for Research Involving Humans, for example, concluded that as written the code (1) might enhance protection for research participants in some areas but not others, (2) would allow some types of research to be conducted without unreasonable constraints but not others, and (3) would not provide an effective mechanism to review ethical requirements and enhance researchers' accountability.

Selected Country Codes Governing the Ethical Conduct of Human Subject Research

In this section we provide a brief summary of the ethical codes and regulations from selected countries including Australia, Canada, the United Kingdom, and the United States. For each country, we summarize the guiding principles for researchers governing ethical conduct of research and briefly review the codes in terms of specific regulations and/or policies focused on (1) research involving youth and (2) research conducted in international settings. The regulations for countries reviewed are listed in Table 2.2 along with information regarding the author, original date of issue, and dates of revisions to the codes.

United States

In the United States, the Belmont Report (National Commission for the Protection of Human Subjects of Biomedical and Behavioral Research, 1978) provides three general guiding principles governing human subject research. The first principle is respect for persons, implying that individuals should have autonomy and that persons with diminished autonomy are entitled to additional protections. For investigators interested in international research on resilience and well-being among youth, this principle requires them to assess developmental, contextual, and cultural factors together with how they affect youths'

Table 2.2: Specific Country Guidelines/Regulations for the Ethical Conduct of Research and Other Resources

Code	Author	Original Date of Issue	Dates of Revision/ Follow-up Reports
Code of Federal Regulations 45 CFR 46 (United States) http://ohsr.od.nih.gov/guidelines/45cfr46.html	Department of Health and Human Services	1974	1991 2005
National Statement on Ethical Conduct in Research Involving Humans (Australia) (replaced Statement on Human Experimentation and Supplemental Notes, 1992) http://www.nhmrc.gov.au/publications/synopses/e3 5syn.htm	National Health and Medical Research Council	1999 2001	
Human Research Ethics Handbook http://www.nhmrc.gov.au/publications/synopses/e4 2syn.htm		2003	
Values and Ethics: Guidelines for Ethical Conduct in Aboriginal and Torres Strait Islander Health Research (replaced Guidelines on Ethical Matters in Aboriginal and Torres Strait Islander Health Research, 2003) http://www.nhmrc.gov.au/publications/synopses/e52syn.htm			
Code of Conduct for Research Involving Humans (Canada) http://www.ethics.ubc.ca/code/	Tri-Council Working Group	1997	2000 2002 2005 2008
Research Ethics Framework (United Kingdom) www.esrc.ac.uk/ESRCInfoCentre/Images/ESRC_Re _Ethics_ Frame_tcm6-11291.pdf	Economic & Social Science Research Council	2005	

capacity to fully understand the study protocol and make an informed decision regarding their participation. The second principle, benefi-cence, implies that persons should be treated in an ethical manner, not only by respecting their decisions and protecting them from harm, but also by making efforts to secure their well-being. Given the potential vulnerabilities of youth who have experienced trauma, researchers' evaluation of potential risks can be challenging (Thompson, 1992) and should take into account factors such as the age of the participant, the recency and severity of the trauma, what service the youth has received, and his/her coping skills. The third principle is justice and acknowledges that people should be treated equally and thus share the burdens and benefits associated with research. In international studies of resilience, researchers have particular obligations towards youth, who are most vulnerable and unable to protect their own interests. Investigators must ensure that they are not exploited for the advance-ment of knowledge.

The specific regulations that these principles embody are contained in the Code of Federal Regulations, Title 45 Part 46, detailing the pro-tection of human participants. Part A of these regulations is also known as the Common Rule, given that they have been adopted by all U.S. federal agencies as the standards governing research with human subjects. Subpart D of these regulations is specific to youth, defined as persons who have not attained the legal age for consent to treatments or procedures involved in research, under the applicable law of the jurisdiction in which the research will be conducted. Thus studies involving youth require consent from the youth's parent(s) or guardian, in addition to the youth's agreement to participate in research. There are, however, no specific federal regulations devoted to research conducted in international settings. Given that the application of the requirements of parental consent and youth assent can be extremely difficult if not impossible in conducting international studies of youth resilience, investigators need to work closely with their research ethics review boards to ensure that the consent proce-dures used balance the principles of respecting youth and protecting them from potential risks.

Australia

The *National Statement on Ethical Conduct in Research Involving Humans* is Australia's set of ethical principles governing the conduct of human subject research (National Health and Medical Research Council, 1999, 2001). It was developed by the Australian Health Ethics Committee, a principal committee of the National Health and Medical Research Council. The overall purpose of the *National Statement* is to protect the welfare and rights of research participants and to promote research that is, or will be, of benefit to the researcher's community or to humankind. The *National Statement* contains four overarching principles governing ethical conduct of human research: (1) respect for persons, (2) research merit and integrity, (3) balancing benefits and risks in research, and (4) justice. The *National Statement* also contains specific guidance for research involving particular kinds of participants, such as young people, and research involving aboriginal and Torres Strait Islander peoples.

The guidelines specific to youth acknowledge the importance and unique role of youth in research, given that information gathered from other individuals often cannot answer questions specific to youth. The guidelines highlight the importance of research methods that are appropriate for young people and that ensure their physical, emotional, and psychological safety. The guidelines also require that consent be obtained from parents/guardians 'in all but exceptional circumstances' as well as from the young participant whenever he or she has sufficient competence to make this decision. Finally, the guidelines state that a young person's refusal to participate in a research project must be respected. These guidelines reflect Panter-Brick's (2002) review and critique of research on street youth. She argues that the existing research often inadequately represents the experiences of youth, frequently uses labels that are stigmatizing to youth, and is conducted from a vantage point that is too limited in scope and results in calls for action that are too limited in focus.

Although the *National Statement* contains no specific guidelines governing research conducted in international settings, it does include specific guidelines governing research conducted within aboriginal and Torres Strait Islander communities, which have relevance to research conducted in international settings. These guidelines are detailed in a document titled *Values and Ethics: Guidelines for Ethical Conduct in Aboriginal and Torres Strait Islander Health Research* (National Health and Medical Research Council, 2003). Requirements contained in the document promote researchers' substantive engagement with aboriginal and Torres Strait Islander communities in ways that are respectful and inclusive of their values and cultures. The document details six values and principles central to ethical research: (1) reci-

procity, (2) respect, (3) equality, (4) responsibility, (5) survival and protection, and (6) spirit and integrity. A community guide has been
developed to support the effective use of these guidelines in research
with aboriginal and Torres Strait Islander communities. The guide sets
out strategies available to assist researchers in the practical application
of these guidelines.

Canada

In 2005, the Canadian Tri-Council issued an updated policy statement
regarding ethical conduct for research involving humans. This policy
statement identifies eight guiding principles for researchers, based in
part on 'statements from the international community' (p. i.5): (1)
respect for human dignity, (2) respect for free and informed consent,
(3) respect for vulnerable persons, (4) respect for privacy and confidentiality, (5) respect for justice and inclusiveness, (6) balancing harm
and benefit, (7) minimizing harm, and (8) maximizing benefit. These
principles are consistent with those from other countries and from
international entities.

Although the Tri-Council policy statement does not contain a specific section related to youth in research, they are considered within the
category of vulnerable persons. Accordingly, youth are afforded
special protections against exploitation, abuse, and discrimination that
are 'often translated into special procedures to protect their interests'
(p. i.5). The section on inclusion, however, clearly states that the exclusion of potential study participants on the basis of age is unacceptable
'unless there is a valid reason for doing so' (p. 5.2).

The policy statement also includes a section specific to research
involving aboriginal peoples that has potentially important implications
for international research. The policy recognizes that aboriginal individuals 'have a unique interest in ensuring that accurate and informed
research concerning heritage customs and communities' (p. 6.2) is conducted. Given this, researchers and Research Ethic Boards (REBs)
should give special consideration as to whether the community is sufficiently engaged in the research to ensure these obligations are met.

United Kingdom

The *Research Ethics Framework* was established by the Economic and
Social Research Council (2005) to guide researchers in the United
Kingdom, ensuring that research involving humans is conducted

using the highest ethical standards. Like most ethical guidelines, the framework is based on six key principles: (1) integrity and quality, (2) full disclosure, (3) protection of confidentiality, (4) voluntary participation, (5) avoidance of harm, and (6) independence of the research from conflicts of interest.

With respect to issues involving youth in research, section 1.1.2 notes that such research would typically be considered as research involving greater than minimal risk. The guidelines further emphasize that researchers should use every effort to ensure consent is received through dialogue with both the youth and his/her parents.

Section 1.14.8 of the framework focuses on research conducted outside the U.K. In short, researchers are required to determine if local ethics reviews are needed and how issues such as inequities in research resources and political and cultural considerations should be handled within an international context.

A Synthesis of Ethical Issues

Balancing Inclusion and Exclusion of Youth

Ethical transgressions against youth throughout history have created shifts in moral discourse and emerging ethical positions on whether youth should be included, may be included, or–a more recent positioning–must be included in research. This section is organized into six areas that reflect this shifting terrain: (1) evolving perceptions of the status of youth as they emerge from the historic roots of exploitation in research; (2) the need for protection and governance; (3) justifications for the inclusion of young people in research; (4) necessary justification for exclusion; (5) challenges and considerations of customs and legalities of a society, and disparities of power that create a potential for exploitation; and (6) the perceived benefit of the voices of youth being included in research.

VARIANCES IN THE STATUS OF YOUTH AND THEIR EXPLOITATION

A society's construction of childhood and youth determines perceptions of the status or position of youth as either dependent and vulnerable or autonomous and competent (Shemmings, 2000). These differences in perception affect how youth are viewed in regard to participation in research. Scholars of young people are typically proponents of one of two perspectives: (1) a developmental lens focusing on judgments or perceptions of the youth's cognitive abilities and social competencies; or (2) a broader social-theoretical lens that views childhood and youth through a collective and contextual perspective (Bogolub & Thomas, 2005) wherein the youth functions with agency (Cocks, 2006). Four research approaches developing from these two perspectives are evidenced in studies where the youth is seen as either the object, the subject, the social actor, or the participant and co-researcher (Christensen & Prout, 2002).

The inclusion of youth in research as object or subject is evidenced by numerous historical studies that unfortunately, and all too often, exploited youth, offering few benefits and heavy burdens (Meaux & Bell, 2001). During the nineteenth century, for example, institutional-ized youth were intentionally infected with microbes of leprosy, syphilis, gonorrhea, and tuberculosis in order to develop diagnostic measures and vaccines for these diseases (Meaux & Bell, 2001). In the 1930s thousands of young people, volunteered by their parents, died after being administered live polio virus as a method of testing the new vaccine. In spite of the American Public Health Association's real-ization that youth needed to be protected as research subjects, such experiments continued to occur through the 1970s. The Willowbrook State Hospital Study in New York, in which children were intention-ally infected with hepatitis in order to develop a vaccine, is yet another example of exploitation of youth in research (Meaux & Bell, 2001). Pediatrician William Silverman described this perception of youth as the property of parents or institutions as the 'ethos of the time' (Attitudes and Practices 1944–1974 section, Department of Energy [DOE], 1994).

THE NEED FOR PROTECTION AND GOVERNANCE
Despite the fact that internationally accepted standards for protecting subjects while conducting research were established as early as 1947 with the Nuremberg Military Tribunal, and later by the *Declaration of Helsinki* in 1964, misuse of human subjects in research continued. Con-sequently, in the United States for example, the National Commission for the Protection of Human Subjects of Biomedical and Behavioral Research (1978) was charged with identifying basic principles and guidelines that should be followed to ensure that research is con-ducted in accordance with ethical principles. The principles of the resulting Belmont Report required research including youth to demon-strate respect of persons, balance of risk and benefit, and justice or

fairness in the distribution of burden and benefits (Meaux & Bell, 2001).

Another important shift in regard to the governance of research with youth was not seen until 1989, at the United Nation's Convention on the Rights of the Child (Cocks, 2006). Scientists in the international research community began viewing young people less as dependents and property and more as competent agents participating in a broader social context (Bogolub & Thomas, 2005). This is reflected in the development of Article 12, which states: 'Parties shall ensure to the child who is capable of forming his or her own views the right to express those views freely in all matters affecting the child, the views of the child being given due weight in accordance with the age and maturity of the child.'

JUSTIFICATION FOR INCLUSION
In the face of historical horrors committed on young people as objects or subjects in research, there remains powerful justification for including youth in research. Exclusion of youth can limit our ability to detect important differences between youth and adults, which in turn can lead to incorrect assumptions and conclusions. Exclusions lead to biases in the knowledge base that create a form of 'manufactured ignorance' around a particular concern; excluded youth become like 'therapeutic orphans' (Leonard et al., 1996). The excluded are unable to derive the benefits of advancements in science and potential treatment options, as is evident in the current paucity of research on the effectiveness of psychopharmacology in youth (Hoagwood, Jensen, & Fisher, 1996).

For example, in the United States, the American Academy of Pediatrics raised concerns that only a small fraction of all drugs marketed in that country had had clinical trials performed in pediatric patients and limited scientific evaluation of treatments (National Institutes of Health [NIH], 1998). Accordingly, the NIH issued guidelines and a policy mandate for the inclusion of young people in research unless there is a strong and explicit justification for not doing so, in order to produce adequate data to inform medical treatments for disorders and conditions of childhood. Similarly, article 5.1(a) of the Tri-Council policy statement notes that researchers should not exclude individuals on the basis, of among other attributes, age (Canadian Tri-Council Working Group, 2005).

While these policies promote the inclusion of youth in research, their focus is primarily on youth participating in intervention studies where they may receive some direct benefit. Although they clearly permit youths' participation in research involving minimal risk, even when there is no direct benefit to that group, other regulations governing the conduct of human subject research designate youth as a 'vulnerable population' and provide them with additional protections (DHHS, 2001, 45 CFR 46).

Despite the United States' federal policy on the inclusion of youth in research, a ruling by the Maryland Court of Appeals concluded that parents cannot consent to the participation of their minor children in research that posed even minimal risk of harm if the research was 'non-therapeutic' and offered no direct benefit to the youth (*Grimes v. Kennedy Krieger Institute*, 2001). Although the court subsequently clarified its ruling, making it more consistent with existing federal regulations (Mastroianni & Kahn, 2002), the case exemplifies the tension between the goals of science and the protection of participants from risk (Glantz, 2002).

By contrast, in an effort to improve the delivery of services to British youth, the United Kingdom formalized a document within the Children's Act of 2004, entitled 'Every Child Matters.' The goal of this initiative is to champion the interests and concerns of young people through research and provide an arena to promote the voices of youth (Cocks, 2006).

JUSTIFICATIONS FOR EXCLUSIONS

In the United States, the NIH (1998) guidelines stipulate that youth be included in all research involving human subjects unless one or more of the following exclusionary circumstances are demonstrated:

- The research topic to be studied is irrelevant to youth.
- The level of risk is higher than is permitted for young people.
- The knowledge being sought in the research is already available for youth and would be redundant.
- A separate, age-specific study in youth is warranted and preferable.
- The disease or disorder is relatively rare in youth, as compared to adults.
- The number of youth is limited because the majority are already

accessed by a nationwide pediatric disease research network, so that requiring inclusion of youth in the proposed adult study would be both difficult and unnecessary.

- Issues of study design preclude direct applicability of hypotheses and/or interventions to both adults and youth (including different cognitive, developmental, or disease stages or different age-related metabolic processes).
- Insufficient data are available in adults to judge potential risk in youth.
- Study designs are aimed at collecting additional data on pre-enrolled adult study participants (e.g., longitudinal follow-up studies that did not include data on young people).

The underlying premise justifying exclusion of youth is based on the principles of justice or fairness in the distribution of burden and benefits. As such, subjects who do not have vulnerabilities should be recruited and asked to assume the risks of research. The Canadian Tri-Council policy statement, although not specifically detailing exceptions, does note that the stated ethical imperative for inclusion of youth in research must be interpreted in the context of the safeguards related to the youth's competence and ability to freely assent (Canadian Tri-Council Working Group, 2005). An argument against these positions is noted by researchers in the United Kingdom and Europe, embracing the personalization of ethics and responsibility of social scientists to give voice to people (Christensen & Prout, 2002). These authors propose that symmetrical strategies be employed for both youth and adults. Research designs and methodologies utilized for adult subjects are contextualized in the 'adult world' with an emphasis on selection and exclusion. The counterpart are methods for youth adapted to the 'child's world' with an emphasis on inclusion and in line with youths' interests, experiences, values, and daily lives (Christensen & Prout, 2002). The challenge for researchers to practise inclusion that is age sensitive and reflexive is not unlike the ethical responsibility of providing accommodations for special needs or various cultural differences in adult populations. Strategies or methodologies that are *youth-led*–such as using a tape recorder where the youth may pretend to be on the radio, or photo dairies using disposable cameras where the participant would be documenting the world around him/her–are examples of research activities that diminish imposition of adult frameworks (Young & Barrett, 2001).

CHALLENGES AND ETHICAL CONSIDERATIONS

The three general considerations in developing requirements for including minors in research are: (1) minors do not have legal capacity to consent; (2) children and adolescents may have difficulty understanding the research process; and (3) youth may perceive that they lack power to refuse to participate (Putnam, Liss, & Landsverk, 1996). Ungar and Liebenberg (2005) expanded these ethical concerns after a team of international researchers reported on issues they confronted during studies of youth exposed to high risk and adversity. These authors note the following areas: (1) confidentiality and safety; (2) obtaining consent; (3) coercion; and (4) review of the research locally by an ethics board. Perhaps the issues of confidentiality and safety are the most critical when considering the inclusion of youth in the majority world facing instances of war, gang, or tribal conflicts (Ungar & Liebenberg, 2005). The potential for retaliation against participants for colluding with outsiders or disclosing personal stories is an area of great ethical concern for those working with individuals who live day to day in areas with high levels of exposure to violence. There are additional concerns for those vulnerable to psychological, medical, economic, and social difficulties, with a potential for re-traumatization or increased stigmatization (Newman & Kaloupek, 2004).

Alderson (1995) offers further considerations when researching youth with additional vulnerabilities, emphasizing the importance of avoiding the harm of exploitation, but also raises concern for the magnitude of harm being done by protecting youth so much that they are silenced and excluded from benefit. The problem of harm and exploitation remains when working with special populations of youth who are generally socially excluded from the dominant culture. This is seen in a study of youth who are both hearing and visually impaired. Here, a researcher reported that staff had noted how a youth flourished during the project, achieving a level of friendship and intimacy rarely experienced. Once the project was completed and the researcher gone, the participant regressed into a place of distance again (Cocks, 2006). Cocks presents similar concerns regarding exclusion in her own studies with autistic youth, where assent was acknowledged by staff caring for youth. In one particular instance, staff had noted that the youth was typically aggressive and would abruptly remove himself from the area and not look at an outsider. The staff operationalized assent of the youth as evidenced by (1) remaining close, and (2) sharing a beloved object with the researcher. These examples bring to light the need for balance of risk and benefit where the potential of exploitation for research purposes exists.

BENEFITS OF INCLUSION: THE VOICES OF YOUTH

In their effort to embrace the complexities of human issues, researchers can gain much from the voices of youth, which offer us insight to their experience and a developmental perspective of our current world problems. Grover (2003) highlights the importance of youth voices in a Save the Children study (Donnestad & Sanner, 2001) conducted in Norway involving 100 youth in the child welfare system. The final outcry, and title, of this study was: 'Hello, is anyone there – someone who can help us bring about some change?' Grover notes that excluding youth perspectives in research may perpetuate representations imposed upon them by adults, especially in those youth who are marginalized due to status.

In summary, it is important to recognize that assumptions made about the capability of youths are primarily determined by the dominant construction of childhood and adolescence in a society (Bogolub & Thomas, 2005). These assumptions are further clouded by the horizontal contextual factors of power differentials between the psycho/medical community and the researched (Draucker, 1999).

There is evidence that withholding the opportunity of inclusion in research participation and excluding youths' perspective not only maintains biases in the knowledge base, but also adds to misrepresentations about youth imposed upon them by adults. Exclusion not only violates the principle of autonomy, but also disallows direct benefits received through therapeutic studies and the advancements of science, as well as indirect benefits from sharing information that may help others (Newman & Kaloupek, 2004).

Finally, perhaps the two most challenging aspects for researchers in practising inclusion of youth from varying contexts of adversity lies in, first, providing for their safety and confidentiality after disclosure and participation, and second, selecting the strategies and procedures to be used in terminating research with those socially marginalized due to disabilities or social position. Both of these challenging areas require close examination of the potential long-term implications for youth involved in research.

Balancing Risk and Benefit

As previously noted, one of the foundational principles detailed in the Belmont Report concerns beneficence–the researchers' obligations to protect participants from harm. Although risk is often thought of only in terms of physical risks, such as drug side effects that might occur during clinical trials, there are other types of risk that are more relevant to mental and behavioural health research. For example, research in these areas is likely to more often present legal risks to research participants, such as possible arrest or prosecution that could result from disclosure of criminal activity or issues of abuse and victimization. Research participants could also experience social risks, such as stigma resulting from participation in studies related to mental illness. Finally, there can be psychological risks such as stress or anxiety that could result from being asked sensitive questions.

This section explains the concepts of 'minimal risk' and 'benefit,' the risk/benefit ratio, adverse reactions to psychological risks, persistence of distress, participant perceptions of risks, and finally, their desire to participate in future studies.

MINIMAL RISK

Minimal risk is defined in 45 CFR 46.102(i) 'as the probability and magnitude of harm or discomfort to the subject anticipated in the research are not greater in and of themselves than those ordinarily encountered in daily life' (DHHS, 2001). This definition closely parallels the definition of minimal risk detailed in section C1 of the Canadian Tri-Council policy statement (Canadian Tri-Council Working Group, 2005). Risk consists of two components: (1) the probability or prevalence of risk and (2) the magnitude or severity of the risk. Probability concerns the likelihood that a certain event will occur, while magnitude refers to the seriousness of harm should it occur. Consent disclosures in social/behavioural sciences seldom include specific details about the prevalence or magnitude of psychological risks. One reason for this is that little is known about the probability and severity of these risks. Hoagwood, Jensen, and Fisher (1996) note that one challenge faced by researchers is the paucity of literature regarding what constitutes harm to youth and how to adequately evaluate it. In the social and behavioural sciences, information has not been routinely collected from study participants about their experiences and is therefore not readily available (Boothroyd & Best, 2003). As Boothroyd (2000) points out, 'few investigators have specifically examined the emotional reactions experienced by study participants' (p. 213) when responding to the kinds of questions often included in mental and behavioural health studies.

A second reason for the failure to include information on risks in consent forms is that participation in behavioural and social science research is generally considered by most to constitute minimal risk. Herjanic, Hudson, and Kotloff (1976) attempted to establish guidelines for assessing the risks involved in administering structured interviews to youth. Follow-up surveys completed by parents and youth led them to conclude the risks were low; approximately one in sixty-three. Professional organizations have attempted to provide guidance to investigators studying youth. For example, the Society for Research in Child Development (SRCD, 2002) stipulates that investigators are obligated always to use the least stressful research procedure. Although the SRDC acknowledges that psychological harm is difficult to define, they maintain that investigators are nonetheless responsible for defining and determining means for reducing or eliminating any possible harm.

Given that research on resilience involves youth who have experienced adversity, these studies may not meet the requirements associated with minimal risk studies and thus will be reviewed closely by research ethics boards.

BENEFIT

The second Belmont principle is beneficence. Major principles of research explicated in the World Medical Association's *Declaration of Helsinki* (1964, 2004) states: 'research involving human subjects cannot legitimately be carried out unless the importance of the objective is in proportion to the inherent risk to the subject.' The guiding principles from this document are that research must have sufficient importance, scientific soundness, respect for autonomy, beneficence, utility, and justice (King & Churchill, 2000).

The two general rules used to operationalize the principle of benefit are: (1) do not harm, and (2) maximize possible benefits and minimize possible harms. Under this principle, researchers are not only obligated to protect research participants from harm, but are also responsible for enhancing subjects' well-being when they knowingly are in a position to do so with minimal risk, inconvenience, or expense. The primary argument or justification for allowing a minimal level of risk in research relates to potential benefits. Direct benefits to participants may be seen in clinical trials where participation in a treatment may bring beneficial results to the involved participant. Indirect benefits from participation are the expected contributions of research findings to the well-being of others in the future.

RISK-BENEFIT RATIO

As previously stated, minimal risk is defined in 45 CFR 46.102(i) 'as the probability and magnitude of harm or discomfort to the subject antic-ipated in the research are not greater in and of themselves than those ordinarily encountered in daily life or during the performance of routine physical or psychological examinations or tests' (DHHS, 2001). The difficulty with this definition is that the reference to daily life does not take into consideration a reference point for 'whose daily life' (Glantz, 2002): a 'street child' growing up in São Paulo, Brazil, or a youth living in Bearsden, one of the most affluent areas of Glasgow, Scotland? The interpretation of this could expose certain research par-ticipants living in environments with greater exposures to health hazards to greater risk than those living in more benign environments (Wendler et al., 2005).

Furthermore, the idea of what constitutes risk has recently been challenged. In the U.S. legal case of *Grimes v. Kennedy Krieger Insti-tute*, the issue of an acceptable level of risk for non-therapeutic research involving youth for the purpose of potential benefits to the broader public's health has brought to light ethical concerns of exploitation (Mastroianni & Kahn, 2002). The courts attempted to clarify risk as 'any articulable risk beyond the minimal kind of risk that is inherent in any endeavor' (Glantz, 2002). To offer further clar-ification of minimal risk in the absence of empirical data, an analy-sis of physical risks present in the daily lives of youth was con-ducted, utilizing a cumulative index of risk, based on participation in sports activities, and mortality, based on average amounts of car travel, bathing, and swimming. The data revealed that daily life poses up to a 1 in 250 risk of injury and 1 in 100,000 risk of mortal-ity for youth in the United States aged fifteen to nineteen years of age (Wendler et al., 2005). Even with this analysis many institutional review boards still categorize studies as posing more than minimal risk, although most studies do not pose the risk of an average daily life as quantified above (Wendler et al., 2005). These issues are cer-tainly germane to the international study of youth and resilience, as most resilience research is non-therapeutic in design and by defini-tion involve youth who experience adversity. This underscores the need for continued research to better understand the magnitude and prevalence of risk and the overall impact of non-therapeutic research on participants.

PSYCHOLOGICAL AND EMOTIONAL RISK: ADVERSE EMOTIONAL REACTIONS

There is a small but growing literature summarizing the type and degree of emotional risk experienced by participants in response to studies asking sensitive questions about sexual behaviours, substance abuse, and victimization (Henderson & Jorm, 1990; Jacomb et al., 1999; Jorm et al., 1994; Turnbull et al., 1988; Zimmerman et al., 1994). Boothroyd's (2000) synthesis of these studies suggests about 2% of respondents became depressed, about 5% experienced some level of distress, and nearly 13% felt uncomfortable being asked personal questions. By contrast, in a series of studies reported by Wendler and colleagues (2005) on 6,064 youth ranging from age five through eighteen years, approximately 27% report sometimes feeling scared or afraid in daily life, with 26% worrying about what will happen to them.

PERSISTENCE IN DISTRESS OVER TIME

There are even fewer studies on minors experiencing distress following disclosure of information on sensitive issues. Existing data do suggest that youth disclosing information on one-time maltreatment experience less distress than those reporting long-standing incestuous relationships, where 25% remain symptomatic for weeks to months after disclosure (Putnam, Liss, & Landsverk, 1996). There is also limited research on long-term effects of adult disclosure of adverse childhood experiences. A six-year follow-up study found that 31% of participants reported having a negative experience at the time of interview, but that at the time of follow-up only 2% still reported a negative experience (Martin et al., 2001).

PARTICIPANTS' PERSPECTIVES ON RISK/BENEFIT RATIO

Newman and Kaloupek (2004) found that trauma exposed participants reported both direct and indirect benefits from participating in the research. Direct benefits described by participants include the usefulness of reflecting on previous experiences and lasting relief, as well as the development of insight from processing traumatic events or other life challenges. Mishna and colleagues (2004), for example, discuss the practical benefit youth experience in a study conducted by Mauthner in 1997 on bullying. Because the construct of being a victim of bullying was not very developed at the time, definitions of non-physical forms of violence and direct forms were discussed during the study. Participants reported feeling empowered after understanding what constitutes bullying and the sequela accompanying such exposures.

An indirect benefit includes participants' perceptions regarding the importance and meaningfulness of contributing to research that may benefit others. A participant in a study of single teenage daughters of mothers on welfare, for example, noted the potential future benefit for other teenagers: 'They need a study like this. Study needs to be continued so that us [teenage girls] can help the girls behind us/the next generation, to stay off of Welfare' (Best & Boothroyd, under review). Here we see the anticipation of benefit, and an expectation that the power differential can be bridged with care and information. The comment reflects participants' beliefs surrounding researchers' access to power to right the wrongs and to utilize research to improve the living situations of women and youth.

WHAT IS THE LIKELIHOOD OF FUTURE STUDY PARTICIPATION?
As a likely proxy for perception of benefit outweighing risk for participants, we propose exploring participant interest in future participation. There is currently limited empirical evidence concerning why participants may be likely to continue to participate in longitudinal studies. Yet, such information would certainly suggest perceived benefits by participants and thus a motivation to participate in future studies. Best and Boothroyd (under review) found, in a recent study assessing adverse emotional reactions to research, that of those participants (58%) reporting any adverse emotional reaction, 89% stated they would participate in future studies.

A combination of both direct and indirect benefits was found when participants reported that it was useful to reflect on previous experiences because reflection provided a lasting sense of relief and contributed to the development of insight from processing traumatic events or other life challenges, and cited the meaningfulness of contributing to research that may benefit others (Newman & Kaloupek, 2004).

The potential confounder is a perceived therapeutic effect from participation generated by having an opportunity to talk to someone outside of family members about distressing events (Mahon et al., 1996). Certainly, there is no justification for utilizing research as a means for participants to experience a potential therapeutic effect; nevertheless, there are indications that both adults and youth participating in research perceive potential access to power with which to make right the wrongs they have been exposed to as well as noting therapeutic benefit (Mahon et al., 1996). For example, Walker and colleagues (1997) found that female trauma survivors, knowing what the survey experience was like, would in retrospect indeed participate again in the study. Similarly, a study of acute physical and sexual assault victims reported that they would be quite willing to participate in a similar study in the future (Griffin et al., 2003).

This section has emphasized the importance of balancing risk and benefit without discounting participants' perceptions of benefit and distress. Utilizing the self-report of participants' desire to participate in future studies and reports of both direct and indirect benefits permits further understanding regarding how to balance this equation.

Practising beneficence when conducting research must include such things as conveying information on important findings to research participants during the study, as well as any unintended negative outcomes or risks. Research should also be sensitive to potential motivations for participation, as in a therapeutic effect from establishing an alliance with an outsider with potentially more power. An illustration of this would be researchers providing disposable cameras to street youth to develop a photo dairy. Young and Barrett (2001) discuss the perceived benefits of fun research activities for Kampala street youth who developed a plan for economic gain: they reported wanting to sell the photographs or parts of the camera.

Informed Consent/Assent

HISTORICAL VIEW

'Informed consent' has been a hallmark of ethics in research for centuries; however, a more formal focus on consent to research is a relatively recent phenomenon. The Nazi research atrocities documented by the Nuremburg trials were able to occur because principles of informed consent for research were not as deeply ingrained in our modern culture as we might have liked to believe. The trials ultimately prompted Andrew Ivy's 'Nuremburg Code' that placed much emphasis on the right of individuals to control their own bodies, and which was incorporated into the judgment by the war crimes tribunal at Nuremberg. The first Nuremburg principle lays out the basic requirements of valid informed consent:

> 1. The voluntary consent of the human subject is absolutely essential. This means that the person involved should have legal capacity to give consent; should be so situated as to be able to exercise free power of choice, without the intervention of any element of force, fraud, deceit, duress, over-reaching, or other ulterior form of constraint or coercion; and should have sufficient knowledge and comprehension of the elements of the subject matter involved as to enable him to make an understanding and enlightened decision. (Nuremberg Code, 1949)

These three requirements continue to be widely accepted today around the world and are often referred to as 'knowledge', 'voluntariness,' and 'capacity.' If informed consent is necessary in a particular situation and any of the three requirements is not met, the consent is considered to be not valid.

KNOWLEDGE

For consent to be 'knowledgeable,' there must be (1) a reasonable and full disclosure of the purpose, benefits, risks, and consequences of providing consent and (2) appropriate understanding or comprehension of the disclosure. The mode or method of disclosing information can be quite broad, including verbal (e.g., written documents or active discussion), visual (e.g., videos or pictograph documents), and experiential (e.g., walking a potential subject through the research process). The content of the disclosure should provide enough information for the potential participant to make a truly informed decision (or, as the Nuremberg Code suggests, an 'enlightened decision'). The 'Common Rule' (US federal regulations governing the protection of human subjects – 45 CFR 46) (DHHS, 1991) lists several specific elements to include in the information disclosure (see discussion of the federal rules below), including reasonably foreseeable risks, potential benefits, alternatives to participation in the research, confidentiality of research records, compensation for participation, clarification that participation is voluntary, and contact information to answer questions.

Consent is not just a document or information, however; it is a process through which a potential research participant makes an informed decision whether or not to participate in the research proposed. Thus, disclosure of information is only half the requirement for the knowledge element of informed consent. The information not only must be disclosed but must be understood or comprehended by the research participants or their proxies (e.g., parents or guardians). The disclosures must be communicated in an understandable manner or mode, in the language appropriate to the potential participant (or, for youth, their parent or guardian). A wonderful presentation of the consent information may be provided, but if the potential subject does not comprehend the information, then any 'consent' or agreement to participate is invalid. There are many techniques designed to increase understanding of consent disclosures, such as enhancement of the consent form or material (e.g., making sure that the reading grade level is at an appropriate level and creating graphical enhancements to the standard consent form) and improvement of the consent process (e.g., providing a third-party facilitator to improve understanding and training persons obtaining consent to be more sensitive to comprehension issues). Many investigators also now use a 'quiz' approach to assess whether a potential subject is making an informed decision – if they don't do well on a brief quiz about the disclosures, then they likely don't understand what they are agreeing to.

VOLUNTARINESS

The 'voluntariness' element of consent is often misunderstood as a fairly simple concept. Making sure that someone is not forced into participating in research would seem pretty straightforward. Particularly with youth subjects, forcing a parent to agree to include their child in research would be easy to recognize, right? Not necessarily.

Coercion and perceived coercion are often very subtle and not obvious to the outside observer. Furthermore, coercion is pervasive in all societies, and researchers must be sensitive to it during the consent process. Sometimes it can be a friend or relative's influence (e.g., 'Come on grandma, it's just a little test ...'), or it can lie in the circumstances of how the consent is obtained (e.g., youth in juvenile detention may agree to many things they would otherwise refuse to do if they were not incarcerated). It can be the provision of compensation that makes participation too rewarding financially to refuse (e.g., offering poor individuals $25 to complete a ten-minute survey). Or it could be the researchers re-asking for participation multiple times until a potential subject 'gives in' (e.g., some say that the 'Dillman method' [Dillman, 1978] of multiple survey waves is coercive or even harassment). The bottom line is that all researchers must use good judgment in assessing whether a particular agreement to participate is the product of coercion. The legal systems of most countries refuse to recognize or enforce actions that are the product of coercion or force (Reisner, Slobogan, & Rai, 1999). If a person would not have participated had the coercion not been present, that calls into question whether the consent is truly voluntary and valid.

The Willowbrook State School hepatitis study (Goldby, 1972), mentioned above, exemplifies questionable voluntariness in research. In an attempt to develop a vaccine for hepatitis, researchers purposely infected over seven hundred institutionalized youth with mental retardation with hepatitis. Early subjects were fed extracts of stools from infected youth, and later subjects received injections of purified virus preparations. The study was scientifically approved, because hepatitis was rampant in the institution and the youth would likely contract it anyways – thus it would be better for them to be infected under carefully controlled research conditions. Parents consented to their children's participation, so the study seemed non-coercive. However, admission to Willowbrook State School was closed due to overcrowding, and many parents could have their children admitted to the school only if they consented to their participation in the study. In addition, consenting parents were told that their children were receiving a vaccine for hepatitis, and were not well informed of the possible health risks to the youth.

CAPACITY

To satisfy the 'capacity' or 'competence' element, a person must possess the capacity to receive, comprehend, and utilize information provided to make a decision about research participation. By definition (see 'age of consent' below), youth do not possess the capacity to validly consent – thus their parents or other legally recognized representative must provide consent before a young person can be enrolled in a study (unless consent has been waived). Generally, in order for a decision to be competent, the person making the decision should be able to (1) understand relevant information about the decision; (2) appreciate the situation and the consequences of accepting or declining to participate; (3) manipulate information rationally ('weigh' the information); and (4) communicate a choice (Grisso & Appelbaum, 1995a, 1995b).

The principle of informed consent is reflected in all published national and international codes, regulations, and guidelines pertaining to research ethics (National Bioethics Advisory Commission, 1998). Even resource-poor countries recognize the importance of consent in the research process. However, there are also cultural considerations that are related to the capacity element of consent. For example, some cultures believe that consent should only be provided by a village elder and not the actual villager who is engaged in the research. The village elder acts on the behalf of the other villagers similar to the way a parent acts on behalf of a young person or a proxy decision maker can act on behalf of another person who does not have the capacity to consent. Such cultural considerations need to be explored and included in the consent process.

FEDERAL RULES ON CONSENT

Federal regulations in the United States (i.e., 45 CFR 46) as well as those found in the Tri-Council policy statement (Canadian Tri-Council Working Group, 2005) offer a framework for providing adequate disclosure of information to research subjects so that a knowledgeable decision can be made. They also provide for waiver of all or portions of the consent elements as well as documentation of consent. Finally, both the U.S. federal regulations and the Tri-Council policy statement provide for specific protections for youth, including guidelines regarding assent. The requirements of the U.S. federal regulations are to be followed by every institution that accepts federal research funds and thus has an Institutional Review Board (IRB). Similar requirements exist in Canada regarding reviews by Research Ethics Boards (REBs). However, because of the widespread use of concepts contained in the rules, these regulations are essentially the minimum standard of care that researchers (at least in the United States) must follow – whether the rules officially apply or not. Many regulatory schemes in other countries follow similar frameworks.

At a minimum, the U.S. federal regulations require the following be disclosed: a statement of research (the purpose of the research); a description of the risks; a description of the benefits; alternative treatments (if any); a description of confidentiality safeguards; a description of compensation (if any) and assistance if injured; contact information (for questions, concerns, etc); and a statement of voluntariness (e.g., no penalty for non-participation). Furthermore, the regulations list several more types of information that should be disclosed, if appropriate (e.g., any danger to pregnant women, consequences of withdrawal, the approximate number of subjects, etc). If any of the above elements are not to be disclosed in the consent process, or if consent is not going to be obtained at all, a waiver or alteration of the consent elements may be obtained from the IRB provided appropriate justification is documented (DHHS, 1991, 45 CFR 46.116).

There is a concept in the children's research literature referred to as 'passive consent' (see, for example, Carroll-Lind et al., 2006). The idea is that rather than obtaining formal active consent from parents or guardians, a researcher can send a notice to parents, and if a parent does not object or actively 'dissent' then it is considered that the parent 'consented' to the research study involving his or her child. This approach has been justified by some under the United Nations Convention on the Rights of the Child, articles 12 and 13, which emphasize the right of youth to form their own views and to express those views (United Nations, 1989). Unfortunately, 'passive consent' is a misleading title, because this approach is not valid consent (consent is an affirmative agreement, not a lack of action) – and thus requires that the consent requirement be waived. As mentioned above, consent can be waived, but appropriate justification is required in order to deny parents the right to know and agree to how their children are involved in research.

The signature of the subject (or parent in the case of youth) on a consent form is the default method of consent documentation. However, documentation of consent can also be waived under certain circumstances – for example, when the consent form is the only thing linking the subject to the research (DHHS, 1991, 45 CFR 46.117). Processes for obtaining assent from youth are also detailed in the federal regulations (DHHS, 1991, 45 CFR 46.408). Assent will be discussed in more depth below.

AGE OF CONSENT, AND WHO CAN CONSENT

Generally, the ability of a person to consent to participate in research is age based and culturally informed. The age at which one can consent to research in the United States is typically eighteen (with some exceptions, such as for emancipated youths and when local law specifically allows youth to consent with no parental involvement to procedures [such as STD testing in most US states]). Similarly, according to the Tri-Council policy statement, youth are considered to be incompetent to consent because of immaturity. Other countries have similar ages, but may have local variations. Before any protocol is implemented domestically or internationally, a researcher should be sure to check local laws and customs regarding age of consent to research. It should be noted that the UN Convention on the Rights of the Child gives weight to the views of the youth, but not legal competence to grant consent.

Similarly, who can provide valid consent varies depending on the local laws and customs. Generally, a biological or adoptive parent may consent to his or her child's participation in research. Legal guardians (or state authorities for state wards) can also typically provide such consent; however, some jurisdictions require that the court specifically give the guardian the power to consent to research in the guardianship order. It is presumed that parents and guardians have the best interest of the youth in mind (which unfortunately is sometimes not the case), but unless there are specific local legal exceptions to the consent requirements for youth, or an oversight board (such as an IRB or REB) explicitly waives the consent requirement, researchers must not include youth without appropriate legal consent from the recognized parent or guardian. Local customs can also dictate authority to provide consent. For example, as mentioned above, some cultures believe that consent should only be provided by a village elder and not the actual villager (including youth) who is engaged in the research.

ASSENT

Because youth are, by definition, incompetent to provide consent to research, the concept of 'assent' has developed to make sure that all research subjects are participating as willingly as possible. Assent is a 'child's affirmative agreement to participate in research' (DHHS, 1991, 45 CFR 46.402[b]). Although the Nuremberg Code did not address the assent of minors (or other incompetent persons), subsequent international documents such as the *Declaration of Helsinki* (WMA, 1964, 2004) have discussed the issue. The concept of assent requires affirmative agreement – failure to object should not be construed as assent. The Canadian Tri-Council policy statement has a similar requirement stating that 'those who may be capable of assent or dissent include: (a) those whose competence is in the process of development, such as children whose capacity for judgment and self-direction is maturing' (p. 2.10).

Professional associations in the United States have provided guidelines for when and what type of assent is appropriate (e.g., American Association of Pediatrics, 1995), and indeed assent can be assessed and documented in several ways. Many IRBs across the United States accept that in general, children around the age of seven should be considered old enough to provide at least verbal assent to research procedures, and youth about twelve years of age can usually provide written (signed) assent. The age and form of assent for particular studies greatly depends on the complexity of a study, the maturity and abilities of the youth, and the risk involved. The U.S. federal rules allow the IRB to determine what kind of assent is needed and at what age it must be obtained (DHHS, 1991, 45 CFR 46.408).

Turning to the cross-cultural dialogue on the topic of assent and fiduciary relationships with parents, there is a reported transatlantic disconnect on the part of British scholars, who adhere more closely to the 'new sociology of childhood' informed by the 1989 United Nations *Convention on the Rights of the Child,* which gives weight to the views of youth in accordance with age and maturity. Conversely, the United States perspective, a more protectionist current, is based upon individual developmental psychology, in which youth are viewed as 'human becomings rather than human beings' (Qvortrup in Bogolub & Thomas, 2005). Ultimately, across international contexts ethical guidelines of most governing entities suggest that the age and form of assent for particular studies greatly depend on the complexity of a study, the maturity and abilities of the youth, and the risk involved.

Privacy and Confidentiality

The concept of preserving the confidentiality of personal information provided to professionals (including researchers) has existed in the biomedical and social-behavioural context for centuries, with the aim of fostering trust, reducing stigma and embarrassment, and encouraging individual autonomy through protecting privacy (DHHS, 1999). Confidentiality has developed as a duty of professionals, and clients in a professional's care have a right to expect that it be preserved. The preservation of confidentiality in the research context has paralleled this evolution.

Some governments have formalized the concept of confidentiality. Most provisions for its protection are promulgated on the local or state level – thus, depending what jurisdiction you are in, there may be more stringent governmental protections. For example, the Canadian Tri-Council policy statement states that 'when a research subject confides personal information to a researcher, the researcher has a duty not to share the information with others without the subject's free and informed consent' (p. 3.1).

Similarly, on the U.S. federal level, it is recognized that protection of the privacy of research subjects is highly important, and the U.S. code even offers the following:

> The Secretary may authorize persons engaged in biomedical, behavioral, clinical, or other research (including research on mental health, including research on the use and effect of alcohol and other psychoactive drugs) to protect the privacy of individuals who are the subject of such research by withholding from all persons not connected with the conduct of such research the names or other identifying characteristics of such individuals. Persons so authorized to protect the privacy of such individuals may not be compelled in any Federal, State, or local civil, criminal, administrative, legislative, or other proceedings to identify such individuals. (42 U.S.C. §241(d))

This provision is the basis for the issuance of Federal Certificates of Confidentiality, discussed below.

DISCLOSURES: WHEN CAN CONFIDENTIALITY BE BROKEN?

Confidentiality is generally considered an absolute right or expectation – and with all absolute rights there can be exceptions. That is, there are times when it is appropriate, and indeed sometimes mandated, that confidentiality be broken. These exceptions are typically included in a consent disclosure process (including any written form) so that the potential research participant is aware of the limits of confidentiality during the study.

DISCLOSURES REQUIRED BY MANDATED REPORTING LAWS

The United States and Canada as well as the governments of many other countries around the world have mandated reporting of certain suspicious activity or events in order to protect vulnerable individuals from abuse and neglect. Thus, child abuse and neglect laws have become a part of the fabric of most modern societies. Although definitions of abuse and neglect may vary, the requirement that at least certain professionals (and sometimes anyone, professional or not) report any suspected abuse and neglect is almost universal. Researchers are no different. Even if they are not mandated by law to report abuse or to intervene, all ethics codes would require that they ensure the safety of any youth who is being abused or neglected.

DISCLOSURES TO IRBS AND DSMBS

Any oversight boards and data-monitoring committees, such as IRBs and data safety monitoring boards (DSMBs), will necessarily need to have access to human study data to ensure that subjects are protected. They are bound by the same confidentiality obligations as the study investigators.

DISCLOSURES TO PARENTS/GUARDIANS

Disclosures of study information to parents and guardians about their child(ren) can be a very sensitive issue. Some studies, particularly social-behavioural studies with older youth, may be greatly affected if adolescent subjects think that their parents will come to know what they have revealed to the investigator. Although in most modern cultures parents generally have a right to know what is going on with their child, some information may be protected by local or state law (e.g., sexually transmitted disease testing laws). Nevertheless, if a parent wants disclosure of research information provided by his or her child, the parent may be able to compel disclosure through legal action and/or remove the young person from the study – especially if the information pertains to other legal involvement of the youth (e.g., he/she is charged with a crime). Because this can be so sensitive and can lead to conflict, whether information is disclosed or not, it is important to clarify up front how the investigator intends to handle information disclosure to parents in the consent process with the parent and in the assent process with the youth.

OTHER DISCLOSURES

Emergencies: It is commonly accepted across cultures that if an emergency is occurring, confidentiality may be broken to protect the subject or other potentially harmed third parties. Such situations can include medical emergencies (e.g., the subject is having chest pains or breaks a bone), behavioural emergencies (e.g., the subject is threatening to lethally harm himself or another person), and social/criminal emergencies (e.g., the subject reveals plans to commit a major crime). Many jurisdictions specifically protect the person disclosing information during such emergencies from legal liability from the person whose information was disclosed.

Freedom of Information Act: In the United States and other international jurisdictions, 'freedom of information' rules have been implemented whereby legislatures, in the interest of open government, allow wider access to publicly supported information. Some researchers have become concerned that data collected in governmentally funded research could be subject to disclosure under these rules. However, at least in the United States, there is no case law or other evidence to suggest this would happen. Regardless, any court examining a disclosure request under these rules would balance the research participant's right to privacy with the public benefit from releasing the information, which makes release of information unlikely.

Requests under Legal Process (Research and Legal Privilege): There has recently been more discussion of whether information or data collected during research studies should be 'privileged' (e.g., McLaughlin, 1999). Privilege is a legal rule that protects certain information from disclosure in legal proceeding that would otherwise be available. For example, 'attorney-client privilege' is well established in common law democracies where disclosure of communication between a client and his or her attorney cannot be compelled. Should there be a researcher-subject privilege? Benefits would include more trust between researchers and subjects, and possibly increased accuracy and reliability of research data (McLaughlin, 1999). However, at this point, at least in the United States and Canada, no researcher-subject privilege has been consistently recognized – that is, all research data are potentially subject to disclosure if a court deems it necessary in a particular case (Lowman & Palys, 2001). One potentially strong remedy for compelled disclosures in the United States is the Certificate of Confidentiality (described below).

PROTECTING CONFIDENTIALITY THROUGH
RESEARCH DESIGN

Clearly, one of the most powerful ways to preserve the confidentiality of subjects is to not collect any information that could allow for the identification of the subjects. Such de-identification is done regularly with surveys and other social-behavioural research with youth. In some studies, it may not be prudent to de-identify data (e.g., clinical trials); however, if a low-risk study can be conducted using a design where subjects are anonymous or at least de-identified, that design would generally be preferable.

PROTECTING CONFIDENTIALITY THROUGH DATA SECURITY

If data are identifiable, the investigator needs to provide security for the information collected that is appropriate to the sensitivity of the information. This is applicable to both paper documentation and electronic files containing such data. Securing data with physical security (e.g., locked file cabinets and doors) and technological security (e.g., network firewalls and data encryption) is critical and expected when conducting research in the twenty-first century. Researchers who do not provide appropriate security for data are at risk for liability if inadvertent disclosure of information occurs.

PROTECTING CONFIDENTIALITY THROUGH A CERTIFICATE
OF CONFIDENTIALITY

In the United States, researchers may obtain a Certificate of Confidentiality from many federal agencies in order to provide added protection against involuntary disclosure of research information. These certificates 'allow the investigator and others who have access to research records to refuse to disclose identifying information on research participants in any civil, criminal, administrative, legislative, or other proceeding, whether at the federal, state, or local level. Certificates of Confidentiality may be granted for studies collecting information that, if disclosed, could have adverse consequences for subjects or damage their financial standing, employability, insurability, or reputation' (NIH Certificate of Confidentiality Internet Kiosk, 2007).

These certificates have not yet been successfully challenged (that is, information disclosure has not yet been compelled when researchers had obtained a certificate), and therefore are strong protection when collecting sensitive research information. Federal funding is not a prerequisite to receive a Certificate of Confidentiality; however, IRB approval is necessary, and the researcher must inform subjects of the certificate in the informed consent process.[1]

HIPÀA AND MEDICAL INFORMATION

In the United States certain medical information must receive special protection under the Health Insurance Portability and Accountability Act of 1996 (HIPAA). Rules implementing HIPAA have been established by the U.S. Department of Health and Human Services, and all 'covered entities' (e.g., hospitals, physicians, and many other medical service providers) must implement systems to protect sensitive health information. This affects research when a study uses protected health information. Special authorizations must be obtained from the individuals whose medical information will be used unless an explicit waiver of authorization is obtained from an oversight board. Guidelines for de-identifying data and using 'limited data sets' have also been implemented.[2]

Therapeutic versus Non-therapeutic Research

Classifying research as therapeutic versus non-therapeutic based solely upon the overarching concepts of medical versus social-behavioural research naively assumes that medical treatments are in the best interest of the youth and are thus therapeutic. However, many medical research protocols include control groups or placebo groups that, when utilized, offer no direct personal benefit to the youth enrolled in those groups. Thus, primarily due to research design, the distinction between therapeutic and non-therapeutic research is not without difficulties. In this section we will explore the premises of both therapeutic and non-therapeutic research together with current arguments.

THERAPEUTIC RESEARCH

Research conducted to provide actual or potential personal benefit to each participant is considered therapeutic research. In general, proxy consent by a parent is given for a young person in significant need with risks reasonable and acceptable, given the diagnostic assessment of the youth (Grover, 2003). The primary ethical challenge here is the 'therapeutic misconception' when youth are placed in placebo groups and active treatment is not included in the protocols (Hoagwood et al., 1996). Mann (2002) suggests that a therapeutic components approach or a risk-benefit analysis be utilized to derive the health-related bene- fits of a therapeutic study and the relative risk of injury or mortality (see Wendler et al., 2005, for a full explanation).

The following are seven universally applicable principles for con- ducting clinical or therapeutic research (Emanuel, Wendler, & Grady, 2000): social value, scientific validity, fair selection of patients, favourable risk-benefit ratio, independent review, informed consent, and respect for potential and enrolled patients.

NON-THERAPEUTIC RESEARCH

Often the emphasis in non-therapeutic research is on non-malfeasance rather than beneficence. It is assumed that any direct personal benefits will at best be a positive side effect, not a primary aim, due to the future-oriented goal of research 'to do good' by promising benefit to society and bringing changes to practices and policies. Mann (2002) takes this notion further by describing the assessment of risk in non- therapeutic research as conducting a risk-knowledge calculus, as we justify risk in relation to acquiring valuable knowledge.

The justification for conducting non-therapeutic research with young people is that the objectives cannot be accomplished by ques- tioning adults (Kotch, 2000). The value of the expanding knowledge base on risk and protective factors associated with general health sup- ports the benefit of conducting non-therapeutic research with children in assisting scientists in developing effective health preventative strategies (Helweg-Larsen & Boving-Larsen, 2003). Such measures further promote the well-being of youth and families by generating knowledge on sensitive issues surrounding mental and behavioural health (Kotch, 2000). Some may interpret this as presenting a trade-off of direct risk to participating individuals and families as findings are developed for the larger population (Bogolub & Thomas, 2005; Glantz, 1996). Current U.S. regulations permit youth to be involved in non- therapeutic research 'that does not provide direct benefits for them if the research poses no more than minimal risk' (DHHS, 45 CFR 46, revised 2001).

In summary, there are critical arguments against non-therapeutic research. Article 5 of the Charter for Children in Hospital, for example, states: 'Every child shall be protected from unnecessary medical treatment and investigation' (see Alderson, 1995). Authors such as Grover (2003) further argue that despite the good intentions of ethical review boards, non-therapeutic research that is not directly in the 'best interest' of the youth should not be justified as ethical based solely on an analysis that the study poses minimal risk to the youth. Yet as scientists we remain conflicted by two competing value systems: protection of human welfare and scientific responsibility (Hoagwood et al., 1996). It remains true that we have limited data on the perceived benefits of participants, and thus perhaps the notion of 'best interest' remains a subjective experience.

From Challenges to Emerging Solutions: Making Moral Progress with Universal Principles and Protective Strategies

While the standard of care for conducting resilience research with youth has been defined in various international declarations, Benatar and Singer (2000) note succinctly that declarations, like constitutions, need to be interpreted. This notion of interpretation of guidelines and principles is not an easily solved puzzle when adapting standards of research across the globe with differing groups, differing languages, differing world views, and tremendous inequities in health issues. For example, in resilience research, what are the investigator's responsibilities for knowing what local resources are available to assist participating youth in coping with their adversity and informing them how to access such resources? If no resources are known or available, should the research even be conducted? Will the potential benefits of the findings from such a study outweigh the potential risk to a given participant?

Recall the framework we proposed at the beginning of this chapter: that researchers assess the existing ethical guidelines by asking whether they must, may, or should act or respond in a specific manner. We further propose that researchers at a minimum should utilize the following in conducting international research on resilience in youth:

- Full assessment of the target country and group, utilizing community and participant consultations (Fisher, 2002)
- Culturally relevant and respectful informed consent and assent procedures
- Development of sensitive confidentiality and disclosure polices

- Ongoing review of outcomes to readjust protocols
- Obligation of public dissemination (Mann, 2002) and distribution of knowledge and resources flowing from research back to the community (Benatar, 2002)

Protective Strategies

Due to the softness of existing guidelines and vagueness of definitions regarding harm and risk, investigators continue to grapple with the ethical challenges of balancing risk and benefit. In response, more recently researchers have begun to develop systematic assessment tools to measure participant reactions to protocols (Kassam-Adams & Newman, 2002). At a minimum, during the design of a study investigators need to ask themselves:

- What are the severities of risks of participating in a non-therapeutic study?
- How do we know that these studies pose minimal risk?
- How can we best inform participants about potential risks?
- How do participants view the risk-benefit ratio?

To improve participants' understanding of possible emotional risks, Boothroyd (2000) has provided recommendations for researchers working specifically with youth. First, investigators need always to ensure that individuals participate only because they want to. Participation resulting from an ill-informed decision or coercive incentives is never acceptable. In international contexts, investigators might consider the use of a local adult to serve as an advocate for youth to be enrolled in the study and to ensure that they are adequately informed of what the study is about.

Second, Boothroyd (2000) suggests that researchers inform potential participants, as part of the consent disclosure process, about the nature of the questions to be asked as well as any potential discomfort that might be associated with answering these questions. Investigators interested in youth resilience should certainly inform youth if they intend to talk about their traumatic experiences. Boothroyd even suggests that examples of potentially sensitive questions be included in the consent form. In this regard, Singh and Paling (1997) have in their consent forms successfully used the 'Paling Perspective Scale,' a graphical representation that depicts the risk of an adverse event occurring relative to the risks involved in daily activity. However, before social scientists can incorporate this suggestion, the prevalence and severity of emotional risks such as becoming anxious or upset need to be much better documented (Boothroyd & Best, 2003). Helweg-Larsen and Boving-Larsen (2003) have also recommend that survey research conducted on sensitive topics be accompanied by an offer of counselling for those in need, to be included in the research budget. To further justify an offering of services, Best and Boothroyd (under review) utilized this approach after an adverse event when a participant made a targeted threat to physicians.

Third, Boothroyd (2000) suggests that researchers provide ongoing reminders to participants regarding the purpose and intent of the study, providing opportunities to ask questions. Evidence supporting this recommendation was found during a longitudinal study in which one in five adolescents was unaware of study goals despite their mothers' reports of being clear about the study goals (Boothroyd, 2000). This suggests that perhaps more time is needed during the consent process with youth, summarizing and reiterating what the study is about.

Investigators also need to consider that readability contributes to participants' comprehension of consent disclosures (Mitchell, Handelsman, & Martin, 1992; Taub, Baker, & Sturr, 1986), even though some researchers have failed to demonstrate a link between the reading level of material and comprehension (Duffy & Kabance, 1982). Despite the lack of consensus on this issue, there is little cost associated with incorporating the suggestions of others, such as ensuring that consent forms are written at or near an eighth-grade level (Taub et al., 1986), or using shorter sentences, improving the organization of information, using familiar terminology, and defining technical language in layman's terms (Young, Hooker, & Freeberg, 1990).

Stiles and colleagues (2001) found that the provision of iterative feedback to potential research participants during the consent process improved their comprehension of consent disclosures. Similarly, Drake, Becker, and Anthony (1994) found the use of 'research induction groups' an effective means of informing prospective study participants about the nature of a study. Their forty-five-minute research induction groups used a psychoeducational approach, in which discussion leaders described to potential participants the research project, study procedures, interviews, and details about consent and confidentiality. The resulting discussion assisted group leaders in ensuring study participants thoroughly understood the project. More than 83% of the group members reported that their participation in the group helped them make a more informed decision about whether to participate in the study. In resilience research, a similar strategy could be used in terms of a facilitated group discussion with youth and possibly caregivers to describe the proposed study.

Turnbull and colleagues (1988) also recommended the use of a 'bail-out' mechanism that establishes criteria for interviewers to stop their interview when they are concerned about distress exhibited by participants during questioning. For example, in a study conducted two and three weeks post assault, participants with exposures to rape and/or physical assault were assessed by a trained clinician to offer a full debriefing, inquire about coping and adverse reactions, and provide a referral sheet for services available in the community (Griffin et al., 2003).

Finally, Boothroyd (2000) has advocated that researchers provide participants with contact information, such as a toll-free telephone number they can call with any questions or concerns that might arise after the interview has been completed.

Conclusion

Perhaps we have offered no clear and precise prescriptions for conducting resilience research in international settings with youth, but we do propose that we as researchers can make moral progress by acknowledging our ethical obligations and adhering to sensitive and flexible protocols that take into consideration the nation, tribe, culture, and values of the targeted group. The current challenge is to remain reflective during the research process with culturally knowledgeable teams that will continually review the outcome data to assess where adjustments must be made, may be made, or should be made to further progress towards ethically sound research with youth in the international community.

Notes

1 Application of Confidentiality should be made to a particular federal entity (e.g., a specific NIH institute). For more information, visit the NIH Certificate of Confidentiality Internet Kiosk:
http://grants.nih.gov/grants/policy/coc/index.htm

2   For more information about HIPAA generally, visit the HIPAA Information website: http://www.hhs.gov/ocr/hipaa/. For more information on how HIPAA affects researchers, visit the researcher information website: http://privacyruleandresearch.nih.gov/.

References

Alderson, P. (1995). *Listening to children: Children, ethics and social research.* London: Barnardo's.

American Association of Pediatrics. (1995). Informed consent, parental permission, and assent in pediatric practice. *Pediatrics, 95,* 314–17.

Benatar, S.R. (2002). Reflections and recommendations on research ethics in developing countries. *Social Science and Medicine, 54,* 1131–41.

Benatar, S.R., & Singer, P.A. (2000). A new look at international research ethics. *British Medical Journal, 321,* 824–26.

Best, K.A., & Boothroyd, R.A. (under review). Reactions to research participation: Risk and benefits.

Bogolub, E.B., & Thomas, N. (2005). Parental consent and the ethics of research with foster children: Beginning a cross-cultural dialogue. *Qualitative Social Work, 4*(3), 271–92.

Boothroyd, R.A. (2000). The impact of research participation on adults with severe mental illness. *Mental Health Services Research, 2*(4), 213–21.

Boothroyd, R.A., & Best, K.A. (2003). Emotional reactions to research participation and the relationship to understanding of informed consent disclosures. *Social Work Research, 27,* 242–51.

Canadian Tri-Council Working Group. (2005). *Code of conduct for research involving humans.* Ottawa: Canadian Institutes of Health Research, Natural Sciences and Engineering Research Council of Canada, & Social Sciences and Humanities Research Council of Canada.

Carroll-Lind, J., Chapman, J., Gregory, J., & Maxwell, G. (2006). The key to the gatekeepers: Passive consent and other ethical issues surrounding the rights of children to speak on issues that concern them. *Child Abuse & Neglect, 30,* 979–89.

Christensen, P., & Prout, A. (2002). Working with ethical symmetry in social research with children. *Childhood, 9*(3), 321–95.

Cocks, A.J. (2006). The ethical maze: Finding an inclusive path towards gaining children's agreement to research participation. *Childhood, 13*(2), 247–66.

Council for International Organizations of Medical Sciences. (2002). *Interna-*

tional ethical guidelines for biomedical research involving human subjects.
Geneva: Council for International Organizations of Medical Sciences.

Department of Energy (DOE). (1994). Nontherapeutic research on children
(chapter 7). Advisory Committee on Human Radiation Experiments
(ACHRE Report). Retrieved 16 October 2002 from
http://www.eh.doe.gov/ohre/roadmap/achre/chap7.html.

Department of Health and Human Services (DHHS). (1991). 45 CFR 46,
Federal Register (6/18/91). Washington, DC: Department of Health and
Human Services.

Department of Health and Human Services. (1999). *Mental health: A report of
the Surgeon General.* Rockville, MD: U.S. Department of Health and Human
Services, Substance Abuse and Mental Health Services Administration,
Center for Mental Health Services, National Institutes of Health, &
National Institute of Mental Health.

Department of Health and Human Services. (2001 [revised]). *Protection of
human subjects, 45 CFR 46.* Retrieved 16 October 2002 from
http://ohrp.osophs.dhhs.gov/humansubjects/guidance/45cfr46.htm.

Dillman, D. (1978). *Mail and telephone surveys: The total design method.* New
York: John Wiley.

Donnestad, E., & Sanner, M. (Eds.). (2001). *Hello, is anyone there? – Young mes-
sages from another reality.* A report to the United Nations General Assembly
Special Session on Children in New York in September 2001. Kristiansand:
Forum for the Convention on the Rights of the Child.

Drake, R.E., Becker, D.R., & Anthony, W.A. (1994). A research induction
group for clients entering a mental health research project. *Hospital and
Community Psychiatry, 45,* 487–9.

Draucker, C.B. (1999). The emotional impact of sexual violence research on
participants. *Archives of Psychiatric Nursing, 13,* 161–69.

Duffy, T.M., & Kabance, K. (1982). Testing a readable writing approach to text
revision. *Journal of Educational Psychology, 74,* 732–48.

Economic and Social Research Council. (2005). *Research ethics framework.*
Swindon, England: Economic and Social Research Council.

Emanuel, E., Wendler, D., & Grady, C. (2000). What makes clinical research
ethical? *Journal of the American Medical Association, 283,* 2701–11.

Fisher, C.B., Hoagwood, K., Boyce, C., Duster, T., Frank, D.A., Grisso, T., et al.
(2002). Research ethics for mental health science involving ethnic minority
children and youths. *American Psychologist, 57*(123), 1024–40.

Glantz, L.H. (1996). Conducting research with children: Legal and ethical
issues. *Journal of the American Academy of Child and Adolescent Psychiatry, 35,*
1283–89.

Glantz, L.H. (2002). Nontherapeutic research with children: *Grimes v. Kennedy Krieger Institute. American Journal of Public Health, 92,* 1070–3.

Goldby, S. (1972). Experiments at the Willowbrook State School. In J. Katz (Ed.), *Experimentation with human beings: The authority of the investigator, subject, professions, and state in the human experimentation process.* (p. 1007). New York: Russell Sage Foundation.

Griffin, M.G., Resick, P.A., Waldrop, A.E., & Mechanic, M.B. (2003). Participation in trauma research: Is there evidence of harm? *Journal of Traumatic Stress, 16*(3), 221–7.

Grimes v. Kennedy Krieger Institute. (2001). 366 Md 29: 782 A2d 807. Retrieved 16 October 2002 from http://www.courts.state.md.us/opinions/coa/2001/128a00.pdf.

Grisso, T., & Appelbaum, P. (1995a). Comparison of standards for assessing patients' capacities to make treatment decisions. *American Journal of Psychiatry, 152,* 1033–7.

Grisso, T., & Appelbaum, P. (1995b). The MacArthur treatment competence study, III: Abilities of patients to consent to psychiatric and medical treatments. Law *and Human Behavior, 19,* 149–74.

Grover, S. (2003). On the limits of parental proxy consent: Children's right to non-participation in non-therapeutic research. *Journal of Academic Ethics, 1,* 349–83.

Helweg-Larsen, K., & Boving-Larsen, H. (2003). Ethical issues in youth surveys: Potentials for conducting a national questionnaire study on adolescent schoolchildren's sexual experiences with adults. *American Journal of Public Health, 93*(11), 1878–82.

Henderson, A.S., & Jorm, A.F. (1990). Do mental health surveys disturb? *Psychological Medicine, 20*(3), 721–4.

Herjanic, B., Hudson, R., & Kotloff, K. (1976). Does interviewing harm children? *Research Communications in Psychology, Psychiatry and Behavior, 1,* 523–31.

Hoagwood, K., Jensen, P.S., & Fisher, C.B. (Eds.). (1996). *Ethical issues in mental health research with children and adolescents.* Mahwah, NJ: Lawrence Erlbaum.

Hyder, A.A., Wali, S. A., Khan, A.N., Teoh, N.B., Kass, N.E., & Dawson, L. (2004). Ethical review of health research: A perspective from developing country researcher. *Journal of Medical Ethics, 30,* 68–72.

Jacomb, P.A., Jorm, A.F., Rodgers, B., Korten, A.E., Henderson, A.S., & Chistensen, H. (1999). Emotional response of participants to a mental health survey. *Social Psychiatry and Psychiatric Epidemiology, 34*(2), 80–4.

Jorm, A.F., Henderson, A.S., Scott, R., Mackinnon, A.J., Korten, A.E., &

Christensen, H. (1994). Do mental health surveys disturb? Further evidence. *Psychological Medicine, 24,* 233–7.

Kassam-Adams, N., & Newman, E. (2002). The reactions to research participation questionnaires for children and for parents (RRPQ-C and RRPQ-P). *General Hospital Psychiatry, 24,* 336–42.

King, N.M.P., & Churchill, L.R. (2000). Ethical principles guiding research on child and adolescent subjects. *Journal of Interpersonal Violence, 15*(7), 710–24.

Kirigia, J.M., Wambebe, C., & Baba-Moussa, A. (2005). Status of national research bioethics committees in the WHO African region. *BMC Medical Ethics, 6*(10). Retrieved 13 March 2007 from http://www.pubmedcentral. nih.gov/articlerender.fcgi?tool=pubmed&pubmedid=16242014.

Kotch, J.B. (2000). Ethical issues in longitudinal child maltreatment research. *Journal of Interpersonal Violence, 15*(7), 696–709.

Leonard, H., Jensen, P.S., Vitiello, B., Ryan, N., March, J., Riddle, M., & Beiderman, J. (1996). Ethical issues in psychopharmacological treatment research with children and adolescents. In K. Hoagwood, P.S. Jensen, & C.B. Fisher (Eds.), *Ethical issues in mental health research with children and adolescents* (pp. 73–88). Mahwah, NJ: Lawrence Erlbaum.

Lowman, J. & Palys, T. (2001). The ethics and law of confidentiality in criminal justice research: A comparison of Canada and the U.S. *International Criminal Justice Review, 11,* 1–33.

Luthar, S.S., Cicchetti, D., & Becker, B. (2000). The construct of resilience: A critical evaluation and guidelines for future work. *Child Development, 71*(3), 543–62.

Mahon, A., Glendinning, C., Clarke, K., & Craig, G. (1996). Researching children: Methods and ethics. *Children and Society, 10,* 145–54.

Mann, H. (2002). Research ethics committees and public dissemination of clinical trial results. *The Lancet, 359,* 406–8.

Martin, J., Perrott, K., Morris, E.M., & Romans, S.E. (2001). Participation in retrospective child sexual abuse research: Beneficial or harmful? What women think six years later. In L.M. Williams & V.L. Banyard (Eds.), *Trauma & Memory* (pp. 149–59). Thousand Oaks, CA: Sage.

Mastroianni, A.C., & Kahn, J.P. (2002). Risk and responsibility: Ethics, *Grimes v. Kennedy Krieger,* and public health research involving children. *American Journal of Public Heath, 92*(7), 1073–6.

McLaughlin, R.H. (1999). From the field to the courthouse: Should social science research be privileged? *Law and Social Inquiry, 24,* 927–66.

Meaux, J.B., & Bell, P.L. (2001). Balancing recruitment and protection: Children as research subjects. *Issues in Comprehensive Pediatric Nursing, 24,* 241–51.

Mishna, F., Antle, B.J., & Regehr, C. (2004). Tapping the perspectives of children: Emerging ethical issues in qualitative research. *Qualitative Social Work, 3*(4), 449–68.

Mitchell, M., Handelsman, M.M., & Martin, Jr., W.L. (1992). Effects of readability on the impact and recall of written informed consent material. *Professional Psychology: Research and Practice, 23*(6), 500–3.

Morrow, V., & Richards, M. (1999). The ethics of social research with children: An overview. *Children & Society, 10*, 90–105.

National Bioethics Advisory Commission. (1998). *Research involving persons with mental disorders that may affect decision making capacity. Vol. 1: Report and recommendations from the National Bioethics Advisory Commision.* Retrieved 11 July 2006 from http://www.georgetown.edu/research/nrcbl/nbac/capacity/Assessment.htm.

National Commission for the Protection of Human Subjects of Biomedical and Behavioral Research. (1978). *Ethical principles and guidelines for the protection of human subject research* (Belmont Report). Washington, DC: Government Printing Office.

National Health and Medical Research Council. (1999). *National statement on ethical conduct in research involving humans.* Canberra: National Health and Medical Research Council.

National Health and Medical Research Council. (2001). *Human research ethics handbook.* Canberra: National Health and Medical Research Council.

National Health and Medical Research Council. (2003). *Guidelines for ethical conduct in aboriginal and Torres Strait Islander health research.* Canberra: National Health and Medical Research Council.

National Institutes of Health (NIH). (1998). *NIH policy guideline on the inclusion of children in research.* Bethesda, MD: National Institutes of Health. Retrieved 16 March 2007 from http://grants1.nih.gov/grants/guide/notice-files/not98-024.html.

Newman, E., & Kaloupek, D.G. (2004). The risks and benefits of participating in trauma-focused research studies. *Journal of Traumatic Stress, 17*(5), 383–94.

NIH Certificate of Confidentiality Internet Kiosk, (2007). Bethesda, MD: National Institutes of Health. Retrieved 19 February 2007 from http://grants.nih.gov/grants/policy/coc/index.htm.

Nuffield Council on Bioethics. (2005). *The ethics of research related to healthcare in developing countries.* London: Nuffield Council on Bioethics.

Nuremberg Code. (1947). In A. Mitscherlich & F. Mielke (Eds.), *Doctors of infamy: The story of the Nazi medical crimes* (pp. xxiii–xxv). New York: Schuman.

Nuremberg Code. (1949). Trials of war criminals before the Nuremberg Military Tribunals under Control Council Law No.10, 181–2.

Palys, T. (1997). *Bulldozers in the Garden: Comments submitted to the Tri-Council Working Group regarding its July 1997 draft* Code of conduct for research involving humans. Vancouver: Simon Fraser University.

Panter-Brick, C. (2002). Street children, human rights, and public health: A critique and future directions. *Annual Review of Anthropology, 31*, 147–71.

Punch, S. (2002). Research with children: The same or different from research with adults? *Childhood, 9*(3), 321–95.

Putnam, F.W., Liss, M.B., & Landsverk, J. (1996). Ethical issues in maltreatment research with children and adolescents. In K. Hoagwood, P.S. Jensen, & C.B. Fisher (Eds.), *Ethical issues in mental health research with children and adolescents* (pp. 113–32). Mahwah, NJ: Lawrence Erlbaum.

Reisner, R., Slobogin, C., & Rai, A. (1999). *Law and the mental health system: Civil and criminal aspects* (3rd ed.) (American Casebook Series). St. Paul, MN: West Group.

Shemmings, D. (2000). Professionals' attitudes to children's perspectives in decision-making: Dichotomous accounts and doctrinal contests. *Child and Family Social Work, 5*, 235–43.

Singh, A., & Paling, J.E. (1997). Informed consent: Putting risks into perspective. *Survey of Ophthalmology, 42*, 83–6.

Society for Research in Child Development (2002). Ethical Standards for research with children. Ann Arbor, MI: SRCD. Retrieved 16 March 2007 from http://www.srcd.org/contact.html.

Stiles, P.G., Poythress, N.G., Hall, A., Falkenbach, D., & Williams, R. (2001). Improving understanding of research consent disclosures among persons with mental illness. *Psychiatric Services, 52*, 780–5.

Taub, H.A., Baker, M.T., & Sturr, J.F. (1986). Informed consent for research: Effects of readability, patient age, and education. *Journal of the American Geriatric Society, 34*, 601–6.

Thompson, R.A. (1992). Developmental changes in risks and benefits: A changing calculus of concerns. In B.L. Stanley & J.E. Sieber, *Social research on children and adolescents: Ethical issues* (pp. 31–64). Newbury Park, CA: Sage.

Turnbull, J.E., McLeod, J.D., Callahan, J.M., & Kessier, R.C. (1988). Who should ask? Ethical interviewing in psychiatric epidemiologic studies. *American Journal of Orthopsychiatry, 58*(2), 228–39.

United Nations. (1989). *Convention on the rights of the child*. Retrieved 16 March 2007 from http://www.unicef.org/crc/fulltext.htm.

United States Department of Health and Human Services, Office for Human

Research Protections. (2007). *International compilation of human subject research protections*. Washington, DC: DHHS, Office for Human Research Protections.

Ungar, M., & Liebenberg, L. (2005). The International Resilience Project: A mixed-methods approach to the study of resilience across cultures. In M Ungar (Ed.), *Handbook for working with children and youth: Pathways to resilience across cultures and contexts* (pp. 211–26). Thousand Oaks, CA: Sage.

Walker, E.A., Newman, E., Koss, M., & Bernstein, D. (1997). Does the study of victimization revictimize the victims? *Psychiatry and Primary Care, 19,* 403–10.

Wendler, D., Belsky, L., Thompson, K.M., & Emanuel, E.J. (2005). Quantifying the federal minimal risk standard: Implications for pediatric research without a prospect of direct benefit. *Journal of the American Medical Association, 294*(7), 826–32.

World Medical Association (WMA). (1964, 2004). *Declaration of Helsinki*. Ferney-Voltaire, France: World Medical Association.

Young, L., & Barrett, H. (2001). Issues of access and identity: Adapting research methods with Kamplaa street children. *Childhood, 8*(3): 383–95.

Young, D.R., Hooker, D.T., & Freeberg, F.E. (1990). Informed consent documents: Increasing comprehension by reducing reading level. *IRB: A Review of Human Subjects Research, 12*(3), 1–5.

Zimmerman, M., Farber, N.J., Hartung, J., Lush, D.T., & Kuzma, M.A. (1994). Screening for psychiatric disorders in medical patients: A feasibility and patient acceptance study. *Medical Care, 32,* 603–8.

QUALITATIVE RESEARCH

3 Participatory Action Research

JACKIE SANDERS AND ROBYN MUNFORD

Young people have always been a topic of intense interest in the academy, the media, and popular discourse. At the boundary between childhood and adulthood their increased physical presence and their more active and direct engagement with adults holds both promise and threat (Lesko, 2001). When we engage in participatory action research with young people, we draw on a number of important theoretical and methodological tools, and it is the application of these in a concrete sense that is the central concern of this chapter. We will first briefly traverse some of these key intellectual frameworks, as they provide the context within which our work is located, before we consider our case study. Our work is constructivist and interpretive; the participatory action approach emphasizes active engagement of research participants, and we take an ecological perspective that requires that we consider not only the young person but also the other individuals, groups, and contexts with which young people function.

While participatory action research approaches draw upon both qualitative and quantitative methodologies, our discussion in this chapter focuses upon the application of qualitative methodologies in one particular project. It is important to note that the participatory action approach is used in a diverse range of disciplines spanning applied areas such as development, rehabilitation and disability studies, education, and health and management studies, as well as in more traditional academic disciplines such as anthropology, sociology, and psychology. It should be noted that most often participatory action approaches have operated at the group or community level. They have typically involved projects that have a development or community development character. In this chapter we explore a case example that operated most strongly at the micro, individual level although there were community development characteristics as well. Readers are encouraged to review the extensive participatory action literature to gain a full appreciation of the potential these methods hold. In this chapter we are interested in exploring the not always appreciated potential for participatory action methods to work at the micro level. There have been several significant reviews of the participatory action approach in the health field in particular, and there is a large body of literature concerning the application of these methods in a range of fields (see, for example, Agency for Healthcare Research and Quality, 2001, 2003; Boutilier, Mason, & Rootman, 1997; Lantz et al., 2001; Potvin et al., 2003; Wallerstein et al., 2003). The project that we are reporting on concerns the use of the participatory action approach in a social work setting with young people in the context of their families and community.

In the literature, participatory action research is referred to in a range of ways, including *action methods, community-based participatory action,* and *community-based research.* A key characteristic of all these approaches is the location of decision making and control within the participating groups rather than the research team. What they share in common is the vesting of power and decision making in the population or community under study. In our discussion we explore these issues in terms of the engagement of one young man, his mother, and the community agency that worked with them both. Our illustrations consider the application of the participatory approach in terms of each of these key actors.

Historically, academic interest has primarily constructed young people as a problem to be solved, or at least as representing issues to be controlled. Typically viewed through the lens of developmental and psychopathological discourse, we have come to understand young people as the quintessential 'other' (Valentine, 1996). This creates challenges when adults seek to address the 'problems' young people are commonly argued to create because we begin from an oppositional position and one that implicitly denies their personhood. Rather than actively embracing their agency, the preferred script of adults emphasizes control and overwriting of young people's reality with adult-constructed stories.

At the end of the previous century, newer theories that challenged this oppositional position began to emerge concerning youth, adolescence, and resilience. For instance, recognizing this significant shift in focus, in 2000 the journal *Reclaiming Children and Youth* changed its subtitle from *The Journal of Emotional and Behavioural Problems* to *The Journal of Strengths-Based Interventions*. These newer theories, together with the methodologies and social practices that grew from them, have allowed us to traverse the difficult waters between ourselves as adult practitioners and researchers and the youth we now seek to understand.

A key feature of the newer approaches to understanding youth and adolescence is the central importance placed on giving youth a voice – not only as participants in research but as partners in investigations and as partners in the application of research findings. These characteristics have clear synergies with those of participatory action research. Far from a democratic nicety, the notion of 'giving voice' has a strong foundation in the emancipatory movements of the 1970s and 1980s that brought about serious criticism of research conducted *on* rather than *with* participants (Denzin & Lincoln, 2005; Lather, 1991). Emerging in fields such as disability, women's, and cultural studies, the inclusion of children and young people as a silenced population occurred relatively late in this process.

Issues of voice and inclusion have profound epistemological implications because they cut to the heart of our beliefs about how knowledge is created and whose interests it serves (Crotty, 1998). These issues also remind us that knowledge generation is a profoundly political act, concerning the power to define and to shape how resources are created and shared. In the New Zealand context, recognition of the significance of youth involvement achieved expression in state policies during the early 2000s that championed a positive youth development orientation (see for instance, the Ministry of Youth Affairs' [2002] *Youth Development Strategy*). In local practice, these sentiments have taken shape in service providers' efforts to engage young people in decision making around service delivery. Examples include the use of family conferences in child welfare and youth justice settings that involve young people in decisions on care and protection issues. However, debate remains about the extent to which ideas embodied in high-level documents such as the *Youth Development Strategy* actually inform and change adult approaches to young people. It can be argued that such documents exist more as rhetorical, positional devices than effective guides that help change the nature of the spaces in the social and political landscape available to young people. While the *Youth Development Strategy* represents an aspirational ideal, many state policies, practices, and organizational guidelines directly contradict these values. This means that researchers and practitioners who do seek a more profound level of engagement with young people still find themselves a minority voice searching for the gaps in policies that can be creatively shaped with young people to better serve their interests.

Our chapter begins with an overview of the theoretical and methodological context of our use of participatory action research approaches in a social work context. This discussion provides a foundation upon which we can consider the learning from a research project involving a study of well-being, resilience, and young people that is covered in the second part of the chapter. We conclude with a discussion about the contribution participatory action research can make to our developing knowledge about what constitutes resilience for young people.

The Theoretical and Methodological Context

Constructionist and interpretive theories have made major contributions to both social work practice (Cooper, 2001) and contemporary understandings of young people (Ungar, 2004). Proponents argue that reality is socially constructed, emerging out of and through the complex interactions between people. Reality, in general terms, and the ways in which specific issues such as those presented by troubled and troubling young people are understood, are a reflection of the interpretations we give to the behaviours we observe. Crotty (1998) offers the following definition of social constructionism, which we have found useful in guiding our approach to collaborative research with young people:

> It is the view that all knowledge, and therefore all meaningful reality as such, is contingent upon human practices, being constructed in and out of interaction between human beings and their world, and developed and transmitted within an essentially social context. (p. 42)

A strong strand in participatory action method's genealogy traces its origins to critical theory; issues of power and the ability to control resources such as knowledge are key concerns in participatory action research (Heron, 1996). Critical theory works well with constructivist and interpretive approaches. It provides analytical tools that help us explain why particular types of explanations of, for instance, the behaviour of young people who live roughly have discursive power while others are marginalized (Crotty, 1998; Healy, 2000).

The participatory action approach requires researchers to be explicit about the values they use, the positions they occupy, and the decisions they make regarding the focus of their research. Relationships become a central concern for action researchers because they must perform their work alongside others in everyday-life settings. In these ways participatory approaches share characteristics with the qualitative research tradition. The works of key writers such as Giddens (1976, 1984) in structuration theory, Habermas (1984) in the theory of communicative action, and Bourdieu (1977) in his work on structure and habitus provide important insights into how this different sort of research endeavour might proceed. The central concerns of social constructionism, critical theory, and the participatory action approach come together to provide strong epistemological and ontological frameworks for engaging in research with young people. Giddens (cited in Coenen & Khonraad, 2003, pp. 439–40) clarifies that the task of social science is to interpret an already interpreted reality in which participating humans have vested interests:

> Social actors give meaning to existing social and natural conditions, but they also try to exert their influence to change these conditions ... human activity is bound up both with interpretation and power.

The new strengths or resilience theories articulated in social work research and practice are featured in our work. Constructionist and interpretive in nature, strengths theories like critical theory provide us with the analytical capacity to explore from a range of angles the nature and capacities of young people. Far from denying the difficulties and challenges that marginalized young people may face or the harm that they may do, the theories allow us to examine these challenges. At the same time they provide commentary upon the resourcefulness and capacity of these young people and help to identify the constitutive forces in their lives (Ungar, 2004). It is these types of resources that can be drawn upon when we work with youth to reduce harm or redirect them to more constructive activities and to heal. We are also inspired by the works of theorists such as Friere (1970, 1994), who encourage us to approach our work through the lens of liberation theory; the recognition that understanding is power and that the knowledge we create as researchers can be used to help change the material and social circumstances of vulnerable people.

These theoretical frameworks allow us to raise critical issues around the nature and purpose of research, to inquire into the multifaceted, dynamic, and contradictory forces that shape young people's lives, to examine whose needs and interests research serves, and to interrogate issues of power. They orient us to the ways in which meanings held by others help explain social phenomena. They lend themselves particularly well to the active engagement of youthful research participants. They give us the capacity to gain analytical purchase on what it may mean to be 'the other' (Ungar, 2004).

There are many different types of participatory action research (Beilharz, 2002; Boog, Keune, & Tromp, 2003; Healy, 2001; Munford & Sanders, 2003a, 2003b). However, all models share a common commitment to knowledge sharing, social justice, and the creation of change as a result of cycles of action and reflection. The *action-reflection cycle* provides the framework within which both understanding and change become possible (Roberts & Dick, 2003). Action research grew out of foundation work by writers such as Freire (1970) in education and Lewin (1948) in action theory, both of whom argued for research as part of emancipatory practice, where, armed with knowledge, individuals become able to effect change in their social and material circumstances. The action-reflection cycle is a key dimension of the participatory approach, and it provides for a sequential building and testing of understandings *in situ* as the research progresses.

The intentional focus upon change is a distinguishing feature of the participatory action approach. Participatory action approaches are most often used in community or group work, but also hold important potential to explore single cases in detail. By adopting a range of investigatory techniques such as critical historical methods, structural analysis, and case histories, they can locate single cases in the layered and intersecting individual, relational, and structural (wider social, historical, political) contexts in which they are embedded. Because a key objective of participatory action research is to draw participants into the research process as active partners, there is a greater likelihood that the resulting research (whether it is single-case design or involves large populations) will identify the most effective sites and ways of fostering change that is responsive to the lived realities of participants (Munford & Sanders, 2003). As we discuss below, for example, when Charlie's mother led the development of a local oral history for the research project, she began to make connections between her circumstances, the political and social history of her community, and the circumstances of others around her. This initiated a powerful reflective process that, among other things, contributed to significant change in her individual relationship with her son, Charlie.

Understanding how structure and agency intersect is a major task for social workers (Healy, 2000), and in participatory action research projects practitioners and participants can be drawn into these wider processes of reflection so that private matters can be connected to public issues. In our own qualitative participatory action research projects we have been able to deeply inquire into these intersections because we worked intensely with a small number of cases, drawing all players into the mix. We could track backwards into the past and outwards into the circles of relationships and events around participants. This allowed us to interrogate the wider socio-political and economic forces that shaped participants' lives. We were able to intentionally search for confirming and disconfirming cases that helped us to understand the circumstances under which troubled young people could find themselves able to strive and thrive and under which they could be crushed. In short, we are able to learn how individuals came to be particular sorts of young people in particular places and times. We were able to join with them in an examination of the ways in which they could build their senses of personal agency and enhance their capacities to shape their lives themselves and with their families.

While the young people with whom we work may not be able to alter all of their social, material, and relational circumstances, the action-reflection cycle does provide a context from within which they can become reflexive and gain greater insight into their everyday lives and the types of solutions that may be possible for them. Because of its intentional focus on change, participatory action methods have many similarities with community development and social work practice.

Action research extends the traditional research process in two directions. These directions occur in the early phases of a project, when research issues are identified, and in the final phases of a project, when research findings are disseminated and when participants identify possible strategies for implementing social change. In the early phases the development of the research project is brought into communities as a series of questions that community representatives, practitioners, researchers, clients, agency funders, and others need to resolve prior to finalizing methodology and collecting data. This early phase incorporates strategies for knowledge sharing so that all participants are able to provide a perspective on the issues to be addressed. In the final phases the researcher's brief is extended to include researcher involvement with the implementation of findings, including ways to involve research participants in developing a range of actions and initiatives that flow from the research findings and from other information generated in the project. In this way, research becomes part of wider processes of action and reflection, not a discrete activity that takes place outside of normal practice. Accordingly, the capacity to manage complex research processes and a wide range of relationships throughout all phases of the research project becomes a critical component of researcher skills.

There are many stories to be told about each young person; we are fortunate to have the theoretical frameworks that allow us to take a prismatic approach to understanding the unfolding of young people's life projects. The postmodern frameworks of constructivism and interpretivism help us to understand the different selves that young people choose to project and to protect in different settings. Critical theory, in turn, focuses our attention on the ways in which these different selves may be shaped, pushed, and pulled in different directions by forces outside and beyond young people's control.

Participatory action research located in community contexts can have a structural or community-level focus on change, seeking to draw from collective experience, patterns, and characteristics in the social world that can be changed through collective action. These types of projects focus on policy or political concerns (Healy, 2001). They illustrate how involvement in social change projects can also result in personal change and enhanced self-efficacy (Greene, 2007; Titterton & Smart, 2006). An involvement in social change can enhance ongoing engagement in community life and build positive social capacity (Barry, 2005; Ungar, 2004). By becoming involved in community projects, community members develop an understanding about how they can become active participants in transforming current situations (Houston, 2001). We have reported elsewhere on just such projects where processes of participation in the action-reflection cycle contributed to young people's decisions to engage with local authority planners and decision makers around the development of new facilities (Munford & Sanders, 2005; Sanders & Munford, 2007).

To illustrate the approach to research with youth, we will focus on a project that shows how action methods can work at the micro level. This example will demonstrate how these methods shaped both the development of social work practice with young people and the way in which the method helped change the life course of a young person and his family. The approach allowed us to focus on the development of resilience in young people along with how we might enhance the capacity of social workers to practice. Our case example focuses on the process of engagement between a social worker who was also a researcher in our project and a young man. It uses the field and case notes of the worker/researcher and draws on the reflective material gathered throughout the project. It also draws on material gathered during research meetings that focused particularly on the connections between personal and social change and on the emerging processes of change across a range of contexts. Here we learned how the action-reflection process, an integral part of the participatory action approach, could feed into changes at both micro and macro levels.

The Project

Our research project was a community study of well-being and resilience among young people. Following Mayall (2001) and Gordon (2000), we conceptualized young people as competent and able to effectively articulate their life experiences and to explore with us the many different types of factors that influenced their capacity to be resilient and to experience well-being. We also drew heavily on the works of writers such as Ungar (2004, 2005) and Brown (1983) who, with others, have pioneered the new youth studies that highlight the key contribution research can make in providing vehicles through which youth can achieve greater voices, generating research findings and results grounded in these voices.

Our project located itself within the new youth studies paradigm. As researchers we considered that we had much to learn from young people, both about their own worlds and about the most effective orientations that adults could take to supporting them to effectively confront adversity, to recognize and draw on their own resilience, and to develop their own capacities to experience well-being. Given this, we needed to recruit a diverse range of young people and work with them in ways that provided the space for them to articulate their own stories. Participatory action research provided us with a framework to do this. However, we confronted some important ethical and methodological challenges, particularly in relation to recruiting young people who were facing the most adversity, who daily needed to deal with significant challenges and who, almost by definition, had the fewest resources within their own networks to support them.

Researchers need to give very careful consideration to the processes used to collect essential information while protecting the right to privacy of young people who participate in research. Chapter 2 in this volume deals in detail with these issues. Here we will consider them only briefly.

From a methodological point of view, these young people can be quite hard to locate and recruit; they are not necessarily trusting of adults and can be reluctant to tell their stories to strangers. Young people in these positions have often been abandoned by the adults who are responsible for them. In learning to care for themselves they may have become suspicious of adults who want them to disclose personal matters. Ethically, there are important issues to consider when working with vulnerable young people; in particular, the potential for harm needs careful consideration. Qualitative methods such as those we used in this participatory action project are inherently exposing, laying bare the details of lives is fundamental to developing the rich understanding sought in such research. Researchers need to give very careful consideration to where the boundaries lie between collecting essential information and voyeurism. They also need to attend with care to the ways in which they will respond to learning about illegal behaviour and activities that young people engage in that may shock and outrage them. Finally, it is open to question whether or not research with vulnerable young people can be ethically justified if it is disconnected from whatever support systems are an ongoing presence in young people's lives. Given that researcher involvement in young people's lives usually ends with the completion of the research, can they justify encouraging such young people to reflect upon and expose powerful, damaging, and difficult experiences when they will not be there to deal with the consequences of such reflection?

Navigating through these issues while we were planning the project reinforced for us the value of the participatory action framework. It indicated that our recruitment strategy for a vulnerable population of young people might best be advanced by building a collaborative relationship with a community-based agency (Reid & Vianna, 2001). This approach meant that there was separation between us and the young people until they had agreed to participate. It also meant that youth had access to ongoing support throughout the project. If interviews and other research activities raised painful issues for them, they could readily access support.

Serendipity can play a role in research, and in our project our approach to the community agency coincided with an approach from their community social worker to undertake her masters' studies through our university. She wanted to use action methods to develop her social work practice and to explore its potential for the development of her agency's overall approach to working with young people. What this allowed us to do was to employ a field researcher who was known to and trusted by the young people. This situation raised its own ethical issues, requiring resolution. For instance, we needed to exercise considerable care in ensuring that information she was privy to as a social worker did not become part of the research data. We also needed to ensure that youth did not feel compelled to participate because they were receiving support from the person who was our fieldworker. Resolving these issues took time and slowed down the early phases of the project as we negotiated with the social worker, her agency, and our university's Ethics Committee in developing protocols to protect both the young people and the social worker.

The wider research team, including the community agency and the field researcher, agreed on the protocols, and these were followed consistently throughout the project. The community agency retained control of the recruitment process in the study, talking with the young people about the research, including its purpose and what their involvement would require of them. This measure was in line with, and countered, previously mentioned concerns around risk of emotional upset in participants stemming from unbarred discussion and reflection on their experiences. The research tools to be used were outlined and included detailed discussion about the nature of individual and group interviews. The young people were informed of the ethical protocols that would enable them to have control over what they shared with an interviewer and how this material was to be used. They knew that they could withdraw from a particular research situation at any time and from the study without any consequences for the support they would receive from the agency. It was important that they knew from the outset that receiving services from the agency was not contingent upon being involved in the research project. A key dimension of this project was the engagement of the agency as a research partner that shared in decision making throughout the project.

Once the project was underway we continued to use strategies that reinforced the difference between the research and social work practice. Strategies included holding research interviews in locations chosen by the young people and clearly separating these from any social work support work. Research interviews would not be done at the same time as a social work meeting with a young person, and research information was kept separate from intervention information. The field researcher carefully explained the difference between the research interview schedule and the tools used to gather information for a social work intervention. The field worker had regular supervision with the research team to ensure that research processes were not interrupting support work with young people and to raise any issues about the research and its impact on agency work.

In the end, these careful negotiations and decisions around research protocols produced benefits for the research, the social worker, and her agency, as well as for the young people involved. It allowed us to learn significantly more about the practice of social work with young people, to gather a greater depth of information, and to achieve a greater depth of engagement of the young people in the transfer of research learning into everyday life. Our engagement with the community provider, the social worker, and the young people was deeper and the participatory action components were more focused as a result. Finally, it provided us with the opportunity to observe the ways in which research knowledge can contribute to the development of more effective practice with vulnerable young people.

In the study we were able to work with fifteen young people, their families and key support people. In this sense, our work did not focus solely upon the young people; the ecological approach adopted included in its scope the people and settings that were significant to the young people. As background information to the study, we documented the work of the community agency and met with the support workers to learn about their work with young people. We also met with the young people to talk about our research and what we hoped it would achieve. We invited them to help us in the design of our methods and, if they wished, to assist in understanding research findings. As a result of these conversations, we developed a variety of techniques in conjunction with these young men for creating opportunities for them to share information with us. While the interview was the primary data-gathering tool, young people chose other mechanisms for telling their stories. These included constructing life stories, drawing, writing music and presenting and recording it on a compact disk (which they subsequently marketed and sold), talking with the researcher while being involved in other activities such as sporting events, and using computer technology (Messenger and Word documents) to write their answers to interview questions rather than talking.

We now share the story of Charlie to illustrate the learning from this research project. In doing this we are particularly interested in describing the way in which a research project became embedded in the work of the community centre and the way in which it became part of the process of change for a specific young man and his family. We hope to illustrate the subtle ways in which participatory action research can contribute to the daily lives of youth and their families and to the development of practice. These approaches, combined with community action, encourage social and community workers to reflect on how they work with young people and understand power sharing and collective ownership of knowledge.

The Case Study

Charlie was fourteen when we first met him. He had lived all his life in the same neighbourhood with his father, mother, and two brothers. The area he lived in was often identified as a stressed community; it achieved notoriety from time to time in the local newspaper, which reported on gang violence, criminal activity linked with substance abuse, and family violence. Like many similar areas, the community was profoundly affected by the structural adjustments undertaken by successive governments since the 1980s. These adjustments were driven by a neo-liberal framework that emphasized individual over collective responsibility. Societal impacts that directly affected young people in this area included poverty and social and personal upheaval resulting from the high unemployment of the 1980s and 1990s; dislocation and loss of hope; a growing sense of exclusion; and extreme vulnerability to predatory and violent behaviour of adults. While we used historical and documentary methods to describe and analyse the way in which these changes influenced Charlie's neighbourhood, talking with Charlie, his family, and his friends also enabled them to trace the way in which these major, global forces had shaped their lives and to use this blended understanding to develop their own plans for their futures.

The social and economic context of this community had a particular impact on the lives and opportunities available to young people such as Charlie. He and his family talked to us about the impact of economic restructuring and other social and political events upon their family life. As an action methods project, these factors, far from being blurred background matters of historical interest, needed to be understood as creating the frameworks within which people such as Charlie and his family worked on their life projects (Mayall, 2001). They needed to be placed alongside the familial and individual factors that played a role in shaping the life of his family and those in his neighbourhood. For young people such as Charlie, these factors were generally related to experiences in educational settings, which included disruption of learning through suspension and, sometimes, expulsion from school. The cumulative effects of these often resulted in difficulty securing successful transitions to work or other learning opportunities such as tertiary study.

Charlie presented some significant challenges to local officials, who described him as a 'time bomb,' and who could find nothing to be gained from investing any resources in supporting him. His behaviour increasingly brought him negative attention. The dominant discourse around Charlie constructed him as bad and even beyond hope. The gaze to which Charlie was subjected primarily constructed him as negative, and this shaped the agendas of the agencies that intervened in his life. It was in this context that he met Mikela, the social worker and researcher, as a possible research participant.

The official story of Charlie contained many features that marked him out as 'high risk.' Charlie's relatively short life had been characterized by exposure to significant levels of family and community violence. His childhood memories were punctuated by fear; he learned to hide and run away. As he grew physically, he learned to violently give vent to the anger he bottled up when he was too small to protect himself. Like many of his friends, he was under a court-imposed curfew that confined him to home between 9 p.m. and 7 a.m., to which he paid relatively little attention. Charlie hadn't attended school consistently since he was ten years old, and two weeks after he officially began high school he was expelled. Charlie's father paid little positive attention to him, and as he moved through adolescence his mother became increasingly remote and neglectful towards him.

As we got to know Charlie through Mikela's eyes, we learned about the public face of Charlie. Mikela understood strengths theories and it was to these that she turned as she developed her strategies for working with Charlie (Brendtro, Long, & Brown, 2000). Her clinical supervisor and her agency supported her in her work with Charlie and encouraged her to contribute to the development of more effective strategies for working with young people in this community. The agency was enthusiastic about Charlie's participation in the study, hoping that through his involvement in the research he might become more able to develop a positive sense of direction, and also that they might learn more about how to effectively support those many young people in their community who, like Charlie, had been defined as beyond hope. However, the 'bad' discourse is powerful and pervasive, and this small community agency struggled to gain traction in challenging it. Monday mornings typically brought the litany of 'bad things' that the young men had done over the weekend, and these overshadowed their achievements in other areas and the positive work that they were engaged in. Strengths of young people are not always obvious or easy to locate, and it can be tempting to give in to the discourses that describe them as all 'bad' and beyond hope (Ungar 2004).

In our reflection meetings with the agency, we talked about their work with the police and the welfare authorities, and the strategies that they used to develop different responses to the young people's behaviour. As part of the knowledge-sharing processes we established with the agency, we discussed key resources concerning how to apply strengths and resilience theories in practice with young people (Bergsson, 2000; Brendtro, Long, & Brown, 2000; DeJong & Berg, 2001; Pottick & Davis, 2001; Saleebey, 2002; Ungar, 2004). These helped staff to create a language to talk with and about the young men that was not saturated with the problems and challenges usually associated with speech about them. The strengths language gave staff ways of engaging with other professionals over joint casework that focused on the things these young men did well, that underscored their capacity and potential, and that were fundamentally respectful and recognized their humanity.

Strengths approaches highlight the importance of developing a strong, positive relational framework for work with troubled young people; they put at the forefront the responsibility of workers to build strong, respectful relationships, and remind workers that the investment they make in creating these relationships will produce long-term, sustainable change. They also tune workers into the ways in which the young men use language, not so much in terms of equipping them to adopt the *lingua franca* of the street – something they had accomplished long ago – but more in terms of working to understand the meanings that lie behind the talk. Attending to those meanings can help workers sharpen their practice. For instance, as we discuss below, they tuned in to phrases like 'standing by me' and 'standing for me' as key indicators of relationships that mattered to the young men.

Reviewing our field notes, we noted the amount of time spent in discussion about Charlie's family and his neighbourhood. As external observers we could see how major social, economic, and political realignments that characterized the reforms of the 1980s had flowed through Charlie's life, rendering both his parents redundant. Their subsistence-level state income support had been cut by twenty-five per cent in 1991, and his father and older brothers resorted to drug dealing and the informal economy to generate income. This was a pattern repeated in households up and down Charlie's street. However, for Charlie, these structural factors were refracted to him through personal experiences such as the imprisonment of most of the male members of his extended family, and through increasing exposure to the violence inextricably linked with the drug economy and the sense of exclusion from mainstream society that these experiences precipitated.

Alongside the work of the agency, we began the research process. We were introduced to the young men and raised the idea of their involvement as research partners. As a way of drawing Charlie and the other young men into the research we developed a life-stories project with them. In these personal biographies (Gordon et al., 2005) we worked to draw out a number of different selves that highlighted the constructive, creative, and emotional characteristics, which could be placed alongside destructive dimensions of their lives that brought these young men notoriety. These formed the basis of their early research activity. We were surprised by the enthusiasm that the young men had for this process. Demonstrating the action-reflection cycle, this process was subsequently incorporated into the educational program provided by the community centre. It allowed centre staff to deepen their understanding of the young people who used the centre and provided mechanisms by which the young people could leave a legacy at the centre. The young men developed their own stories that could be used in research reports following the research project. This process also developed into a biography of the centre itself. In developing the history of the centre, the young men took on the role of researchers, interviewing staff and other community stakeholders. Linking back into the strengths approach, this allowed adults in and around the community centre to see the young men in new ways. An unintended outcome of this particular part of the project was that the young men also became more involved in management and decision making at the centre, initiating new activities. For instance, many who had difficulties with reading began to look for ways of increasing their exposure to books. They raised the possibility of the mobile library service visiting the centre. Similarly, their work on biographies drew them into memories of early childhood, and when the local early childhood educators' consortium approached the centre to use its facilities for a 'family fun day,' the young men helped by running games and looking after the children. Through the process of biography writing they began to see themselves as young men with potential to create spaces for other children to have different kinds of childhoods. The ways in which they engaged in the research reflection sessions held at the centre started to change; they became more animated, engaged, and active contributors to both the sessions and the research analysis.

Change is not, however, immutable, and one evening Charlie was arrested late at night for a drunken rampage; he called Mikela. When she arrived at the police station he simply said, 'I knew you would stand by me,' and in her field notes for that day she recognized that Charlie now trusted her. From that night on her interactions with Charlie became more intentionally focused on how they could steer a path through the challenges he faced.

Gradually the balance in Charlie's behaviour began to shift. When interviewed for the research a month after this incident, Charlie expressed interest in returning to school and in actively shaping his future. He also began to seek out leadership roles in the centre in relation to the other young men. As we completed our research fieldwork, we had contact with authorities such as the police who had historically had a high level of involvement in the young men's lives. With Charlie's permission we asked whether or not they had any contact with him. They reported that they were seeing less and less of Charlie; that he had not broken his curfew and that he had not come to their attention in town for the past eight months.

Attending carefully to Charlie's story, creating time and space for him to articulate his needs, and energetically asserting that Charlie was significantly more than the sum total of his violent acts were critical parts of the support that Mikela provided to Charlie. These were also a critical part of the research project; Charlie was able not only to tell his story as part of a healing process, he was able to tell it as part of a story that was shared by many of his friends. Charlie was also able to actively participate in the shaping of it as a research story that could be told and retold in different settings. In this way a small action methods project had the potential to contribute to large effects both for Charlie and for other young people. In building his story as a research story, Charlie was able to develop an outsider's relationship to his own biography; he was able to make connections between his own experiences and those of other young people in similar positions to himself.

But our case study is mostly concerned with explaining the transformative potential of a participatory action approach at the individual level where it provided reflective spaces for Charlie's story to be connected to Mikela's, and where she enacted her commitment to the application of strengths-based practice in challenging settings. The research project also helped to connect these stories to Charlie's mum's story about healing and reconnecting with Charlie by learning to see him first through Mikela's eyes. The action-reflection cycle that is a fundamental part of participatory methods provided new ways of reflecting back to our three key actors the things that were occurring between them.

Participatory research provides structured opportunities for research participants to simultaneously stand inside and outside of their circumstances and to take on other perspectives that can provide alternative interpretations of the issues they are confronting in their daily lives. For instance, as we worked with Charlie to write his story, we were able to include Mikela's positive observations of him; her sense of him as an engaging young man provided him with a new way of seeing himself. Over time he was increasingly able to identify with himself as this nice young man. Similarly, as we worked with Mikela's story, the significance of 'standing by' the young men became apparent, and from this Mikela was able to more intentionally target her work with Charlie, ensuring that she always responded to him when he asked for her help. She was also able to recognize the critical significance of the role his mother's remoteness played in his violent behaviour and the way in which his violent behaviour triggered further remoteness in her. Mikela discovered how Charlie's mum could become involved in a change process that enabled her to confront her challenges so that she could also become available to stand by Charlie. To do this she also needed someone to stand by her. Here, the centre was able to identify ways in which it could begin to work more effectively in harnessing and strengthening the networks of young people like Charlie and their significant others.

Mikela's support for Charlie and the action research project became entwined. Insights gained through working on the research stories fed into the choices she made about how to work with Charlie. They also helped her to pinpoint Charlie's mum as a critical part of the restorative project she was engaged in through the support process. For Charlie, being encouraged gradually to actively author his own story as a research story in its positive and negative dimensions played an important role in shaping his approach to his own life. He wanted the story to have a happy ending. His stance in relation to himself changed notably over the research project's eighteen months, from passive to more active. Through the process of writing his story for the research project he developed the capacity to adopt a reflexive stance in relation to himself. While he still faced challenges, and serious issues remained after eighteen months (such as completing a short custodial sentence, attending a residential alcohol and drug treatment facility, and then attempting to be reintegrated into a mainstream school), his involvement in the action research project helped to prepare him for these challenges.

Conclusions

The participatory action research approach provides researchers with a strong interdisciplinary framework for examining resilience among young people who confront high levels of adversity. Because they privilege research participants' voices, they hold significant potential for us to learn about their 'hidden resilience' (see Ungar, 2004) and to develop interventions that intentionally engage with these positive constructive aspects of their lives. In addition to this, key features of the participatory action approach bring additional benefits to researchers and practitioners working with young people. The action-reflection cycle provides structured opportunities for the sequential building of understanding and the testing of this understanding with participants' interpretations of the research material. The emphasis upon change orients researchers to the potential of their projects to bring benefits to participants and not just to themselves (Healy, 2001).

Our research and the development of interventions and support processes that emerge from it are likely to be more effective as a result. These methods have important potential for the development of strengths-based social work with young people. In concluding this chapter, then, we consider three aspects of the participatory action approach that were particularly fruitful in our research.

The project was structured around the action-reflection cycle. The procedures for working with the action-reflection cycle were established at the beginning of the project and operated at a range of levels, from our engagement with the community centre that employed Mikela as we planned the project and managed the interface between the research and the services provided to Charlie, to our regular research reflection sessions that we held with Mikela as her work with Charlie developed. As a result of the project, Mikela and the community centre also adopted this set of practices in their work with the young men, and in this way the action-reflection cycle influenced not only the way in which the research developed but also the way in which the services were provided to Charlie and his mum. Mikela also adopted the action-reflection cycle in her work with Charlie and his mum, and we saw this in her work with Charlie on his biography and with his mum as they compiled the oral history of their neighbourhood for the research project. These action-reflection processes intersected with and informed each other; they created scaffolding around which the research and the intervention could be constructed. At the end of the process, the cycle of doing and thinking that action-reflection embodies had become part of the process that Charlie used to increase his well-being. He could recount the new ways in which he managed himself and his relationships with his peers, and the choices that he made in terms of an action-reflection cycle. In his journey with Mikela he had developed a more intentional focus upon himself. He became a more active author of his own story, internalizing newer versions of himself. Initially in Mikela, and later in his mum as well, he had an appreciative audience in front of which he could enact these new versions of what it means to be Charlie. The participatory action research had synergies with the intervention process.

As shown, participatory action research is *adaptable* and *flexible*. Indeed, the action-reflection cycle requires a degree of fluidity and the capacity to respond as the research unfolds in much the same way as good-quality social work interventions are flexible and adaptable. In this project, we were able to widen and shift the focus as Mikela's work with Charlie developed. For instance, when Mikela began to voice frustration at the unresponsiveness of Charlie's mum, we could follow her as she shifted emphasis in her work for a time from Charlie to his mum. In doing this we were able to learn about the ways in which social work practice adapts as new information comes to light and also the ways in which social workers need to learn to manage their frustrations and anxieties when they observe significant others undermining the well-being of their clients. The opportunity presented by Mikela's work with Charlie's mum also allowed us to explicitly focus upon the ways in which structural matters such as the major economic reforms of the 1980s and 1990s influenced the daily lives of individuals and communities. The oral history of the neighbourhood provided evidence of the devastation caused to families by these reforms and the cyclical way in which these effects were transmitted across generations. In being adaptable and flexible, participatory action research enables researchers and agencies involved in these projects to work at the micro level, effecting change alongside individuals while at the same time building a process for confronting more intractable community issues such as the effects of social and economic reforms. The knowledge gained from working with individuals as they construct life projects has enabled the community workers associated with the research project to identify localized projects that enable young people and families to address neighbourhood issues. Alongside this, these processes have also provided momentum for the young men to become involved in creating change, such as negotiating for the mobile library to attend the centre and developing active roles in the management of the centre, as well as in the work they did in caring for the younger children who attended the centre's family fun day.

Finally, *initiating change* is a key concern for participatory action research. As we noted in the introduction, action methods research typically focuses on change at an organizational or community level, but in our project we explored its potential in individual practice. At the end of this eighteen-month project Charlie's life had not been transformed: many of the challenges he brought into his involvement with Mikela remained. However, much had changed and, most importantly, his orientation to himself and his future now contained the potential for new opportunities that, despite the adverse circumstances Charlie experienced, held many possibilities for building resilience across contexts.

When we first met him, the local police were a significant feature of his life. At the end of the project he had little contact with them. Charlie had also decided to enrol in a residential rehabilitation program for young people with alcohol and drug addiction, and at the end of the project was planning this next phase in his life. So while challenges remained for Charlie, his engagement in the research project had provided him with opportunities to adopt a reflexive stance in relation to his life story. He had become increasingly interested in the way in which this story about himself would develop.

In a similar way, Mikela commented that the action methods approach intensified her focus on understanding the details of Charlie's life and the way in which different facets of his complex social world intersected. The oral history she completed with Charlie's mother, something she would not have done had she not been engaged in the research project, provided her with a context for understanding not only Charlie's situation, but also those of the other young men with whom she worked. The strengths literature that she gained access to as part of the research also provided her with a conceptual framework to engage not only with Charlie, but with the other agencies involved in Charlie's life. The work she did in the action-reflection process as part of the research team gave her a framework she could use to critically reflect on her practice decisions and to evaluate the usefulness of the theoretical frameworks she used to inform her practice. She was engaged in knowledge creation as she worked through the research to record the voices of Charlie and his mum differently, and the reflective use of her conceptual frameworks enabled her to engage not only with Charlie but with the other agencies involved in his life. In this way she was able to become a more effective advocate for Charlie and to create the possibility that other professionals would see Charlie in new ways.

The synergy between participatory action research and strengths-based practice holds great potential for encouraging researchers (and practitioners) to develop alternative interpretations of the connections between practice and theory development. It provides us with opportunities to learn how the micro level interacts with the wider context of lives as they are lived. It opens up possibilities for young people and their families to interpret their contexts and to discover how individuals can actively engage in their social worlds and develop their capacity to create change. As Ungar (2004, p. 87) argues:

Through teenagers' performance individually and collectively, with us adults playing the roles of both audience and supporting actors, high-risk youth construct for themselves powerful identities negotiated with others based on the health resources to which they share access.

Thus, the use of participatory action research in strengths-based practice can enhance the development of effective interventions with those young people who daily confront a high level of adversity.

References

Agency for Healthcare Research and Quality. (2001). *Community-based participatory research: Conference summary.* AHRQ W.H. Kellogg Foundation, Office of Minority Health, U.S. Department of Health and Human Services, Office of Behavioral and Social Sciences Research, National Institutes of Health. Retrieved 22 September 2007 from http://www.ahrq.gov/about/cpcr/cbpr/cbprack.htm.

Agency for Healthcare Research and Quality. (2003). *Creating partnerships, improving health: The role of community-based participatory research.* U.S. Department of Health and Human Services. Retrieved 22, September 2007 from http://www.ahrq.gov.

Barry, M. (2005). Introduction. In M. Barry (Ed.), *Youth policy and social inclusion: Critical debates with young people* (pp. 1–8). London: Routledge.

Beilharz, L. (2002). *Building community: The shared action experience.* Bendigo, Australia: St Luke's Innovative Resources.

Bergsson, M. (2000). From deficit to competence: Changing our paradigm. *Reclaiming Children and Youth, 8*(4), 203–6.

Boog, B., Keune, L., & Tromp, C. (2003). Action research and emancipation. *Journal of Community and Applied Social Psychology, 13*(6), 419–25.

Bourdieu, P. (1977). *Outline of a theory of practice.* Cambridge: Cambridge University Press.

Boutilier, M., Mason, R., & Rootman, I. (1997). Community action and reflective practice in health promotion research. *Health Promotion International, 12,* 69–78.

Brendtro, L., Long, N., & Brown, W. (2000). Searching for strengths. *Reclaiming Children and Youth: The Journal of Strengths-Based Interventions, 9*(2), 66–7.

Brown, W. (1983). *The other side of delinquency.* New Brunswick, NJ: Rutgers University Press.

Coenen, H., & Khonraad, S. (2003). Inspirations and aspirations of exemplarian action research. *Journal of Community and Applied Social Psychology, 13*(6), 439–50.

Cooper, B. (2001). Constructivism in social work: Towards a participative practice viability. *British Journal of Social Work, 31,* 721–37.

Crotty, M. (1998). *The foundations of social research: Meaning and perspective in the research process.* St Leonards: Allen and Unwin.

DeJong, P., & Berg, I.K. (2001). Co-constructing cooperation with mandated clients. *Social Work, 46,* 361–70.

Denzin, N., & Lincoln, Y. (2005). *The Sage handbook of qualitative research* (3rd ed.). Thousand Oaks, CA: Sage.

Friere, P. (1970). *Pedagogy of the oppressed.* Trans. M.B. Ramos. New York: Seabury.

Friere, P. (1994). *Pedagogy of hope: Reliving pedagogy of the oppressed.* Trans. R.R. Barr. New York: Continuum.Giddens, A. (1984). *The constitution of society: An outline of the theory of structuration.* Cambridge: Polity Press.

Giddens, A. (1976). *New rules of sociological method.* Cambridge: Polity Press.

Gordon, T. (2000). Tears and laughter in the margins. *NORA: Nordic Journal of Women's Studies, 8,* 149–59.

Gordon, T., Holland, J., Lahelma, E., & Thomson, R. (2005). Imagining gendered adulthood: Anxiety, ambivalence, avoidance and anticipation. *European Journal of Women's Studies, 12,* 83–103.

Greene, S. (2007). Including young mothers: Community-based participation and the continuum of active citizenship. *Community Development Journal, 42*(2): 167–80.

Habermas, J. (1984). *The theory of communicative action.* Trans. T. McCarthy. Cambridge: Polity Press.

Healy, K. (2000). *Social work practices: Contemporary perspectives on change.* London: Sage.

Healy, K. (2001). Participatory action research and social work: A critical appraisal. *International Social Work, 44*(1), 93–105.

Heron, J. (1996). *Co-operative inquiry research into the human condition.* London: Sage.

Houston, S. (2001). Beyond social constructionism: Critical realism and social work. *British Journal of Social Work, 31,* 845–61.

Lantz, P., Viruell-Fuentes, E., Israel, B., Softley, D., & Guzman, R. (2001). Can communities and academia work together on public health research? Evaluation results from a community-based participatory research partnership in Detroit. *Journal of Urban Health, 78*(3), 495–507.

Lather, P. (1991). *Getting smart: Feminist research and pedagogy with/in the postmodern.* New York: Routledge.

Lesko, N. (2001). *Act your age: A cultural construction of adolescence.* New York: Routledge-Falmer.

Lewin, K. (1948). *Resolving social conflicts: Selected papers on group dynamics.* New York: Harper Brothers.

Mayall, B. (2001). Introduction. In L. Alanen & B. Mayall (Eds.), *Conceptualising child-adult relations* (pp. 1–10). London: Routledge-Falmer.

Ministry of Youth Affairs. (2002). *Youth development strategy: Action for child and youth development.* Wellington, NZ: Ministry of Youth Affairs.

Munford, R., & Sanders, J. (2003a). Action research. In C. Davidson & M. Tolich (Eds.), *Social science research in New Zealand: Many paths to understanding* (2nd ed., pp. 263–74). Auckland: Pearson Education.

Munford, R., & Sanders. J., with Andrew, A., Butler, P., & Ruwhiu, L. (2003b). Action research with families/whanau and communities. In R. Munford & J. Sanders (Eds.), *Making a difference in families: Research that creates change* (pp. 93–112). Sydney: Allen and Unwin.

Munford, R., & Sanders. J. (2005). Borders, margins and bridges: Possibilities for change for marginalized young women. *Community Development Journal.* Retrieved 12 July 2006 from http://cdj.oxfordjournals.org.

Pottick, K.J., & Davis, D.M. (2001). Attributions of responsibility for children's mental health problems: Parents and professionals at odds. *American Journal of Orthopsychiatry, 71,* 426–72.

Potvin, L., Cargo, M., McComber, A., Delormie T., & Macaulay, A. (2003). Implementing participatory intervention and research in communities: Lessons from the Kahnawake schools diabetes prevention project in Canada. *Social Science and Medicine, 56,* 1295–1305.

Reid, P., & Vianna, E. (2001). Negotiating partnerships in research on poverty with community-based agencies. *Journal of Social Issues, 57*(2), 337–54.

Roberts, G., & Dick, B. (2003). Emancipatory design choices for action research practitioners. *Journal of Community and Applied Social Psychology, 13*(6), 486–95.

Saleebey, D. (2002). The strengths perspective: Possibilities and problems. In D. Saleebey (Ed.), *The strengths perspective in social work* (3rd ed., pp. 264–86). Boston: Allyn and Bacon.

Sanders, J., & Munford, R. (2007). Speaking from the margins: Implications for education and practice of young women's experiences of marginalisation. *Social Work Education, 26*(2), 185–99.

Titterton, M., & Smart, H. (2006). Can participatory research be a route to empowerment? A case study of a disadvantaged Scottish community. *Community Development Journal.* Retrieved 5 September 2006 from http://cdj.oxfordjournals.org.

Ungar, M. (2004). *Nurturing hidden resilience in troubled youth.* Toronto: University of Toronto Press.

Ungar, M. (Ed.) (2005). *Handbook for working with children and youth: Pathways to resilience across cultures and contexts.* Thousand Oaks: Sage.

Valentine, G. (1996). Angels and devils: Moral landscapes of childhood. *Environment and Planning D: Society and Space, 14*(5), 581–99.

Wallerstein, N., Duran, B., Aguilar, J., Joe, L., Loretto, F., Toya, A., Yepa-Waquie, H., Padilla, R., & Shendo, K. (2003). Jemez Pueblo: Built and social-cultural environments and health within a rural American Indian community in the Southwest. *American Journal of Public Health, 93,* 1517–18.

4 Not Just the Master Discourse: A Case for Holistic Case Studies of Youth Resilience

ELI TERAM AND MICHAEL UNGAR

> The case to be studied is a complex entity located in a milieu or situation embedded in a number of contexts or backgrounds. Historical context is almost always of interest, but so are cultural and physical contexts. Other contexts often of interest are the social, economic, political, ethical and aesthetic. (Stake, 2005, p. 449)

A book about researching youth across cultures and contexts would not be complete without considering case study as a method for understanding resilience. Elsewhere we argued that 'to successfully deliver the message of youth to professionals and policymakers, we must facilitate communicative processes between those most informed about a particular problem and those who have to address it' (Ungar & Teram, 2005, p. 159). The development of this perspective requires research methodologies that pay equal attention to individuals and to the political, social, and cultural contexts of their lives; well-designed case study research suits this purpose. As suggested by the quotation above, case study is used when the researcher wants to understand contextual conditions that are relevant to the phenomenon under study (Yin, 2003). It is a comprehensive research strategy, ideal for studying 'phenomenon within its real-life context, especially when the boundaries between phenomenon and context are not clearly evident' (Yin, 2003, p. 13). Youth resilience is unmistakably such a phenomenon.

Current thinking about resilience has moved away from a focus on the capacity of individuals to cope with adverse life circumstances to a focus on the interactions between youth and their environments

(Lerner, 2006; Ungar, 2005). However, this conceptual shift has not been fully reflected in research methodologies that account for the relationship between micro resilience practices and the macro processes and structures in which they are embedded. The best-known studies of resilience have tended to compartmentalize individual and environmental factors into distinct lists. Better-designed quantitative studies are finding such dichotomous thinking inaccurate, with some individual characteristics being shown to cluster with environmental factors and some environmental factors grouping with individual traits (Thoeokas & Lerner, 2006; Ungar, 2008). It is no longer possible to discern purely individual qualities like self-efficacy or intellectual capacity. The traits we attribute to the inner sphere of individuals are not independent of external factors that shape the extent to which each influences positive development under stress.

Even qualitative researchers who appreciate this link cannot always resist the temptation or pressure to develop what Clarke calls 'the master discourse, that which usually trumps the others' (2005, p. 175).[1] Although case studies of youth resilience may not offer the breadth of the master discourse, they carry the depth and immediate relevance that comes with understanding the minute dynamics of resilient practices within a particular context. Moreover, these studies can be designed according to the contextual specificity that interests the researchers and their sponsors, and to the resources at their disposal.

This chapter begins with a brief account of the qualitative component of the International Resilience Project (IRP). The IRP is a multisite study of resilience that is seeking to discern culturally diverse understandings of positive development under adverse circumstances. The IRP's purpose is to contrast conventional understandings of resilience, most often developed in Western contexts, with those of individuals in non-Western countries and marginalized peoples living in the West (visible minorities, aboriginal peoples, etc.). The project has used a unique 'ground-up' approach to research design that has resulted in an iterative mixed-methods study. Over the course of phase one of the project, more than fifteen hundred youth from around the world participated in one or more aspects of the research. Since the main purpose of the IRP was the exploration of methodological issues, it provides an ideal starting point for this chapter, which was stimulated by the critical reflections facilitated by the project's methodology and outcomes.

The second section presents two examples that demonstrate how case studies advance practical knowledge about resilience within particular contexts. Since the suggested case study approach locates resilience narratives at the centre, the third section presents an example that highlights the potential contributions of personal narratives to resilience research. The fourth section addresses key research design issues. We define the case, or unit of analysis, as the resilience process experienced by youth rather than resilient youth. The core data for each case are the narratives of the focal youth about their experience, and the accounts of key informants about the involvement of the youth with formal support systems. Although this section also discusses case selection and data collection and interpretation, readers planning to use the approach outlined in this chapter are advised to consult resources that deal in more detail with the methodologies of case study (e.g., Ragin & Becker, 1992; Stake, 2005; Yin, 2003) and narrative inquiry (e.g., Chase, 2005; Josselson, Lieblich, & McAdams, 2003; Lieblich, Tuval-Mashiach, & Zilber, 1998).

The IRP Qualitative Research[2]

Qualitative research methods fit well with the current understanding of resilience. Unlike quantitative methods that are driven by particular conceptual frameworks and rely on standardized measures, qualitative methods explore the uniqueness of individual youth and the way in which they negotiate their environments. Qualitative studies provide opportunities for youth to share with researchers their own definitions of resilience and the strategies they use to access the resources required for their well-being (Ungar, 2003). The insights generated by these studies can help us shape interventions in ways that are relevant for youth rather than preserving irrelevant institutionalized arrangements (e.g., Ungar, Teram, & Picketts, 2001). They are also useful for gaining a different understanding of what we consider ordered or disordered behaviours (e.g., Ungar & Teram, 2005). Well-designed qualitative studies attempt to understand the ability of youth to thrive while considering the cultural, economic, social, and political conditions that construct their mental health. This contextual specificity is particularly relevant when the study of resilience expands to communities and countries in which Eurocentric perspectives of youth resilience and mental health do not apply.

A clear understanding of the rationale for qualitative resilience research drove the conception and design of the IRP. The essence of the qualitative component part of the study was eighty-nine interviews with youth in fourteen sites in eleven countries (for a full account of the methodology see Ungar & Liebenberg [2005] or the website at www.resilienceresearch.org). The fourteen communities participating in the study highlighted social, geographic, or cultural variations; children in each community were believed to be exposed to different kinds and levels of risk. The number of interviews in each site ranged from two to twenty-four; they lasted between thirty minutes and two hours. The data were analysed using the common procedures for generating grounded theory (Strauss & Corbin, 1998).

The analyses of the interviews identified seven tensions that seem to be present in all participating sites. These tensions may be understood as themes that are relevant to the participants across different cultures. Each theme, while potentially of influence, varies in the impact it exerts on the decisions youth make regarding how best to adapt to adversity. These seven tensions are:

1 *Access to material resources:* Availability of financial, educational, medical, and employment assistance, resources, or opportunities, as well as access to food, clothing, and shelter
2 *Relationships:* Association with significant others, peers, and adults within one's family and community
3 *Identity:* Personal and collective senses of purpose, self-appraisal of strengths and weaknesses, aspirations, beliefs and values, including spiritual and religious identification
4 *Power and control:* Experiences of caring for oneself and others; ability to effect change in one's social and physical environment in order to access health resources
5 *Cultural adherence:* Adherence to one's local and/or global cultural practices, values, and beliefs
6 *Social justice:* Experiences related to finding a meaningful role in community and social equality
7 *Cohesion:* Balancing one's personal interests with a sense of responsibility to the greater good; a feeling of being a part of something larger than one's self socially and spiritually (Ungar et al., 2007).

Using these tensions as a conceptual map, the findings were summarized as follows:

Findings show that *youth who experience themselves as resilient, and are seen by their communities as resilient, are those that successfully navigate their way through these tensions. Resilient youth find a way to resolve all seven tensions simultaneously according to the strengths and resources available to the youth individually, within their family, community and culture.* It is the fit between the solutions youth try, and how well their solutions address the challenges posed by each tension, within the social and political constraints of their community, that contribute to a young person's experience of resilience. (Ungar et al., 2007)

Although this framework may appear as a 'master discourse,' Ungar and his colleagues try to avoid the trumping of other discourses by emphasizing the differential manifestation of these tensions in each site. They also stress that there are many equally good ways to resolve these tensions. Focusing on the fit between tension management strategies and the context within which they are used, Ungar et al. highlight the interactive nature of resilience. Thus, this framework adheres to the current conception of resilience, offering a framework for thinking about it without negating the unique ways resilience may be expressed in different contexts. However, notwithstanding its flexible application, this overarching framework has elements of a 'master discourse' in the sense that it pays more attention to the proposed conceptual map than to the details of resilience stories. Ungar et al. demonstrate this well when they apply their framework to the story of a Palestinian boy. The process they follow serves as a reminder that the extraction of general ideas from data, with the use of specific details as illustration, background, or qualification, does not advance the exploration of unique differences (Flyvbjerg, 2001).

The development of the seven tensions framework advances a common understanding of pathways to resilience *across* cultures. However, it does not help us understand the uniqueness of resilience processes *within* particular cultures and their theoretical and practical implications.[3]

Two local analyses can help us to further explain this distinction and the potential contribution of case studies.

The Value of Case Studies in Resilience Research

'Resilience in the Palestinian Occupied Territories' (van Teeffelen, Bitar, & Al-Habash, 2005), a chapter in an edited book based on the IRP (Ungar, 2005), presents the interrelated stories of Saleem and the

Palestinian Youth Association for Leadership and Rights Activation (PYALARA). Saleem is a young man who found his source of re-silience within PYALARA, a youth media–and-communications-oriented non-governmental organization (NGO). Saleem's story is effectively used to demonstrate how PYALARA's strategies of engag-ing youth fit the broad political and cultural contexts of the Israeli–Palestinian conflict. The chapter introduces us to the concept of *sumud*, or steadfastness, which reflects much of Palestinian cultural ways of coping. Although *sumud* has been criticized for its inflexibility, for van Teeffelen and his colleagues it 'captures the essential elements of endurance and refusal to give up without which no account or analysis of Palestinian society will be valid' (p. 422). PYALARA, like other NGOs working with Palestinian youth, attempts to strengthen *sumud* and contribute to healing through activities that challenge despair and negativity.

Saleem's story is limited mainly to his involvement with PYALARA and how it changed his life and encouraged him to become a journal-ist and writer (Saleem is also a co-author of the chapter). Nevertheless, it illuminates both PYALARA's contribution to strengthening the resilience of Palestinian youth and an important part of one person's pathway to resilience. Although Saleem's other life circumstances, family, and friends remain unknown to us, van Teeffelen et al. effec-tively situate his resilience within the resilience of the Palestinians' struggle for national independence. Saleem's story demonstrates the complexity of the relationships between individual agency and struc-ture, while highlighting the historical context that made PYALARA an effective mediator between youth and the needs of the Palestinian society at a particular time in its history. In his words,

In 1997 I got to know about a new idea of a newspaper for young people – all made by young people. Since I loved writing and I could not find a place to publish my writings but my notebooks and computer, I was excited to get involved. At that time, during the years after the Oslo agreement was signed, it was a duty to help develop Palestinian society. A whole new bunch of creative and fruitful ideas were evolving, and the process of development was being remodeled into a more vibrant momentum ... My experience with PYALARA has changed a lot about who I am without changing my principles and beliefs. PYALARA has given me the space and tools to grow, yet without being forced into a certain shape. Having the tools for change, you end up in a cycle of creating change: not only do you create change amongst others, but further, they exert change within your life as well; it is a cycle. (pp. 427–8)

The connection between Saleem's desire to become a writer, the Oslo agreement, and the birth of organizations like PYALARA is the kind of integration between actors and structures that is typically found in case studies.

Within a very different Canadian context, Ungar, Teram, and Picketts (2001) use official files and personal work experience with two young offenders to demonstrate a similar integration. In two case studies, they track and contrast the organizational careers of Paul and Cameron to argue for deliberate and tight collaboration between institutions and communities. The authors show that Paul, who was removed from his community at an early age, did not have the roots that ease the transfer from institutional care back to community life. Thus, Paul could not benefit from the same community support and continuity in care providers offered to Cameron, whose relative success was built largely on the alliance between his community and different parts of the formal helping system. By highlighting how institutions can pave very different paths for two boys with remarkably similar risk factors, Paul and Cameron's stories raise questions about the current operation of these institutions. As Ungar, Teram, and Picketts (2001) explain:

The two cases demonstrate the essential elements of best and worst scenarios of identity rebuilding. In Cameron's case, institutional care was part of a process of identity construction and used effectively as he moved in and out of custody. With the occasional upheavals as Cameron adjusted to the community taken into account, the institution was an accessible and flexible resource for Cameron and his caregivers, providing the controlled environment for the intensive therapy he required. In several instances, continuity in his identity construction was facilitated when workers shared responsibility for his care both inside and outside placement. In Paul's case, placement in the institution was used by the community and its service providers to disengage from participation in his identity construction. Given this disengagement, Paul chose to assert himself through physical violence towards his institutional caregivers. Ironically, the assessment of Paul as a dangerous offender was based largely on his behaviour in the institution rather than in the community that feared him. Thus, the script for Paul was written by his performance in the institution whereas the script for Cameron was written by the community, reflecting its tolerance and acceptance of him. (p. 38)

These detailed case studies contrast the very different roles institutions can play in the lives of two similar young offenders. The use of case studies in this way fits well with two conclusions reached by Luthar and Bidwell Zelazo (2003) based on their integrative review of resilience research. The first is the need to emphasize that the study of resilience is about a process or phenomenon rather than about the personal attributes of children. The second is the importance of focusing on what adults can do to boost the capacities of children and support their efforts to overcome adversities rather than on what at-risk youth can do for themselves. In this regard, the focus of van Teeffelen, Bitar, and Al-Habash (2005) on PYALARA, rather than Saleem, may reflect this understanding, particularly in poorly resourced, conflict-ridden, and confined environments like the Occupied Palestinian Territories.

If we agree that the ideal purpose of resilience research is to gain insights about our helping practices, carefully designed case studies are suited to serve this purpose. Although some case studies can be designed with limited input from youth (e.g., Ungar, Teram, & Picketts, 2001), youth are probably most informed about the questions we need to ask, including what they find most and least useful, when and why they use or do not use the resources we allocate to them, and how these resources can be arranged to maximize their effective use. Thus, we suggest that the narratives of youth about their experiences should be the core data of resilience case studies. As we will see in the following section, a narrative approach also fits well with our interest in both agency and context.

What Personal Narratives Offer

Joyce Carlson Clouston's recent experiences with methodological choices help us demonstrate the rational for a narrative approach to the study of resilience.[4] Joyce's dissertation focuses on the experiences of Aboriginals caring for children with developmental disabilities. After interviewing twenty-one caregivers, she attempted to analyse the data following the constant comparative data analysis methods of grounded theory research. Joyce found the process frustrating because she felt that the analysis did not effectively represent the lives of the people she interviewed. Like the contributors to Daiute and Light-foot's (2004) edited book, Joyce found narrative analysis more appeal-ing because it provided her with analytical tools to articulate the holis-tic nature of the caregiving experience.

Thus, she turned away from her earlier attempts to identify common themes across participants' experiences to narrative analyses that connect their individual stories to the broad realities of being an Abo-riginal in Canada. Her current analysis is organized around the story of Mary, a mother and grandmother who adopted two children affected by fetal alcohol syndrome.[5] Mary's story not only covers most of the themes in other interviews, but also connects her personal expe-riences with the broad and historical contexts of Aboriginal life. It takes us through abuse in residential schools and its intergenerational traumatic impacts, alcoholism, healing, and the negation and reclaim-ing of traditional values and culture.

Closer to the study's focal interest, Mary's story articulates Aborigi-nal spiritual and cultural values that consider *all children* as 'gifts' from the Creator, whose lives have purpose and value. Mary's daily care for her children is rooted in spirituality and marked by a strong commit-ment to *taking responsibility*. This responsibility includes accessing the best possible resources for her children through the formal social, health, and education systems and *sharing responsibility*[6] for their care with agencies and professionals in these systems. In her attempts to access supports, Mary's story also demonstrates the ambivalence of people whose community is in transition from being self-sustaining and autonomous to becoming increasingly dependent on Western-style formal support.

In a meeting convened to share a summary of the interviews, other interviewees confirmed that Mary's story captures their experiences; they viewed her as a leader who, having been through cycles of anguish, despair, recovery, and triumph, can understand and express the struggles experienced by many caregivers. The voices, words, and stories of other participants are used to complete the picture of what it is to care for a child with a disability, with Aboriginal values, in Canada. Some of them enrich the dimensions revealed through Mary's story; others add new dimensions that are not captured by her experience.[7]

Mary's story demonstrates how personal narratives can capture the logic of personal actions within environmental constraints. As the Per-sonal Narratives Group concludes:[8]

> Personal narratives are particularly rich sources because, attentively interpreted, they illuminate both the logic of individual courses of action and the effects of system-level constraints within which those courses evolve. Moreover, each life provides evidence of historical activity – the working out within a specific life situation of deliberate courses of action that in turn have the potential to undermine or perpetuate the conditions and relationships in which the life evolved. (Barbre & Personal Narratives Group, 1989, p. 6)

More importantly, Mary's story directs us to the actions required to alter the conditions and relationships that constrain her choices and those of other Aboriginals who care for children with disabilities. Their collective story points to interventions that might enable intergenerational recovery from trauma. Specifically, it suggests that mainstream educational, health, and social service agencies have to structure their interventions around Aboriginal values. This implies the facilitation of initiatives within First Nation and Metis communities that build on their cultural orientation to support caregivers and their families as they 'take responsibility' for their children's care. Where family and community supports are fragmented or absent, we need to facilitate the negotiation of 'shared responsibility' between caregivers and mainstream agencies in a way that minimizes the shame and guilt that may be associated with seeking support outside the Aboriginal community.

Mary and Saleem's stories, as well as those of Paul and Cameron, have the three common key features Elliott (2005) associates with narrative in social research: they are chronological, meaningful, and inherently social. She identifies these features following Hinchman and Hinchman's proposition that

> narratives (stories) in the human sciences should be defined provisionally as discourses with a clear sequential order that connect events in a meaningful way for a definite audience and thus offer insights about the world and/or people's experiences of it. (1997, p. xvi, quoted in Elliott [2005])

Similarly, Czarniawska (2004) sees a narrative 'as a spoken or written text giving an account of an event/action, or series of events/actions, chronologically connected' (p. 17).

An important element of narrative inquiry that makes it particularly relevant for studying youth resilience is the emphasis on locating the narrative within the opportunities available to the narrator. As suggested by Chase (2005):

> Narrative researchers view stories as both enabled and constrained by a range of social resources and circumstances. These include the possibilities for self and reality construction that are intelligible within the narrator's community, local settings, organizational and cultural and historical location. (p. 657)

The narratives of people like Mary and Saleem are thus not just a way to learn about them but also about what caused them to make certain choices. Understanding the rationale for these choices can in turn help us design our interventions in ways that are most useful for youth facing similar adversities in similar locations. Mary's story, for example, directs us to ways to ease the difficulties experienced by Aboriginals who have to share the responsibility of caring for their children with formal mainstream organizations. Similarly, although narrated by others, Paul and Cameron's stories highlight the need to conceptualize institutions for young offenders as an extension of community resources rather than as incarceration facilities.

Thus, narrative inquiry offers an effective way to understand youth, the resources they need and have, the ways they use or do not use these resources, and how these resources can be arranged to maximize their contribution to paving different paths to resilience. As Chase (2005) points out, many researchers 'approach *any* narrative as an *instance* of the possible relationships between a narrator's active construction of self, on the one hand, and the social, cultural, and historical circumstances that enable and constrain that narrative, on the other' (italics in the original) (p. 667). This approach to narratives fits well with case study research, as both emphasize the link between the phenomenon under study and its context. However, since case study research is not limited to personal narratives, it may be better suited to address the editors' interest in methodological flexibility and linking research to effective interventions. The following section explores how case studies of resilience, with personal narratives as the core data, offer methodological flexibility for developing practical knowledge.

Designing Holistic Case Studies of Resilience[9]

One of the most challenging matters in case study research is to define our unit of analysis or decide what the case is (Ragin & Becker, 1992; Yin, 2003). Although not research based, the chapter on PYALARA demonstrates how the answer to this question can shape the research design and focus of the study. Van Teeffelen and his colleagues state at the outset of their paper that their specific interest is in how PYALARA 'creates conditions that bolster resilience among Palestinian youth.' They go on to say:

> This discussion will show that resilience is as dependent on how, struc-
> turally, organizations respond to the needs of youth, providing them
> opportunities for meaningful participation in their communities, as it is
> on the individual qualities each youth has when confronting adversity.
> (van Teeffelen, Bitar, & Al-Habash, 2005, p. 417)

Thus, they approach PYALARA as a holistic single case, with Saleem's story being a small part of the bigger narrative of an organization that contributed to his resilience. With PYALARA as the unit of analysis, their interest in Saleem's life is limited to his history with PYALARA. However, if Saleem had been defined as the holistic single case, PYALARA's story would have been part of the bigger tale of his resilience. PYALARA could have also been studied using an embedded single-case design. In this design, PYALARA as a whole would have remained the main unit of analysis but we would also pay attention to a sub-unit or sub-units within it. Examples of embedded units of analysis include specific programs the organization offers and youth like Saleem who were served by the organization.

Case study research is not limited to single cases. Based on our interest and resources, we can also develop holistic or embedded multiple-case designs. The selection of Paul and Cameron as holistic case studies reflects part of the logic of multiple-case designs. It was intended to contrast the two extremes of effective and ineffective use of institutional resources. Stake (2005) refers to cases that are studied to provide insight into a particular issue or a generalization as *instrumental*, highlighting their use in supporting a particular point rather than an *intrinsic* interest in the case itself. Van Teeffelen, Bitar, and Al-Habash (2005) seem to have an intrinsic interest in PYALARA, although they use their case to demonstrate a more general point.

Chart 1

PYALARA: A holistic single case	PYALARA: An embedded single case	Saleem: A holistic single case
Interest in Saleem is limited to his history with the organization	The stories of selected youth are sub-units of analysis Specific programs offered by PYALARA are also sub-units of analysis	Interest in PYALARA is limited to its involvement with Saleem

Multiple-case studies tend to be more clearly instrumental, as they are designed to investigate a particular phenomenon, population, or condition (Stake, 2005).

Our interest in holistic case studies is instrumental. Similarly, our suggestion to use personal narratives as the core data falls into the domain of studies in which the narrative is employed for investigating a particular research question (Lieblich, Tuval-Mashiach, & Zilber, 1998).[10] While a holistic case study can contribute to our understanding of resilience within a particular context, multiple holistic case studies within the same context are required to comprehend the full complexity of the process. Single or multiple holistic case studies within different contexts and cultures can advance our understanding of the differences and similarities between the experiences of resilience in these locations, and may advance our understanding of it as a universal phenomenon. But what are our cases and how should we select them?

The most obvious approach would be to define our cases as selected youth who had been through the process of overcoming adverse conditions in their lives. However, by taking this approach we once again put individuals at the centre of the analysis and indirectly reinforce the sense that resilience is about personal qualities and actions. If we accept the idea that resilience is a process, and agree that it would be helpful to know more about what adults can do to bolster the ability of youth to overcome adverse life circumstances (Luthar & Bidwell Zelazo, 2003), our case should be the resilience process. The purpose of the analysis would be to understand this process through gathering information from individuals who experienced it in different roles. This can be done effectively through holistic, single or multiple, cases designed to explore the perspectives of selected youth and those who facilitated or hindered their resilience process. To the best of our knowledge, there are no studies of youth resilience that take this approach. Therefore, it is important to provide more details about this proposed research strategy.

Case Design

With the resilience process of a particular youth as our case, or unit of analysis, each case can be designed around the personal narratives of youth about their experience. These narratives guide the identification of key informants from the youth's 'formal support network' and formal documents that can facilitate a holistic understanding of the process. Key informants in each case will include people who in their formal capacity played an important role in the resilience process (e.g., teachers, social workers, youth workers, community leaders).

Family members and significant others who interacted with these officials will also be asked about their experiences with the formal system. The limitation of their input to 'formal experiences' signifies that the narratives of the focal youth are considered the only relevant account of those youths' private lives. Asking others about the same private spheres would also be ethically problematic, because there is no easy way to manage diverse narratives of the same interpersonal dynamics, and the consequences of their disclosure in our interpretations. Accepting the reality of multiple, partial, and incomplete 'truths' (Denzin & Lincoln, 2005, p. 189), our interest is in the youth's construction of his/her story rather than in the impossible task of sorting out 'the truth.' As Chase (2005) points out, researchers are well aware that narrators do not construct unitary, fixed, or authentic selves; thus, they 'treat narratives as socially situated interactive performances – as produced in this particular setting, for this particular audience, for these particular purposes' (p. 657).

Our interest in hearing the perception of the officials who were part of the resilience process is to gain a better understanding of how they see their contribution, and what can be learned from their experience. We want them to tell us about their theory of intervention with the focal youth; it is clearly not a professional version of, or a commentary on, the youth's resilience story, but akin to a narrative on their work with that person. This information will make our understanding of the case more complete and help us understand the social, organizational, and policy contexts of the case. More importantly, it will help us generate useable knowledge for those who are in a position to bolster youth resilience. As demonstrated by Teram, Schachter, and Stalker (2005), professional practice can be effectively influenced by knowledge generated collaboratively with input from both clients and professionals.

When deciding which officials to include in the case and what documents to review, our choices should not be limited to the 'good' characters in the resilience story or to 'success' documents. Officials who were not helpful or presented obstacles in the resilience process should also be included in the study of the case. Similarly, we should include documents that provide accounts of interventions that were not helpful or did not work. The inclusion of this 'negative' information is essential to having a more complete understanding of intervention theories, social values, and society's attitudes towards youth. More importantly, they can help us understand the perspectives of those who mediate between youth at risk and society. As suggested by Hardin (1990), professionals 'are mediators between their clients' or patients' needs and social constraints imposed by policy. The conflict of interest is one between each client and the larger society, not between the professional and the client. But it is mediated through the professional' (p. 538).

Similarly, Hasenfeld (2000) writes about the actions taken by human service organizations as moral practices in the sense that they confer on clients a judgment of their social worth, the cause of their problems, and the desired outcomes of interventions. Thus, the full potency of social values is expressed through these organizations, the professionals they employ, and their interactions with youth. Like in the story of Mary, we can discover the clash between cultures and the need to work differently with people who have experienced a long history of oppression.

Researchers can make these discoveries by attending explicitly to issues of power and its manifestation in narratives about the contact between youth and the systems designed to facilitate their development and growth. The juxtaposition of the narrative of youth about their resilience process with the narratives of interventions in the same case can be an effective way of attending to these power differentials, and of bringing the voices of youth to professionals, managers, and policy makers. A careful selection of cases and contexts can facilitate an effective change process to make interventions more relevant to the realities of youth.

The Selection of Cases

Defining the case as the resilience process experienced by a particular youth means that we don't have to label youth as 'resilient' or 'not resilient.' Instead, it can be assumed that all youth with adverse life circumstances struggle to overcome obstacles on their paths to meaningful lives. This assumption will guide the selection of cases based on their potential to advance knowledge, answer our questions, and generate required changes (Flyvbjerg, 2001; Stake, 2005; Yin, 2003). Specifically, the case selection should be driven by our interest in gaining an understanding of what can be done to bolster the ability of youth to overcome the adverse circumstances of their lives.

According to Yin (2003), the logic of selection in multiple-case studies is similar to that of replication in multiple experiments. However, while in experimental research conditions can be either duplicated or altered in the lab, when selecting cases the researcher looks for variations that generate similar duplications or alterations in real-life situations (e.g., Campbell, 1969). Thus, each case has to be selected so that it predicts either similar results (a literal replication) or contrasting results for predictable reasons (a theoretical replication) (Yin, 2003, p. 47). Although replication and prediction may not be appealing concepts for qualitative researchers, this logic of case selection provides useful ways for thinking about the kind of variations we need in the selected cases. Possible alterations may be related, for example, to race, ethnicity, culture, immigration, size and type of communities, formal support systems involved in the case, and the risk factors faced by the youth. The choice of cases based on these and other variations has to derive from current knowledge about youth resilience, and from opportunities to observe how these variations are played out. The cases of Paul and Cameron were selected based on the same logic, building on an opportunity to contrast the resilience process of two similar young offenders, with the variation being the way institutional care was used in each case.

Flyvbjerg (2001) expands on the above logic in his discussion of four types of cases used in information-oriented selection: extreme/deviant cases, maximum variation cases, critical cases, and paradigmatic cases. Unlike random selection, which enhances representation, information-oriented cases are selected to maximize the information on a given problem or phenomenon. Extreme cases for our purpose can be, for example, youth resilience processes that worked extremely well, or extremely poorly, in terms of facilitating the management of multiple adverse life circumstances. Given the need for cases that maximize variations, it would be unfortunate if researchers avoid cases that may lead to important insights because they are afraid to indirectly label youth as non-resilient. We hope that defining the case as the resilience process rather than the resilient youth will encourage researchers to explore extreme cases of both successful and unsuccessful processes.

Critical cases have strategic importance in relation to the focal issue and can generate 'information which permits logical deductions of the type "if this is (not) valid for this case, then it applies to all (no) cases"' (Flyvbjerg, 2001, p. 79). Thus, for example, a critical case of youth resilience may be one that involves intensive interventions by all formal support systems in a particular community. Such cases can help demonstrate the operation of these systems, the way they work or don't work together, and how their practices influence particular resilience processes. The intensive activation of formal systems and interorganizational processes in this case exposes their best or worst practices. These critical cases may lead to deductions like *If this is the way these systems facilitated the resilience process for this youth, they are likely to work in similar ways in other resilience processes in this community*, or alternatively, *If these systems could not work together when the need for collaboration was so obvious, they are not likely to collaborate in cases in which this need is not so obvious.*

Paradigmatic cases are intended to develop a metaphor or establish a school of thought related to the study's domain. As such, their choice is problematic because it is difficult to determine in advance the metaphorical or prototypical value of a case (Flyvbjerg, 2001). This value is determined by interrelated factors that include the strategic selection of the case, its execution, the reaction to it, and its validity claims in scientific and, sometimes, public discourses. Thus Flyvbjerg concludes that researchers can only use their experience and intuition to assess whether a given case has the potential to become paradigmatic. He also notes that the same case 'can be simultaneously extreme, critical, and paradigmatic' (p. 81).

Data Collection and Interpretation

Although the literature on resilience research provides a sense of what stories of resilience may sound like, it is important to suspend this knowledge as much as possible and focus on listening (Chase,

2003). One way of thinking about the story we want to hear is to consider it as the *interviewee's own theory of his/her way of making it against all odds*. This includes an account of these odds, how they were overcome, insights about the experience, what and who was helpful or not helpful, and how it or they were helpful or not helpful. While an orientation to listen and follow the interviewee's lead is important, we concur with Chase's (2003) suggestion to develop an interview guide. Like Chase, we expect most of the questions to be answered naturally by following the interviewee's response to the broadest question about the resilience story. A question like *Tell me how you made it to where you are in spite of all the difficulties* is likely to provide a general frame for inviting the story. However, it is important for the interviewer to anticipate the domains the story is likely to cover (Chase, 2003) based on current knowledge of youth resilience. Knowing these domains may be useful for probing and exploring areas that the interviewees did not cover in the initial articulation of their resilience story. The exploration of these possible gaps should be left to the final parts of the interview, allowing the interviewees to first tell their stories without interference and guidance. The expression of interest in hearing about unexplored domains is intended to expand the story rather than lead it in a particular direction. For example, asking interviewees about the role of parents, siblings, or teachers in their stories brings these significant others into the story, without directing or influencing their responses.

The interviews with officials can be organized around a broad question like *Tell me how you and your organization made a difference in the life of [name of focal youth]*. If the interviewees do not remember the focal youth, they should be asked to refresh their memories by reviewing his/her official files. With the consent of the youth, these files should also be reviewed by the researcher prior to the interview. Similar to the interviews with the youth, professionals should first be given an opportunity to tell their account of the focal youth's resilience and then be asked to fill in gaps related to areas identified in the official files. The researcher should arrange a group meeting with all the officials involved in the case to share with them the interpretation of the case and its theoretical and practical implications.

Special consideration has to be given to making the interview process comfortable for children. Eder and Fingerson (2002) present a compelling rationale for group interviews with youth, as they have a natural connection with their peer culture and collective construction of meanings. They argue that, when conducted with existing groups, these interviews emulate the natural conversations that go on in these settings. Eder and Fingerson also refer to other strategies of creating a natural context for the interviews, including conducting interviews within a larger, familiar activity, and the use of children as interviewers.

Although group interviews may have some advantages, their use for collecting narratives of resilience may be inappropriate because youth should be able to tell their stories without the self-censorship imposed when peers are present. More accurate accounts, which may be one product of group interviews (Eder & Fingerson, 2002), are less important in the study of narratives than the ability of individuals to express themselves as authentically as possible.[11] Thus, strategies that make personal interviews more comfortable, such as being around youth in their hangouts or using interviewees they know and trust, are preferable to group interviews. Ungar (1995), for example, got closer to the children he was planning to interview by working with them as a counsellor for a few months before inviting them to participate in his study. Boundaries between the two roles were maintained by distinguishing one from the other (Schein, 1987; Snyder, 1992). Youth were interviewed after treatment had ended and payment for their participation signalled a change in their status from client to participant. The youth reported appreciating the opportunity to express themselves. The level of trust built previously provided excellent access to their lives and those of their families in part because of the previous guarantee of confidentiality and familiarity.

Once the stories are gathered, their interpretation can take different forms (see Chase, 2005; Lieblich, Tuval-Mashiach, & Zilber 1998). This interpretation is bound to be related to our interest in the connections between individual resilience practices and broader organizational and social policy contexts. Hopefully, this interest is broad enough to facilitate an accurate representation of the participants' interpretations of their own experiences. However, as Riessman (1993) reminds us:

All forms of representation of experience are limited portraits. Simply stated, we are interpreting and creating texts at every juncture, letting symbols stand for or take the place of the primary experience, to which we have no direct access. Meaning is ambiguous because it arises out of the process of interaction between people: self, teller, listener and recorder, analyst, and reader. Although the goal is to tell the whole truth, our narratives about others' narratives are our worldly creations. (p. 133)

In interpreting cases, the power of resilience researchers is not very different from that of the professionals who mediate between society and clients. Both can represent the realities of young clients in ways that reflect ideological, organizational, professional, and personal biases rather than the realities of people constrained by the choices available to them. Ungar and Teram's (2005) critique of Hemmings' (2000) blaming of the youth she studied, while ignoring the context of their lives, illustrates this point. It is therefore important to involve youth not only in the telling of their stories but in the interpretation and writing process.

Youth can be involved in various ways. For example, Ungar (1995) conducted two rounds of interviews with the youth he studied. In the first interview he explored each participant's search for mental health; in the second interview he shared with them his interpretation of the data and asked them for feedback. Salmon (2007) followed a similar process, engaging in participatory group interviews Aboriginal women with experiences of substance abuse during pregnancy and fetal alcohol syndrome/effects. While the first group interviews focused on the participants' experiences, the second interview was a *dialogic analysis,* building on Salmon's preliminary interpretation of data from the first group interviews. This approach led to discussions about making policy more relevant to women's personal experiences. Teram, Schachter, & Stalker (2005) went a step further by directly connecting health professionals and survivors of childhood sexual abuse to develop guidelines for sensitive practice, using as a starting point the researchers' interpretation of interviews with survivors. The common element of these approaches is respect for the knowledge of research participants, placing their expertise at par with that of professionals, policy makers, and researchers. With this essential idea and examples in mind, the inclusion of youth in influencing the outcome of research can take many forms.

Conclusion: Materializing the Potential for Action

The conception of resilience as a dynamic interaction between youth and their environments to overcome adverse conditions in their life is an improvement over its earlier conception as personal qualities that some children have and others lack. As such, it is going in the right direction by not blaming the victims (Luthar & Bidwell Zelazo, 2003). The case study approach outlined in this chapter takes this idea a step further by considering the task of overcoming adverse life circumstance as the *shared responsibility* of youth, their families, and the formal system that represents society's values and perception of social problems. To follow the full logic of the new conceptualization of resilience, research has to consider both the stories of youth who made it against all odds and the accounts of officials who play a role in these stories. If resilience is indeed an interactive process, we must stop focusing exclusively on youth and include in our studies all key participants in this process.

In order to inform and influence social policy and professional practice, resilience research has to be more than a dialogue between youth and academics, or among academics. Thus, it is important that researchers consider their role as mediators between youth and society, with an emphasis on facilitating a process by which those who can effect change can hear the messages of youth. This directs researchers to humility in determining the scope of the research, the research sites, and the particular cases to be studied. It enjoins attention to settings in which this mediation process is likely to be effective. Examples include organizations or inter-organizational networks that want to understand how to work effectively with youth in their community, or funding bodies that are frustrated with the poor return on their investment in programs for youth. Another example is the exploration of alternative interventions through the resilience processes experienced by the youth who benefitted from them. In these cases, the purpose would be to study the narrative of successful resilience stories as a possible way of facilitating the acceptance and diffusion of initiatives that are well received by youth.

Bringing the voices of youth to those who have to hear them does not mean that we must be invited to do the study by a particular policy-making body, organization, or group. As academics, or students, we are well positioned to initiate research that aims at social improvement by responding to the unmet needs of disadvantaged groups (Greenwood & Levin, 2000). As demonstrated by Teram, Schachter, and Stalker (2005), a well-designed research study can effectively influence professional practice even when the target audience did not initiate the study. As long as the needs are real and the implications of the findings make sense and can be practically implemented, unsolicited low-cost studies can be as influential as large-budget solicited ones. Thus, researchers should not shy away from studying cases of resilience involving disadvantaged youth who are not connected to any formal system. Alternatively, we can take on the study of youth whose resilience process did not lead to the overcoming of the adverse circumstances of their life.

Case studies ought not to be limited to one location and context. As discussed earlier, holistic and embedded multiple cases can offer valuable insights through comparative analyses of the resilience process in different locations and contexts. Notwithstanding the scope of the research, and the number of cases it includes, we should always try to design it in a way that allows each case to consider and respond to its local realities.

One of the advantages of the approach outlined in this chapter is that the study of each case provides opportunities to get close to local realties in all research phases (Flyvbjerg, 2001). Beyond data collection and sharing the interpretation of the case with participants, the study should be designed to contribute to the enhancement of effective resilience processes. Although there is no way to predict the substantial outcomes of the study, the final phase has to bridge the study's implications with local practices related to resilience. This phase should be planned at the outset, considering the political and cultural contexts of the study (Eder & Fingerson, 2002). Otherwise, the full potential of local case studies will not materialize and they will remain an academic discourse that makes no difference to the resilience of youth in particular communities.

Notes

1   Clarke notes that this concept is a play on Everett Hughes' (1971) concept 'of "master status," a particular social status that essentially trumps all others one might possess and requires "marking" in interaction – for example, a *woman* physician or pilot, a *male* nurse, a *black* actor, a *trophy* bride' (Clarke, 2005, p. 179).
2   The first two paragraphs of this section are based on Ungar and Teram (2005).
3   It is noteworthy that the IRP's sample was far too small to make any claim to substantive theory generation about how young people in any of the project's host communities thrive. Instead, the scale of analysis was

global, with an emphasis on seeking a substantive theory to account for diverse experiences among a heterogeneous population of youth. The results are seven themes, or tensions, that are common but have no distinctive patterns to their resolution. The novelty of this finding is that it highlights the need to understand protective processes related to resilience in their complexity, sensitive to the non-linear relationship between individual and environmental determinants of positive development.

4 Joyce Carlson Clouston completed her PhD at the Faculty of Social Work, Wilfrid Laurier University. Eli Teram served as the co-chair of her dissertation committee. The account of her experience is presented with Joyce's approval and permission.

5 The story is drawn from different drafts of Joyce's dissertation.

6 Moroney's (1986) concept of *shared responsibility* refers to the ideal relationships between the state and families who provide care for children with disabilities and frail elderly.

7 For example, moving from rural to urban centres in order to gain access to services for a child with disabilities was recounted by a number of participants, but was not part of Mary's experience.

8 The Personal Narrative Group was a collaborative feminist research project that explored women's lives through their personal narratives. Personal narratives are central in feminist scholarship and research.

9 The discussion in this section follows Yin's (2003) typology of case study designs.

10 In addition to this domain, Lieblich, Tuval-Mashiach, and Zilber (1998) refer to studies in which the narrative is the research object, and studies on the philosophy and methodology of qualitative approaches to research.

11 Gubrium and Holstein (2002) point out that even in an individual interview, we cannot be certain about whose voices we hear and the source of the ideas communicated to us.

References

Barbre, J.W., & the Personal Narratives Group. (1989). *Interpreting women's lives: Feminist theory and personal narratives*. Bloomington: Indiana University Press.

Campbell, D.T. (1969). Reforms as experiments. *American Psychologist, 24*(4), 409–29.

Chase, S.E. (2003). Learning to listen: Narrative principles in a qualitative research methods course. In R. Josselson, A. Lieblich, & D.P. McAdams (Eds.), *Up close and personal: The teaching and learning of narrative research* (pp. 79–99). Washington, DC: American Psychological Association.

Chase, S.E. (2005). Narrative inquiry: Multiple lenses, approaches, voices. In N.K. Denzin & Y.S. Lincoln (Eds.), *The Sage handbook of qualitative research* (3rd ed., pp. 651–79). Thousand Oaks, CA: Sage.

Clarke, A. (2005). *Situational analysis: Grounded theory after the postmodern turn.* Thousand Oaks, CA: Sage.

Czarniawska, B. (2004). *Narratives in social science research: Introducing qualitative methods.* Thousand Oaks, CA: Sage.

Daiute, C., & Lightfoot, C. (Eds.). (2004). *Narrative analysis: Studying the development of individuals in society.* Thousand Oaks, CA: Sage.

Denzin, N.K., & Lincoln, Y.S. (Eds.). (2005). *The Sage handbook of qualitative research* (3rd ed.). Thousand Oaks, CA: Sage.

Eder, D., & Fingerson, L. (2002). Interviewing children and adolescents. In J.F. Gubrium & J.A. Holstein (Eds.), *Handbook of interview research* (pp. 181–201). Thousand Oaks, CA: Sage.

Elliott, J. (2005). *Using narrative in social research: Qualitative and quantitative approaches.* London: Sage.

Flyvbjerg, B. (2001). *Making social science matter: Why social inquiry fails and how it can succeed again.* Cambridge: Cambridge University Press.

Greenwood, D.J., & Levin, M. (2000). Reconstructing the relationships between universities and society through action research. In N.K. Denzin & Y.S. Lincoln (Eds.), *Handbook of qualitative research* (2nd ed., pp. 85–106). Thousand Oaks, CA: Sage.

Gubrium, J.F, & Holstein, J.A. (2002). From the individual interview to the interview society. In J.F. Gubrium & J.A. Holstein (Eds.), *Handbook of interview research: Context & method* (pp. 3–32). London: Sage.

Hardin, R. (1990). The artificial duties of contemporary professionals: The social service review lecture. *Social Service Review, 64,* 528–42.

Hasenfeld, Y. (2000). Organizational forms as moral practices: The case of welfare departments. *Social Service Review, 74*(3), 329–51.

Hemmings, A. (2000). The 'hidden' corridor curriculum. *High School Journal, 83*(2), 1–10.

Hinchman, L.P., & Hinchman, S.K. (1997). Introduction. In L.P. Hinchman & S.K. Hinchman (Eds.), *Memory, identity, community: The idea of narrative in the human sciences* (pp. xiii–xxxii). New York: State University of New York Press.

Hughes, E.C. (1971). *The sociological eye.* Chicago: Aldine Atherton.

Josselson, R., Lieblich, A., & McAdams, D.P. (Eds.). (2003). *Up close and personal: The teaching and learning of narrative research.* (Narrative study of lives.) 1st ed. Washington, DC: American Psychological Association.

Lerner, R.M. (2006). Resilience as an attribute of the developmental system. *Resilience in children: Annals of the New York Academy of Sciences, 1094,* 40–51.

Lieblich, A., Tuval-Mashiach, R., & Zilber, T. (1998). *Narrative research: Reading, analysis and interpretation.* Applied Social Research Methods Series. Vol. 47. Thousand Oaks, CA: Sage.

Luthar, S.S., & Bidwell Zelazo, L. (2003). Research on resilience: An integrative review. In S.S. Luthar (Ed.) *Resilience and vulnerability: Adaptation in the context of childhood adversities* (pp. 510–49). Cambridge: Cambridge University Press.

Moroney, R. (1986). *Shared responsibility: Families and social policy.* New York: Aldine.

Ragin, C.C., & Becker, H.S. (Eds.). (1992). *What is a case?: Exploring the foundations of social inquiry.* Cambridge: Cambridge University Press.

Riessman, C.K. (1993). *Narrative analysis.* Newbury Park, CA: Sage.

Salmon, A. (2007). Walking the talk: How participatory interview methods can democratize research. *Qualitative Health Research, 17,* 982–33.

Schein, E.H. (1987). *The clinical perspective in fieldwork.* Newbury Park, CA: Sage.

Snyder, S.U. (1992). Interviewing college students about their constructions of love. In J.F. Gilgun, K. Daly, & G. Handel (Eds.), *Qualitative methods in family research* (pp. 43–65). Newbury Park, CA: Sage.

Stake, R.E. (2005). Qualitative case studies. In N.K. Denzin & Y.S. Lincoln (Eds.), *The sage handbook of qualitative research* (3rd ed., pp. 443–66). Thousand Oaks, CA: Sage.

Strauss, A.L., & Corbin, J.M. (1998). *Basics of qualitative research: Techniques and procedures for developing grounded theory.* Thousand Oaks, CA: Sage.

Teram, E., Schachter, C.L., & Stalker, C.A. (2005). The case for integrating grounded theory and participatory action research: Empowering clients to inform professional practice. *Qualitative Health Research, 15*(8), 1129–40.

Thoeokas, C., & Lerner, R.M. (2006). Observed ecological assets in families, schools, and neighbourhoods: Conceptualization, measurement, and relations with positive and negative developmental outcomes. *Applied Developmental Science, 10*(2), 61–74.

Ungar, M. (1995). *A naturalistic study of the relationship between the process of empowerment and mental health during adolescence.* Unpublished doctoral dissertation, Wilfrid Laurier University, Waterloo, Canada.

Ungar, M. (2003). Qualitative contributions to resilience research. *Qualitative Social Work, 2*(1), 85–102.

Ungar, M. (2005). *Introduction: Resilience across cultures and contexts.* In M. Ungar (Ed.), *A handbook for working with children and youth: Pathways to resilience across cultures and contexts* (pp. xv–xxxix). Thousand Oaks, CA: Sage.

Ungar, M. (2008). Resilience across cultures. *British Journal of Social Work, 38,* 218–35.

Ungar, M., Brown, M., Liebenberg, L., Othman, R., Kwong, W.M., & Armstrong, M. (2007). Unique pathways to resilience across cultures. *Adolescence, 42*(166), 287-310.

Ungar, M., & Liebenberg, L. (2005). *The International Resilience Project: A mixed methods approach to the study of resilience across cultures.* In M. Ungar (Ed.), *Handbook for working with children and youth: Pathways to resilience across cultures and contexts* (pp. 211–26). Thousand Oaks, CA: Sage.

Ungar, M., & Teram, E. (2005). Qualitative resilience research: Contributions and risks. In M. Ungar (Ed.), *Handbook for working with children and youth: Pathways to resilience across cultures and contexts* (pp. 149–63). Thousand Oaks, CA: Sage.

Ungar, M., Teram, E., & Picketts, J. (2001). Young offenders and their communities: Reframing the institution as an extension of the community. *Canadian Journal of Community Mental Health, 20*(2), 29–42.

van Teeffelen, T., Bitar, H., & Al-Habash, S. (2005). Resilience in the Palestinian Occupied Territories. In M. Ungar (Ed.), *Handbook for working with children and youth: Pathways to resilience across cultures and contexts* (pp. 417–31). Thousand Oaks, CA: Sage.

Yin, R.K. (2003). *Case study research: Design and methods* (3rd ed.). Thousand Oaks, CA: Sage.

5 The Use of Image-Based Methods in Research with Youth

LINDA LIEBENBERG

Traditionally, Western constructions of children and youth have marginalized young people, excluding them from decision-making processes that affect their lives. In recent decades various authors have argued for the legitimacy of youth views and opinions in policy making. Their views have filtered into the field of research, where a move to, at the very least, centre youth voices in the research process has occurred (Bemak, 1996; Dallape, 1996; Kefyalew, 1996; Volpi, 2002; West, 1996; Whitmore & McKee, 2001).

Globally, the degree to which youth have been marginalized in the research process differs extensively. Institutionalized social structuring and its effects on youth – particularly those in high-risk contexts – often problematize the research context. When one is conducting research with marginalized youth, barriers relating to power, trust, and communication, for example, need to be overcome in order to establish meaningful research relationships in which uninhibited exchanges of information can occur (Alldred, 1998; Blackbeard & Lindegger, 2007; Oakley, 1994). At a basic level, language and dialect pose communication problems to researchers who, more often than not, come from contexts different than those of youth participants – especially contexts related to age or culture. Further complicating the research context is the possibility that youth may distort experiences in ways that they believe reflect the story adults want to hear. The need often exists, then, to find ways of accessing youth voices and engaging youth participants in a reflective process that establishes a safe space in which youth can discuss their experiences and the meaning attached to these experiences in honest ways.

The positioning of youth voices in a developing field such as youth resilience is of particular importance. Resilience studies ask of researchers to better understand behaviour sometimes considered deviant, destructive, or illegal, within a healthy outcomes framework that values adaptation. Indeed, the very nature of resilience studies requires engaging with youth who not only are confronted by adversity in a multitude of ways, but are also systemically marginalized, compounding the aforementioned issues of trust and communication. Accessing these voices, then, is of great importance in the development of meaningful resilience theory.

Against the background of concerns regarding the positioning of youth voices in resilience research, this chapter explores photo elicitation and visual narratives as two means of facilitating communication within the youth resilience research context. Both methods incorporate imagery into research interactions with youth, enhancing reflection on experiences and communication. After introducing visual methods in the context of studies with marginalized youth, I explore the benefits of using participant-produced images, as well as the various media with which to create images. This is followed by a discussion of photo-elicitation and visual diaries or narratives as two visual methods that lend themselves to boundary crossing between researchers and marginalized youth.

Visual Methods and the Study of Marginalized Youth

Image-based methods such as photo-elicitation and visual narratives are a means of including participants in research that is reflective of open-ended interviewing. The process is stimulated and guided by images (Harper, 1998, after Collier, 1967), raising the voice of the researched over that of the researcher. Functioning as a bridging tool, images worked into the data collection process facilitate the reduction of traditional barriers to meaningful comprehension of participants' lives, such as culture and language. Researchers attest to the value of incorporating images in interviews, arguing that they enhance the interview process, illuminating taken-for-granted aspects of participants' lives through a period of reflection on the images participants produce (Daniels, 2003; Harper, 1998; Schwartz, 1989). As Schratz, Walker, and Wiedel (1995) have shown, incorporating images into the research process promotes the use of the visual not as a replacement for words, but rather 'to create a context within which to talk and write' (p. 77).

It is for these reasons that photo-elicitation was incorporated into a study exploring the experiences of five coloured[1] teenage mothers in a sub-economic community of Cape Town, South Africa (Liebenberg, 2005). It was anticipated that these young women would have difficulty verbalizing the nuances of their lives as young mothers, given their subordinate status and marginalized position stemming from their race and its connection to historically oppressive legislation, sex and its connection to epistemic and oppressive violence, economic positioning, education (or lack thereof), and 'deviance' as young, un-wed mothers (Daniels, 2003; Fussell & Greene, 2002; Laird, 2003; Lesch & Kruger, 2004; Nsamenang, 2002). As various authors working in this context have argued, many of these young women experience personal disempowerment and silencing (Jewkes et al., 2001; Lesch & Kruger, 2004; Swartz, Gibson, & Gelman, 2002; Varga, 2003; Wood, Maforah, & Jewkes, 1998; Wood & Jewkes, 2006). Such a context is reflective of Spivak's (1993) argument that the *voice* of the subaltern is also suppressed in the multiple layers of the oppressor's world.

The young women were provided with cameras for a period of one week. Participants were asked to 'take pictures of things which are very important to you – good [and] bad' (Graham, 1995, p. 136), with regard to being a mother. Individual, open-ended interviews were then conducted, based on the questions:

• Which images do you like the most/least?
• Which photograph best represents motherhood for you?
• Which photograph least represents motherhood for you?
• Which photographs illustrate what you most and least enjoy about motherhood?
• Is there any other photograph that you would like to discuss?
• Is there any photograph that you would not like to discuss?

All images were discussed at length, allowing the interviewer to probe issues relating to the rewards and difficulties of being a young mother in a specific context, as well as the factors that enable and limit the ability to mother and, simultaneously, develop as an individual. Data analysis resulted in a second week of image production during which time each participant made images in response to individualized topics that had emerged from her own narrative.

By using cameras, participants in this study could construct a visual representation of their daily lives through which they would be able to disclose their experiences and interpretations thereof. These methods allow participants to take the researcher into their private worlds – worlds to which outsiders would ordinarily have limited or no access (see also Karlsson, 2001).

A study that asks participants to produce their own images facilitates the interview process by establishing an opportunity for reflection. As Beloff (1985) explains, photography offers individuals the opportunity to truly 'see what is all around us' (p. 7) – to look at our lives in detail. The experience of making images of motherhood, for example, afforded these young women the opportunity to reflect on their experiences, enhancing the quality of the interviews that followed. In this way, the focus is not so much on the images as on how participants perceive and articulate their lives following a period of reflection.

Interviewing in settings such as the one in which this study took place can often be a difficult and awkward process that does not always make sense to the interviewee. Establishing open communication can be challenging (Alldred, 1998; Blackbeard & Lindegger, 2007; Oakley, 1994). Again, image-based research may assist in reducing some of these challenges. Asking participants to represent their lives through a powerful visual medium shifts power over the research process to them, allowing participants to establish control over their own stories and representations of their world and experiences. This control is brought into the interview, where participants are prepared (by means of reflection) to talk about topics that *they* have highlighted as important (by means of image making), while focusing attention on the content of the images themselves. This focus on the images helps to mitigate feelings that the researcher's attention will be directed at the participants personally. Stated differently, discussion of and focus on images deflects attention away from participants to broader environmental contexts, while simultaneously inspiring collaboration between participants and researchers.

It is perhaps for these reasons that visual methods work well with marginalized groups such as youth, where issues around trust and communication are problematic and may increase the possibility of cultural misunderstandings and misrepresentations. Niesyto (2000) argues that the use of subjective forms of representation provides exactly those people who have difficulties with verbal or written tasks with 'adequate possibilities of expression' (p. 139). In this way, visual methods bring greater depth to conversations about health-related phenomena like resilience, adaptation, and hopefulness, enhancing the quality of data gathered and thickening accounts of participants' experiences. Various other studies have also demonstrated how marginalized youth in a variety of settings can use visual media to depict and better understand their worldviews (Cavin, 1994; Clark, 1999; Hubbard, 1991, 1994; Karlsson, 2001; Larson, 1999; Niesyto, 2000; Orellana, 1999; Rich & Chalfen, 1999; Young & Barrett, 2001).

Young and Barrett's (2001) study, for example, used a series of 'visual action activities' (p. 144), including elicitation interviews, to explore the 'socio-spatial geographies' of youth living on the street in Kampala, Uganda 'in relation to their street environments and survival mechanisms' (p. 142). The researchers found that 'visual methods proved to be particularly important for developing gainful insight into the street child's urban environment from the child's perspective' (p. 142). Specifically, mental maps, drawings, daily time lines, and photographs were used to establish images from which to elicit information from participants. The authors argue that these methods 'introduced a relaxed, fun atmosphere and allowed the children to take control of the process without imposing adult influence' (p. 142).

Participant-Produced Images

Images produced by researchers are very often made to depict aspects of the community in which the research is being conducted. Such images usually range from being constructed independently of participants – to be discussed with them later in interviews – or constructed in collaboration with participants – moving through the community with the researcher capturing data pointed out by participants (see, for example, Collier, 1967; Prosser, 1992; Schwartz, 1989). Even when the latter approach is used, such images represent the vision and perceptions of the researcher, that is, the researcher's interpretation of the participants' social and physical ecology. Consequently, authors such as Collier (2001) and Henny (1986) argue that images made by participants are more revealing than images made by researchers, particularly when conducting exploratory research.

Niesyto (2000) believes that by using participant-produced images, researchers are better able to delve into the subjective modes of participants. Indeed, he goes so far as to argue that qualitative research involving youth and images should *only* be carried out when images have been constructed by youth themselves so as to allow for 'subject-related self-representations.' He asserts that 'if somebody ... wants to learn something about youths' ideas, feelings and their ways of experiencing the world, he or she should give them a chance to express themselves by means of their own self-made media productions' (p. 137).

Similarly, in her study of the spatial manifestation of apartheid discourse in school environments, and the emergence of post-apartheid discourse in that space, Karlsson (2001) explains her decision to incorporate learners in data gathering 'to supplement my outsider/front-stage view' (p. 24). She based her decision on the need to avoid 'objectifying learners as part of the material landscape' (p. 26). She believed that constructing visual representations of school spaces and from this drawing theoretical conclusions pertaining to learner identities, without actively including learners in such representation of their own experience, 'would approximate the colonial gaze on the less powerful "Other"' (p. 26).

Various studies have also demonstrated the value of participant-produced images in establishing a sense of voice among participants (see, for example, Clark, 1999; Hubbard, 1991, 1994; Larson, 1999; Liebenberg, in press; Orellana, 1999; Rich & Chalfen, 1999; Young & Barrett, 2001). This is perhaps best exemplified by a youth participant in the British Cockpit Cultural Studies. This ten-year program used photography and darkroom activities to empower various marginalized groups, situating control over a powerful means of representation with the groups themselves. In 1984 a group of homeless youth living in a local shelter attended the program, culminating in the 'Down But Not Out' exhibition and subsequent publication of their work (Dewdney, Grey, & Minnion, 1994). As one participant said:

> I'm fed up with being asked 'How do you feel about what you do? What are your views on homelessness?' You have all these media people saying let's make a video about you or let's do some pictures or something about homeless people. We will do it for you ... I'd much rather not be interviewed on TV; not be asked, 'How do feel about being homeless?' I'd rather someone gave me a camera and said, 'Show us how you feel.' (Grey, 1995, p. 146)

Asking respondents to focus on an aspect of their lives gives them the opportunity to reflect on both their context and experiences. Beloff

(1985) explains that 'sometimes we have the chance to see what is all around us, but that we've never "seen" because we've never looked at it' (p. 7). By having the opportunity to reflect on experiences before engaging in conversation about them, participants are able to understand their lives before conversing about them, leading to more comprehensive interview narratives.

Indeed, the underlying idea of methods such as photo-elicitation is that particular photographs assist in jarring memories of the participants, triggering improved recall and focus (Banks, 2001; Harper, 2002). Morphy and Banks (1997) argue that 'visual representational systems ... can create emotional states and feelings of identity and separation' (p. 23). By combining ideas of construction and representation by participants themselves in the use of visual methods, images act as a catalyst for transforming thought and understandings of self, culture, and society. Thus, using visual methods in research in a representative manner may result in 'new ways of understanding individuals, cultures and research materials" (Pink, 2001, p. 13).

This understanding of participant-produced images is exemplified in the South African study of teenage mothers. Participants were able to provide detailed and often well-thought-through responses to questions and probes about their experiences as marginalized mothers. Some of the young women even commented on the new understandings and interpretations they had reached about their lives and who they are as a result of the research process. Brenda, for example, outside of the interview context, discussed how she had never realized the positive aspects of her life, believing during the three years preceding the research that everything was just bad. She could also, through the research process, clearly identify risks and challenges in her life, allowing her to better explore ways of overcoming these.

Selecting a Medium

Visual material well suited for use in research includes, but is certainly not limited to, photographs, film, and art (sketches, paintings, collages, etc.). The medium selected, as well as the related technology, together with the manner in which these resources are used, will depend very much on the research context, research question, and subsequent research design. Points to bear in mind when deciding on a visual medium include the fit between research context and research question.

Video, for example, provides a continuous running image as well as the narrative of participants and perhaps others in the visual representation, whilst photographs do not. Pink (2001) believes that video and photographs produce different types of knowledge. Because of the continuous nature of video and its ability to include narrative at the time of the filming, it is sometimes regarded as more intimate than photographs or drawings (Barnes, Taylor-Brown, & Wiener, 1997; Larson, 1999). One could argue, however, that the degree of intimacy will depend on the access the researcher has to sites and on what participants are willing to include on film or not.

So, for example, in the context of the teenage mothers study, participant safety was already a major concern. The community in which the research occurred is notorious for drug and gang-related violence (Dowdney, 2005; Frank, 2005), and women in particular are noticeably victims of male and gang-perpetuated violence (Abrahams, et al., 2004; Jewkes et al., 2001; Wood, Maforah, & Jewkes, 1998). As such, positioning these young women in the community with such an intimate recording device may have added considerably to the daily risks they were already confronting. At the very least, the more valuable equipment would have been at increased risk of being stolen. At the very worst, the act of filming peers might have triggered interpersonal violence.

Conversely, in the study to be discussed in greater detail later in this chapter, Video Intervention/Prevention Assessment (VIA) incorporated the use of video precisely because of its ability to capture intimate narrative in the moment. In this study, originally of children living with asthma in Boston, participants constructed daily visual diaries of their experiences living with the disease (Rich & Chalfen, 1999).

With regard to photography, Stanley (1995), based on her studies with women, believes that because camera technology is still not readily available to marginalized groups in many non-Western, majority world contexts, 'photography provides a new and dynamic way of recording, communicating and understanding aspects of women's lives' (p. 19). Furthermore, in the reality of day-to-day living for people in the majority world, cameras offer a quick and easy means for participants to document their lives. The point-and-shoot convenience of a basic camera, combined with story-telling traditions, may be better suited to communities that place little emphasis on literary skills.

It was very much this consideration that prompted the choice to use photographs in the teenage mothers study. Cameras would be affordable, light and mobile, quick and easy for participants to master and use, and would potentially pose the least risk to participant safety as they could most easily be made to look damaged and of little value. The data recorded would also be the least conspicuous in abusive contexts.

In contrast, drawings are useful in instances where participants are unable to produce photographs or films or where psychological issues are of concern. Diem-Wille (2001) tells us that drawings 'can provide an understanding of a deeper level and make the subject aware of deeper aspects of his or her feelings' (p. 132). As a psychoanalyst, she highlights principles of interpretations worth attending to while participants create these images. In particular she says:

> The context and the explanations of the person who drew the picture are more important than single elements ... there are some important principles to keep in mind: for example, the subject's use of space on the sheet of paper, the order of appearance of elements and the symbols chosen ... The understanding of the drawing is worked out with the interviewee drawing on data from the narrative interview. (p. 129)

Should participants be unwilling to draw images, simply discussing the images they wanted to but could not make may also yield valuable data. As Pink (2001) explains, 'While in many instances ethnographers may never see the photographs informants describe, they provide interesting examples of how informants may visualize certain emotions, values and experiences' (p. 75).

Drawings were part of the original teenage mothers study design. I anticipated that there would be images participants would not be able to capture, for reasons of practicality or personal safety. As such, it was decided that at the end of each interview, participants would be asked if there were any images they would have liked to capture but could not. They were then offered the opportunity to draw a representation of the image. Three of the five participants answered 'yes'. Interestingly, none of the reasons cited for not making the images included safety, but, rather, the practicality of gathering people in a single place to be photographed. Brenda, for example, wanted a photograph of her son with his father. Unfortunately, this was not possible as the father lived more than a day's journey away and they had not seen him for two years. Carol would have liked a group photograph of her mother, her daughter, her boyfriend, and herself. She was unable, however, to find a moment when her boyfriend, her mother, and she were able to be together along with someone who could take the photograph.

Of further interest was participants' response to being asked if they would like to draw the missing photographs. Brenda explained that she was too old and too tired to be drawing, whilst Carol giggled and said she could not draw very well and so would rather not. These are interesting considerations to bear in mind when designing a study.

Researchers making decisions regarding media and technology also need to consider the impact and demands on the lives of participants of incorporating visual methods. For example, what are the implications of asking research participants to master the operation of technology related to digital equipment, as opposed to more simplified point-and-shoot film cameras with automatic flashes? What additional and perhaps unnecessary demands are researchers making on the daily lives of participants when we ask them to master more complicated equipment? Furthermore, is there the time and the financial resources to deal with the realities of training research participants in how to use more technically complicated equipment? Similarly, what are the safety implications for participants in carrying more expensive-looking equipment around with them?

As previously mentioned, in the study of teenage mothers participants were provided with easy-to-use, inexpensive, point-and-shoot film cameras. In a matter of minutes participants were comfortable with using the cameras – they had little to learn, as even the flash was automated. To enhance their own safety, cameras were taped up in an effort to make them look even less valuable (see also Rich & Chalfen, 1999). This served another purpose in that the battery compartment and film casing could not easily be opened, safeguarding both participant ability to make images and the content of the film.

In some research settings a participant may be anxious to make the 'right' image or make images that are technically sound as a result of existing cultural power relations or social desirability. By including a 'delete' option (as in the case of digital cameras) or the ability to record over (with video cameras) during the image-producing process, researchers may find themselves losing much meaningful data. Again, in the teenage mothers study, participants were asked if there were any images they did not want to discuss and why this was. One participant, Carol, selected an image that she explained was a 'mistake' and should not have been made because to her mind, the image was technically flawed in its visual construction (permission for the use of this transcript material was obtained from the participant at the conclusion of the interview):

> I: Why don't you like that photo?
> C: It doesn't look right. She shouldn't have stood like that and ... it's messy there ... Maybe she could have sat and said that he could take the photo or something like that.

Probing revealed that the father of her daughter had snapped a photograph of her cousin (seen standing in a doorway, looking back over her shoulder, eating) without first asking either Carol's permission to use the camera or her cousin's permission to take a photograph of her:

> C: She also didn't know he was going to take the photo, just that she looked around ... and then the thing went off. I also wasn't around there .... When I came in I saw that he had already taken the photo.

When such images are incorporated into interview settings, participants are afforded the opportunity to voice personal opinions about the image, allowing researchers to explore the reasons behind the participant's belief that an image is 'wrong.' This in turn may help increase understanding of various power relations or ideas about self-representation (Blackbeard & Lindegger, 2007; Harper, 1986; Liebenberg, in press). Returning to the image of the cousin, further discussion around Carol's perceptions and emotions related to the photograph highlighted her own feelings of powerlessness in her relationship with this young man. More importantly, how her own mother features in the maintenance of this disempowerment, and how this affects Carol's own role as mother and her own identity, emerged through the discussion of an image that may, given the use of more sophisticated technology, never have been included in the interview.

Photo Elicitation

The variety of images that can be incorporated into a photo-elicitation study is almost limitless. As Harper (2002) points out, 'there is no reason studies cannot be done with ... virtually any visual image' (p. 13). It is what the photograph contains and how this relates to the research participant that is important in photo-elicitation, as opposed to the degree of professionalism of the image. The fact that photographic techniques are not of importance with this method, but rather the image's connection to the participant's culture, allows for the use of photographs that a more proficient photographer may otherwise have considered 'too "boring" or "commonplace" even to consider using' (Harper, 1986, p. 26; see also Harper, 2002). Harper contends that it is ordinarily these very mundane images that bring forth a wealth of information.

Interview questions are not about photographs as records so much as about the ways in which the images are interpreted. Harper (1988) contends that this 'interview process produces information that is more deeply grounded in the phenomenology of the subject. A photograph, a literal rendering of an element of the subject's world, calls forth associations, definitions, or ideas that otherwise go unnoticed' (p. 65).

Echoing issues highlighted by youth and post-colonialist researchers, visual methodologists such as Banks (2001), Collier and Collier (1986), and Harper (2002) believe that interviewing is a difficult and often awkward process that does not always make sense to the interviewee. Incorporating images into the research process may assist the researcher in dealing with differences in power, facilitating the establishment of more open communication. A method such as photo-elicitation, where the researcher and participant discuss photographs produced by youth themselves, provides participants with power by situating them as authorities on their lives and allows them to assume the role of teacher in the research experience (Collier, 1967; Henny, 1986). This is what Harper (2002) has described as 'postmodern dialogue based on the authority of the subject rather than the researcher' (p. 15).

As mentioned earlier in this chapter, the structure of a photo-elicitation interview also results in a less stressful interview setting. Harper (2002; see also Collier & Collier, 1986) believes that 'photo elicitation may overcome the difficulties posed by in-depth interviewing because it is anchored in an image that is understood, at least in part, by both parties' (p. 20). Pressure is diverted from the participant, as both researcher and participant focus on 'the photographs as a kind of neutral third party' (Banks, 2001, p. 88), lessening eye contact and avoiding awkward silences. As Karlsson (2001) writes of her work with school youth in Durban, South Africa, 'by looking constantly at the photographs and being side by side the learner and I reduced anxiety-related eye contact, especially important for younger learners and in cross-cultural situations' (p. 29).

Similarly, Steven Gold (1991) comments on his use of photo-elicitation with Vietnamese refugees that it 'offered a valuable technique for studying ethnic relations ... The use of photographs provoked ample dialogue ... offering information ...The photos gave respondents an object on which they could focus their discussion of [the research question]' (p. 21).

Harper (2003) believes that images function as a 'cultural Rorschach' test (p. 188), 'in which people of different cultures spin out their respective worlds of meaning. This procedure is fuelled by the radical but simple idea that two people standing side by side, looking at identical objects, see different things' (Harper, 2002, p. 22). Because photography can be regarded as a form of 'social exchange' (Beloff, 1985), the discussion of images creates a link between the differing realities of the researcher and the participant (Pink, 2001). This feature of photo-elicitation becomes particularly relevant in cross-cultural research settings, encouraging the redefinition of fieldwork relations as well as approaches to the data.

Visual Diaries

Prosser and Schwartz (1998) regard visual diaries as self-reflective, media-literate chronicles of participants' experiences. With this method, participants make photographs, drawings, or videotaped recordings over a period of time. These images are then incorporated into some form of journal where the participant can record contextual information as well as thoughts and emotions surrounding the images. Journals can be written, audiotaped, or posted on web pages and so forth. As Harper (2003) tells us, 'the sentiments behind the image making must be understood through another mode of expression: a diary, a poem, or other expressive form' (p. 191) such as story telling.

This method is informed by theories such as that of Solomon (1995), who maintains that 'snapshots are part of and create family folklore and mythologies' (p. 11). Similarly, Stanley (1995) believes that 'diaries are a place for subjectively ... portraying personal feelings and external events of significance' (p. 18), and, importantly, are their creator's 'own accounts, where we are not posed or snapped by another' (p. 19). As such, journals become places where we learn about the nuances and meaning of children's lives.

Video Intervention/Prevention Assessment (VIA) offers an example of how visual diaries have been used effectively to cross age and power boundaries, and to inform improvements to medical service provision for youth. VIA began as a multidisciplinary project in child health research, education, and advocacy, and was designed to obtain an understanding of patients' lives, which had been largely inaccessible using other research techniques. The core of VIA involves providing youth participants with small, easy-to-use camcorders. Participants then make video diaries, recording their lives as they perceive them (Rich & Chalfen, 1999).

VIA was originally developed to gain greater understanding of how children with asthma experience the medical services available to them. The children were asked to videotape pre-assigned, 'universal' situations (such as mealtimes, preparing for school, or visiting the doctor). Participants interviewed family, friends, and others with whom they interact for their perspectives on the research question. Perhaps more importantly, participants were asked to set up the camera and speak to it daily, revealing their ongoing inner life as well as their reactions to events of the day. These monologues not only added the internal dimension of lived experience, but also openly acknowledged and capitalized on the material's subjective point of view (Rich & Chalfen, 1999).

Rich and Chalfen (1999) believe that 'by having lives and worlds self-documented by the participants rather than recorded by researchers, VIA seeks to diminish the reactivity of participants to an outside observer' (p. 54). Journals made by participating youth brought new and important perspectives of 'real-world circumstances' (p. 67) to the research question. In their study, the authors found that participants gained a sense of purposeful expression and increased self-awareness through visual communication. The study also demonstrated that young people are capable of visually documenting their own worlds as they see, understand, and live in such worlds: 'Young people in our sample were willing and able to reveal new dimensions of their lives, hitherto unknown realities that are increasingly important and useful to those who can take therapeutic action' (p. 67). Furthermore, as Rich and Chalfen explain, professionals were able to learn from the wisdom of participants: 'Clinicians were literally able to see and feel aspects of asthma that they have never experienced before' (p. 67).

Recent studies have demonstrated the relevance of VIA to understanding a variety of adolescent experiences with illness, including obesity (Corrado, Patashnick, & Rich, 2004), spina bifida (Rich, Patashnick, & Kastelic, 2005), and diabetes (Buchbinder et al., 2005; Chalfen & Rich, 2004). Primary benefits of this method include equal abilities of both parties to play a role in establishing true dialogue as well as the potential to inform change processes (Rich, Polvinen, & Patashnick, 2005).

Data Analysis

How visual data is analysed will depend on the research question. The theoretical framework within which the research is being conducted will also influence the approach taken to data analysis. As Prosser and Schwartz (1998, p. 126) explain, a theoretical 'framework aids management of large amounts of (visual) data by providing logic for sorting, organising, indexing and categorisation.' Harper (1998) too believes that 'to accomplish in-depth understanding one must complete 'immersive' field research driven by *theoretical* questions' (p. 34). He argues that it is only in this way that we can 'learn to see through the lenses of the cultural Other' (p. 34). Harper suggests that if we do not organize and present our data from a sociological or anthropological perspective, 'we may create visual information which will unconsciously reflect our personal taken-for-granted assumptions' (p. 34).

Therefore, because of the marginalized position of young mothers in the South African context, there was a need to explore the interconnectedness among multiple issues, what Collins (1991) refers to as the 'matrix of domination,' from the perspective of participating teenage mothers themselves. Given the need to situate participant perceptions and voices at the centre of the study, grounded theory analysis, together with social constructionism (see Charmaz, 2006), was used to guide the data analysis in the study. In this way reality, as experienced and understood by these young women, was allowed to emerge from the data, rather than existing theoretical frameworks being superimposed on their experiences.

Following grounded theory approaches to data analysis (Charmaz, 2006; Glasser & Strauss, 1967; Strauss & Corbin, 1990), many researchers suggest beginning with analysis while still in the field

(Barnes, Taylor-Brown, & Wiener, 1997; Suchar 1997). Images first produced, discussed, and made meaningful during fieldwork will be given new significance in an academic culture (Morphy & Banks, 1997). Should this initial analysis be skipped, important meanings of the data would be at risk of being omitted in the final analysis.

The primary focus of analysis in the field is the meaning that participants attach to images (Gloor & Meier, 2000; Pink, 2001). Because visual representations are both produced and consumed in a social context (Banks, 2001), contextual meaning is central to the analysis. Research participants bring to the research their own cultural frameworks through which they see images, as do researchers. Contexts are multifaceted, including the academic discipline, research paradigm, and theoretical framework the researcher works within; the extent of disparity between the interpreter's and the image maker's culture, ethnicity, religion, gender, class, and values in viewing the object of the photograph; and the micro-context that shapes the particular dynamic relationship between 'taker' and 'taken.' As Daniels (2003) remarks with regard to her study of women living in an informal settlement in Johannesburg, South Africa:

> Had we analysed these pictures and drawings, we would have interpreted them through our lens of experience and ... we would have compromised the findings. Similar to how we stand the chance of missing the finer nuances and meanings when we communicate through a second language, we could miss the drama, quality or bravery in people's lives when we analyse and interpret the photos without their input. (p. 203)

Elicitation studies facilitate the analysis of participant-produced visual data in that images are discussed in detail with participants before being analysed by researchers. As with grounded theory studies, though, analysis of interview narratives should also be reviewed with participants to ensure accurate interpretation.

In the analysis of the teenage mothers study, initial images and narratives were member-checked with participants in follow-up interviews, resulting in a second period of image production where, as previously mentioned, participants made images in line with a dominant theme emerging from their own individual interviews. These themes were quite diverse, but, interestingly, most centred on relationships. They included explorations of the following topic areas:

- What does your relationship with your son look like?
- How does your mother support you in being a mother yourself?
- How do you define yourself? How is this different from before you were pregnant?
- Now that your son has been born, how do you understand motherhood?
- What do respectful children look like to you? What role does the father of your children play in establishing this respectfulness in your own children?

Initial analysis in the field is best begun with an open-ended viewing, where informants say whatever they wish about the images being viewed. In this process, data is first viewed in its entirety, allowing for discoveries based on feelings and impressions. Here images act as cultural statements that allow the researcher to form a structure within which to continue the fieldwork, generating questions that guide further research and analysis.

An inventory of emerging categories can also be created to structure the analysis and production of detailed descriptions later on. Harper (2001) argues that analysis conducted in this way helps us 'respond to larger patterns within the whole that may reveal the new and unforeseen, that provide significant meaning to otherwise chaotic details' (p. 39). In the teenage mothers study, initial data highlighted the importance of relationships for these young women. Although each of the five emerging research questions differed significantly, later analysis of all five data sets demonstrated the importance of significant relationship dynamics in how these five young women were either empowered or disempowered not only as mothers, but as individuals overcoming multiple challenges in a high-risk environment.

Finally, once images have been removed from the research setting and returned to the academic environment, researchers should incorporate a more formal approach to data analysis. Here researchers search for meaning by returning to the complete visual record. The data should again be responded to in an open manner so that details from the restructured analysis can be placed in a context that defines their significance. After the context has been re-established, conclusions influenced by this final exposure to the whole can be written (Collier, 2001).

In the study of teenage mothers, formal analysis began with a reviewing of each participant's images. Hard copies of photographs were spread out on my desk and studied using Weber's (n.d.) focusing questions, which include:

- What stories do the images tell?
- What is the main 'text' or messages conveyed by the images?
- What are the countertexts or the hidden (implicit) messages?
- How are gender differences and similarities portrayed?
- Who has power or how is power distributed or used?
- What is the relationship between the image-text and the status quo?

Notes of this process were saved as memos to be integrated into the analysis along with initial field and analysis notes. Following review of total image sets, visual data were reintegrated with the relevant participant's interview narrative. The entire data set was then analysed using techniques borrowed from grounded theory.

Conclusion

Visual methods such as photo-elicitation and visual diaries, as well as other methods such as photo-voice, are gaining in strength and popularity. There are increasing numbers of publications documenting their use in studies with marginalized populations, including youth living in high-risk contexts. Their value in accessing voice, identity, and hidden aspects of community, together with their adaptability in terms of technology, medium, and range of use, are gaining recognition.

Important concerns and potential barriers to the use of these methods – particularly with regard to their future application to resilience research – warrant mention. Legitimate concerns regarding participant safety could prevent their use. Whilst this is a serious consideration that should feature in the selection of methods, it is important to bear in mind that youth engaged in resilience research have not only survived in their environments for extended periods of time, but more often than not have thrived in these contexts. As was found with the teenage mothers, they were well aware of the dangers in their community and knew what they could and could not safely photograph. Nevertheless, it was made clear to participants at the outset of the research that no images were worth their personal safety and that they should under no circumstances place themselves in threatening or dangerous positions for either an image or the safety of their cameras.

A second issue that should be considered includes the expense and time that studies involving visual methods can demand. There is little doubt that most visual methods, with the exception of drawings, will add to the cost of field work. Depending on the choice of technology (e.g., disposable cameras vs. digital or video cameras), however, and the way in which equipment is to be worked into the research (e.g., the number of participants using the cameras and whether the timing of use is simultaneous or staggered), costs can most certainly be reduced. Furthermore, visual methods such as photovoice can demand extensive timelines for the study. Wang, Burris, and Xiang's (1996) work with women in rural China, for example, required women to make images over a period of a year. As research funding becomes increasingly limited (Denzin, 2006), the expense demanded in terms of cameras, film, and time in the field would certainly affect the choice to include visual methods.

Such concerns and limitations should not, however, prevent those working with youth from considering the place and value of these methods. Their value lies in the opportunity for participant reflection and heightened communication during the interview process. Of particular importance is the capacity of this process to introduce issues of relevance and importance to research participants rather than topics identified by the researcher through review of literature (see also Liebenberg, in press). Furthermore, combining visual data with phenomenological or critical theory approaches to analysis and presentation of research findings allows the voices of participants to remain centred in research findings and the policies and programs that these findings influence.

Note

1 Racial categories, particularly within the South African context, are recognized as social constructions and remain controversial (Swartz, Gibson, & Gelman, 2002). These categories are, however, important to social research, highlighting the impact of apartheid on specific groups (Shefer, Strebel, & Foster, 2000; Swartz, Gibson, & Gelman, 2002). The category 'coloured' refers to South Africans of mixed racial origins, most noticeably black and white.

References

Abrahams, N., Jewkes, R., Hoffman, M., & Laubsher, R. (2004). Sexual violence against intimate partners in Cape Town: Prevalence and risk factors reported by men. *Bulletin of the World Health Organisation, 82*(5), 330–37.

Alldred, P. (1998). Ethnography and discourse analysis: Dilemmas in representing the voices of children. In J. Ribbens & R. Edwards (Eds.), *Feminist dilemmas in qualitative research: Public knowledge and private lives* (pp. 93–110). Newbury Park, CA: Sage.

Banks, M. (2001). *Visual methods in social research*. London: Sage.

Barnes, D.B., Taylor-Brown, S., & Wiener, L. (1997). 'I didn't leave y'all on purpose': HIV-infected mothers' videotaped legacies for their children. *Qualitative sociology, 20*(1), 7–32.

Beloff, H. (1985). *Camera culture*. New York: Basil Blackwell.

Bemak, F. (1996). Street researchers: A new paradigm redefining future research with street children. *Childhood, 3*, 147–56.

Blackbeard, D., & Lindegger, G. (2007). 'Building a wall around themselves': Exploring adolescent masculinity and abjection with photo-biographical research. *South African Journal of Psychology, 37*(1), 25–46.

Buchbinder, M.H., Detzer, M.J., Welsch, R.L., Christiano, A.S., Patashnick, J.L., & Rich, M. (2005). Assessing adolescents with insulin-dependent diabetes mellitus: A multiple perspective pilot study using visual illness narratives and interviews. *Journal of Adolescent Health, 36*(1), 9–13.

Cavin, E. (1994). In search of the viewfinder: A study of a child's perspective. *Visual Sociology, 9*(1), 27–41.

Chalfen, R., & Rich, M. (2004). Applying visual research: Patients teaching physicians about asthma through visual illness narratives. *Visual Anthropology Review, 20*, 17–30.

Charmaz, K. (2006). *Constructing grounded theory: A practical guide through qualitative analysis*. Thousand Oaks, CA: Sage.

Clark, C.D. (1999). The autodriven interview: A photographic viewfinder into children's experiences. *Visual Sociology, 14*, 39–50.

Collier, J. (1967). *Visual anthropology: Photography as a research method*. New York: Holt, Rinehart and Winston.

Collier, J. (2001). Approaches to analysis in visual anthropology. In T. van Leeuwen & C. Jewitt (Eds.), *Handbook of visual analysis* (pp. 35–60). London: Sage.

Collier, J., & Collier, M. (1986). *Visual anthropology: Photography as a research method*. New Mexico: University of New Mexico Press.

Collins, P.H. (1991). *Black feminist thought: Knowledge, consciousness and the politics of empowerment*. New York: Routledge.

Corrado, S.P., Patashnick, J.L., & Rich, M. (2004). Factors affecting change among obese adolescents. *Journal of Adolescent Health, 34*, 112–24.

Dallape, F. (1996). Urban children: A challenge and an opportunity. *Childhood, 3*, 283–94.

Daniels, D. (2003). Learning about community leadership: Fusing methodology and pedagogy to learn about the lives of settlement women. *Adult Education Quarterly, 53*(3), 189–206.

Denzin, N. (2006). The international congress of qualitative inquiry. *Qualitative Research in Organizations and Management, 1*(2), 130–34.

Dewdney, A., Grey, C., & Minnion, A. (1994). *Down but not out*. Stoke-on-Trent: Trentham.

Diem-Wille, G. (2001). A therapeutic perspective: The use of drawings in child psychoanalysis and social science. In T. van Leeuwen & C. Jewitt (Eds.), *Handbook of visual analysis* (pp. 119–33). London: Sage.

Dowdney, L. (2005). *Neither war nor peace: International comparisons of children and youth in organised armed violence*. Rio de Janeiro: Children in Organised and Armed Violence.

Frank, C. (2005). Young guns: Children in organised armed violence. *Crime Quarterly, 14*. Retrieved 16 September 2006 from http://www.issafrica.org/static/templates/tmpl_html.php?node_id=669&link_id=20.

Fussell, E., & Greene, M.F. (2002). Demographic trends affecting youth around the world. In B. Bradford Brown, R.W. Larson, & T.S. Saraswathi (Eds.), *The world's youth: Adolescence in eight regions of the globe* (pp. 21–60). Cambridge: Cambridge University Press.

Glasser, B., & Strauss, A. (1967). *The discovery of grounded theory: Strategies for qualitative research*. Chicago: Aldine.

Gloor, D., & Meier, H. (2000). A river revitalisation seen through the lens of local community members. *Visual Sociology, 15*, 119–34.

Gold, S. (1991). Ethnic boundaries and ethnic entrepreneurship: A photo-elicitation study. *Visual Sociology, 6*(2), 9–22.

Graham, B. (1995). Mothers of invention. In J. Spence & J. Solomon (Eds.), *What can a woman do with a camera? Photography for women* (pp. 135–42). London: Scarlet Press.

Grey, C. (1995). 'Give me a camera and I'll show you how I feel.' In J. Spence & J. Solomon (Eds.), *What can a woman do with a camera? Photography for women* (pp. 143–52). London: Scarlet Press.

Harper, D. (1986). Meaning and work: A study in photo elicitation. *Current*

Sociology/La sociologie contemporaine: Theory and practice of visual sociology, 34(3), 24–46.

Harper, D. (1988). Visual sociology: Expanding sociological vision. *The American Sociologist, 19*(1), 54–70.

Harper, D. (1998). An argument for visual sociology. In J. Prosser (Ed.), *Image-based research: A source book for qualitative researchers* (pp. 24–41). London: Falmer Press.

Harper, D. (2001). *Changing works: Visions of a lost agriculture.* Chicago: University of Chicago Press.

Harper, D. (2002). Talking about pictures: A case for photo elicitation. *Visual Studies, 17*(1), 13–26.

Harper, D. (2003). Reimagining visual methods: Galileo to Neuromancer. In N.K. Denzin & Y.S. Lincoln (Eds.), *Collecting and interpreting qualitative materials,* 2nd ed. (pp.176–98). Thousand Oaks, CA: Sage.

Henny, L.M. (1986). Theory and practice of visual sociology. *Current Sociology/La sociologie contemporaine, 34*(3), 1–76.

Hubbard, J. (1991). *Shooting back: A photographic view of life by homeless children.* San Francisco: Chronicle.

Hubbard, J. (1994). *Shooting back from the reservation: A photographic view of life by Native American Youth.* New York: New Press.

Jewkes, R., Vundule, C., Maforah, F., & Jordaan, E. (2001). Relationship dynamics and teenage pregnancy in South Africa. *Social Science and Medicine, 52,* 733–44.

Karlsson, J. (2001). Doing visual research with school learners in South Africa. *Visual Sociology, 16*(2), 23–37.

Kefyalew, F. (1996). The reality of child participation in research: Experience from a capacity-building programme. *Childhood, 3,* 203–13.

Laird, S.E. (2003). Evaluating social work outcomes in Sub-Saharan Africa. *Qualitative Social Work, 2*(3), 251–70.

Larson, H. (1999). Voices of Pacific youth: Video research as a tool for youth expression. *Visual Sociology, 14,* 163–72.

Lesch, E., & Kruger, L.M. (2004). Reflections of the sexual agency of young women in a low income rural South African community. *South African Journal of Psychology, 34,* 464–86.

Liebenberg, L. (2005). *The use of visual research methods in the South African research context.* Unpublished doctoral dissertation, Stellenbosch, University of Stellenbosch.

Liebenberg, L. (in press). The visual image as discussion point: Increasing validity in boundary crossing research. *Qualitative Research.*

Morphy, H., & Banks, M. (1997). Introduction: Rethinking visual anthropology. In M. Banks & H. Morphy (Eds.), *Rethinking visual anthropology* (pp. 1–35). London: Yale University Press.

Niesyto, H. (2000). Youth research on video self-production: Reflections on a social aesthetic approach. *Visual Sociology, 15*, 135–53.

Nsamenang, A.B. 2002. Adolescence in Sub-Saharan Africa: An image constructed from Africa's triple inheritance. In B. Bradford Brown, R.W. Larson, & T.S. Saraswathi (Eds.), *The world's youth: Adolescence in eight regions of the globe* (pp. 61–104). Cambridge: Cambridge University Press.

Oakley, A. (1994). Women and children first and last: Parallels and differences between children and women's studies. In B. Mayal (Ed.), *Children's childhoods observed and experienced* (pp. 13–32). London: Falmer Press.

Orellana, M.F. (1999). Space and place in an urban landscape: Learning from children's views of their social worlds. *Visual Sociology, 14*, 73–89.

Pink, S. (2001). *Doing visual ethnography*. London: Sage.

Prosser, J. (1992). Personal reflections in the use of photography in an ethnographic case study. *British Educational Research Journal, 18*(4), 397–411.

Prosser, J., & Schwartz, D. (1998). Photographs within the sociological research process. In J. Prosser (Ed.), *Image-based research: A sourcebook for qualitative researchers* (pp. 115–30). London: Falmer Press.

Rich, M., & Chalfen, R. (1999). Showing and telling asthma: Children teaching physicians with visual narrative. *Visual Sociology, 14*, 51–71.

Rich, M., Lamola, S., Gordon, J., & Chalfen, R. (2000). Video intervention/ prevention assessment: A patient-centered methodology for understanding the adolescent illness experience. *Journal of Adolescent Health, 27*, 155–65.

Rich, M., Patashnick, J.L., & Kastelic, E. (2005). Achieving independence: The role of parental involvement with adolescents with spina bifida. *Journal of Adolescent Health, 36*(2), 129.

Rich, M., Polvinen, J., & Patashnick, J.L. (2005). Visual narratives of the pediatric illness experience: Children communicating with clinicians through video. *Child and Adolescent Psychiatric Clinics of North America, 14*, 571–87.

Schratz, M., Walker, R., & Wiedel, J. (1995). Being there: Using pictures to see the invisible. In M. Schratz & R. Walker (Eds.), *Research as social change: New opportunities for qualitative research* (pp. 65–90). London: Routledge.

Schwartz, D. (1989). Visual ethnography: Using photography in qualitative research. *Qualitative Sociology, 12*(2), 119–54.

Shefer, T., Strebel, A., & Foster, D. (2000). 'So women have to submit to that': Discourses of power and violence in student's talk on heterosexual negotiation. *South African Journal of Psychology, 30*(2), 11–19.

Solomon, J. (1995). Introduction. In J. Spence & J. Solomon (Eds.), *What can a woman do with a camera? Photography for women* (pp. 9–14). London: Scarlet Press.

Spivak, G. (1993). Can the subaltern speak? In P. Williams & L. Chrisman (Eds.), *Colonial discourse and post-colonial theory* (pp. 66–111). New York: Harvester Wheatsheaf.

Stanley, J. (1995). Accounting for our days. In J. Spence & J. Solomon (Eds.), *What can a woman do with a camera?: Photography for women* (pp. 17–27). London: Scarlet Press.

Strauss, A., & Corbin, J. (1990). *Basics of qualitative research: Grounded theory procedures and techniques.* Newbury Park, CA: Sage.

Suchar, C.S. (1997). Grounding visual sociology research in shooting scripts. *Qualitative Sociology, 20*(1), 33–55.

Swartz, L., Gibson, K., & Gelman, T. (Eds.). (2002). *Reflective practice: Psychodynamic ideas in the community.* Cape Town: Human Sciences Research Council.

Varga, C.A. (2003). How gender roles influence sexual and reproductive health among South African adolescents. *Studies in Family Planning, 34*(3), 160–72.

Volpi, E. (2002). *Street children: Promising practices and approaches.* Washington, DC: World Bank Institute.

Wang, C., Burris, M.A., & Xiang, Y.P. (1996). Chinese village women as visual anthropologists: A participatory approach to reaching policy makers. *Social Science and Medicine, 42*(10), 1391–1400.

Weber, S. (n.d.). Analysing visual qualitative data. Retrieved 16 April 2002 from Concordia University and McGill University, *Image and Identity Research Collective* (IIRC), http://www.iirc.mcgill.ca/about.html.

West, A. (1996). Children's own research: Street children and care in Britain and Bangladesh. *Childhood, 6*(1), 145–55.

Whitmore, E., & McKee, C. (2001). Six street youth who could .... In P. Reason & H. Bradbury (Eds.), *Handbook of action research: Participative inquiry and practice* (pp. 396–402). London: Sage.

Wood, K., & Jewkes, R. (2006). Blood blockages and scolding nurses: Barriers to adolescent contraceptive use in South Africa. *Reproductive Health Matters, 14*(27), 109–18.

Wood, K., Maforah, F., & Jewkes, R. (1998). 'He forced me to love him': Putting violence on adolescent sexual health agendas. *Social Science and Medicine, 47*(2), 233–42.

Young, L., & Barrett, H. (2001). Adapting visual methods: Action research with Kampala street children. *Area, 33*(2), 141–52.

QUANTITATIVE RESEARCH

6 Cross-Cultural Resilience Research on Youth: Avoiding Methodological Hazards

ROGER G. TWEED AND ANITA DELONGIS

Cross-cultural studies of youth may waste many hours of participant and researcher time if some common research hazards are not avoided. These hazards can, however, be minimized with careful planning of studies. When well done, research across cultures, whether of resilience-related phenomena or otherwise, promises at least three benefits: identifying pan-cultural findings, identifying culture-specific findings, and increasing awareness of oversimplified truisms. Each of these outcomes may help improve interventions for youth.

By way of introduction, these three possible benefits deserve elaboration. First, cross-cultural research may identify pan-cultural findings such as resilience resources that influence youth well-being in all cultures. These pan-cultural findings in turn could guide international efforts to promote resilience. For example, the evidence may show that particular types of social support interventions bolster resilience among youth in all cultures; this type of finding could guide international efforts to build resilience in both minority-world and majority-world countries.

Second, and just as important, research may elucidate specific aspects of culture, with important implications for development of culturally sensitive clinical interventions with youth at risk. For example, a modular approach to treatment could be implemented, with the choice of modules informed by knowledge of culture-specific needs. Anecdotal evidence, for instance, suggests that maintaining positive relationships in Japan more frequently requires particular skills in indirect management of conflict than would be the case in many other cultures (Lebra, 1984). The veridicality of this claim could be examined in carefully controlled research, and, if supported, provide guidance for evidence-based interventions. Ultimately, a knowledge base of culturally specific observations can increase effectiveness of clinical interventions by facilitating treatment matching. Those planning the intervention would, of course, need to remember that neither the Japanese nor any other cultural group is homogeneous. Within any cultural group, heterogeneity exists, meaning that even culturally targeted interventions will have to be adaptable in order to meet individual needs.

Third, the study of youth across cultures can highlight oversimplifications taught in one's own culture, oversimplifications that the researcher may initially fail to recognize. For example, North Americans are taught that resilience stems from believing in yourself (Twenge, 2006). This culturally based teaching has some elements of truth, as suggested by research on the value of self-efficacy and self-esteem, but the possibility of overstating this cultural truism may not occur to North Americans even though it was well described a century ago by G.K. Chesterton (1994 [1908]), who wrote:

> Once I remember walking with a prosperous publisher, who made a remark which I had often heard before; it is, indeed, almost a motto of the modern world. Yet I had heard it once too often, and I saw suddenly that there was nothing in it. The publisher said of somebody, 'That man will get on; he believes in himself.' And I remember that as I lifted my head to listen, my eye caught an omnibus on which was written 'Hanwell' [an asylum for those with severe mental illness]. I said to him, 'Shall I tell you where the men are who believe most in themselves? For I can tell you. I know of men who believe in themselves more colossally than Napoleon or Caesar. I know where flames the fixed star of certainty and success. I can guide you to the thrones of the Super-men. The men who really believe in themselves are all in lunatic asylums.' He said mildly that there were a good many men after all who believed in themselves and who were not in lunatic asylums. 'Yes, there are,' I retorted, 'and you of all men ought to know them. That drunken poet from whom you would not take a dreary tragedy, he believed in himself. That elderly minister with an epic from whom you were hiding in a back room, he believed in himself. If you consulted your business experience instead of your ugly individualistic philosophy, you would know that believing in himself is one of the commonest signs of a rotter. Actors who can't act believe in themselves; and debtors who won't pay. It would be much truer to say that a man will certainly fail, because he believes in himself.' (p. 8)

Admittedly, Chesterton overstated his own point and lacked the modern social sensitivity of using nonsexist terminology and of speaking with dignity regarding people with mental illness. Nonetheless, his report illustrates the 'aha' experience that can occur when individuals critically consider cultural truisms that they have blindly accepted. Cross-cultural research can make researchers and research consumers more aware that the world can be viewed in ways quite different from their own, and may make them question their culturally conditioned, partially accurate, but dangerously oversimplified theories about young people and how they cope with adversity.

This chapter is designed to help the reader manage the difficulties of researching youth across multiple cultural contexts, and thereby succeed in generating important findings that change lives. Cross-cultural research is difficult to conduct well. The researcher faces both the typical hazards of conducting effective research and the added hazards that emerge when conducting research across diverse settings where values and customs diverge. This chapter will review some hazards of cross-cultural research. It will then review strategies for each of the following: enhancing-translation accuracy, avoiding imposed etic research, recruiting comparable samples, expanding the audience by assessing previously studied dimensions, minimizing cultural distrust effects, minimizing the effect of idiosyncratic rating scale statements, minimizing the reference effect, correcting for nay-saying, correcting for extremism, and using an alternative to statistical corrections for nay-saying. The chapter concludes with a call to apply these principles in order to improve our understanding of and interventions for youth.

Rating scale research will be the focus of our discussion. Admittedly, much important cross-cultural research relies on methods other than rating scales. Our expertise, however, is with rating scale research, and we refer the reader to other chapters in this volume for discussions of aspects of cross-cultural research that share similar threats, albeit expressed in different ways because of other methodological choices. When using rating scales, participants read particular statements and provide their response to each by choosing from a specific set of answers such as: 'strongly disagree,' 'disagree,' 'moderately disagree,' 'neither agree nor disagree,' 'moderately agree,' 'agree,' and 'strongly agree.' As this chapter will illustrate, such methods can be adapted for use globally if the researcher carefully minimizes some common hazards.

Assumption and Analogy Regarding Methodology

We begin with the assumption that threats to research validity can be controlled well enough to produce important cross-cultural research findings. Without such an assumption, we would be left to rely on intuition, supposed common sense, and other sometimes useful but non-empirical resources. Managing threats to research validity is a bit like coping with stress. We can't always remove the source of stress, but we can often learn to manage it sufficiently well to allow us to achieve important personal goals. Likewise, threats to research validity may always be present, but can be managed sufficiently to uncover important findings.

Students with limited knowledge of research methodology may be tempted to dismiss research findings once they uncover a single threat to validity within specific studies (e.g., reliance on self-reports, or hypothetical scenarios, or a non-random sample of participants). However, uncovering a threat to validity should not be surprising even when interpreting a well-designed study. No single study can neutralize all threats to validity (Cook & Campbell, 1979). Researchers always face trade-offs. Strategies for reducing one threat to validity (e.g., using a true experimental design) may simultaneously increase another threat (e.g., ecological invalidity). Likewise, some methodologically ideal procedures are unacceptable for other reasons. For example, ethical requirements for informed consent usually preclude the possibility of a true random selection of participants. Although some threats are more serious than others, threats to validity are ubiquitous. As a result, a single social science study can rarely, if ever, provide absolute proof for a hypothesis. Demanding proof is an unrealistic expectation. We instead seek to provide guidance for designing studies that minimize validity threats in order to provide important and persuasive evidence addressing important questions about youth and their needs.

Cross-Cultural Hazards

Researchers encounter various hazards when studying an issue like resilience across cultures and contexts. We will discuss some of these hazards here with regard to the use of rating scales when conducting research on well-being-related factors with youth.

Nay-Saying

One difficulty with rating scales occurs because cultures differ in their tendency towards nay-saying (Hofstede, 1980). In other words, some cultural groups are more likely to report disagreement on rating scale items than other cultural groups. In our experience, English-speaking North Americans tend to demonstrate more nay-saying than do culturally Chinese participants. As a result, English-speaking North Americans tend to score lower on self-reports of a variety of psychological variables (e.g., personality, learning style, values, anger expression, coping responses). It would not seem reasonable to argue that North Americans simply have lower true scores on all these variables (i.e., less intense values, less anger expression, less intense learning styles, fewer coping responses, and lower scores on most personality variables). Instead it seems that these average differences reflect a response bias. The nay-saying effect can make results difficult to interpret. If, for example, English-speaking North Americans score lower than Chinese on a rating scale for a particular coping response (e.g., seeking social support), one could wonder whether that difference is due to actual differences in coping behaviour or merely a reflection of response bias.

Furthermore, one cannot assume that this is a simple East–West difference. In our experience and that of other researchers, Japanese tend to be more similar to North Americans than to Chinese in their tendency towards nay-saying. Researchers should therefore be prepared in each study to assess and possibly correct for the extent to which one cultural group engages in culture-bound behaviours like nay-saying more than does another cultural group.

Extremism

Some researchers also suggest that cultures differ in their tendency to use the extreme response options. Chen, Lee, and Stevenson (1995), for example, found evidence that Japanese tend to use the 'strongly disagree' and 'strongly agree' response options less frequently than do Americans. This response tendency makes sense when you compare Japanese folk beliefs ('The nail that stands out gets pounded down') to American folk beliefs ('The squeaky wheel gets the grease') (Markus & Kitayama, 1991, p. 224). Nonetheless, this tendency towards difference could potentially make research results difficult to interpret. If one finds, for example, that Japanese moderately agree that membership in a religious community is important to personal well-being, but North Americans more strongly agree, how do researchers discern from this data alone whether this reported difference in beliefs is real or merely due to differential response style? Later in this chapter we will address solutions to such questions.

Reference Effect

A third hazard encountered by researchers results from the reference effect (Heine et al., 2002). Participants compare themselves to a reference group when considering their responses. Thus, responses to rating scales may depend not only on respondents' perception of themselves, but also on the group to which they compare themselves. For example, if the researcher asks a student whether he values his relations with his family, the student may immediately consider how he compares to his peers. If he believes that he values these relations more than his friends do, he may say he strongly values these relations. If not, he may say he moderately values these relations.

Reference effects may help explain counterintuitive findings, such as the fact that, according to their self-reports in cross-cultural questionnaire studies, Japanese groups are often no more collectivistic than American groups (Oyserman, Coon, & Kemmelmeier, 2002). Such findings could result in part because the Japanese in completing questionnaires may be comparing themselves to other Japanese, and the Americans comparing themselves to other Americans.

Reference effects become problematic in cross-cultural research because they may mask cultural differences. It might be reasonable to hypothesize, for example, that youth in Mexico tend to value their family relations more than do youth in England, but even if this were the case, reference effects could shrink the apparent differences on rating scales. Youth in Mexico may compare themselves to their friends, just as youth in England are expected to do. On average, then, both groups as a result may say that they only moderately value their family. If the reference effect shrinks the apparent difference, cultural differences may appear to be statistically insignificant when in fact significant cultural differences exist.

Translation Problems

Many times questionnaires are available in only one language, making translation necessary. Some phrases may not translate well. For example, a questionnaire may ask youth whether it is important to 'pursue their dreams.' Youth raised in North American culture will know that this phrase refers to striving to meet your goals. Translators will have to take care to assure that in the second language, respondents don't think that phrase exclusively refers to following visions seen during one's sleep. The opportunities for mistranslation are frequent and can seriously skew the results of any given study.

Imposed Etic Research

Berry (1989) popularized the term 'imposed etic' research to refer in part to research that relies on measurement instruments created in one culture and used without change in a second culture. This approach assumes that: (1) the variables created in one culture will always make sense in another; and (2) may also indicate an assumption that variables important in the one culture exhaust the list of variables important in the other. The first assumption of imposed etic research is clearly wrong. Concepts that seem coherent to one cultural group may seem like a collection of unrelated ideas to a second group. An example is the Confucian work dynamism construct as discussed by Bond and others (Chinese Culture Connection, 1987). Confucian work dynamism includes valuing hierarchical social relations, thrift, persistence, and a sense of shame. To North Americans, this construct may seem like a loose collection of unrelated concepts, despite being meaningful in a culturally Chinese context. Thus, variables meaningful to one culture may lack meaning in the second culture.

The second possible assumption further demonstrates the problems with imposed etic research. Variables important in one culture do not necessarily match the list of variables important in another. Self-efficacy, for example, is clearly of great importance for supporting the subjective well-being of individuals from individualistic contexts. Individuals from individualistic cultures may seldom, however, consider the importance of communal mastery (the extent to which one believes one's community has efficacy). These same individualistic researchers will probably not assess communal mastery in their studies, though at least one recent study suggests that in some cultural contexts the importance of communal mastery may overshadow the role of self-efficacy (Hobfoll et al., 2002). Thus, researchers from one culture may completely miss variables of great importance in another context if relevance of characteristics is not considered.

Non-comparable Samples

Non-comparable samples can invalidate research findings. Sometimes non-comparability is obvious. For example, a cross-cultural researcher could compare the psychological test scores of a sample of thirteen-year-olds from Spain to those of a sample of fifteen-year-olds from Nigeria. The researcher might be tempted to conclude that group differences are due to cultural influences, but this conclusion would be erroneous. Any observed group differences in this hypothetical study could be due to culture or to age. In this case, the non-comparability is obvious, but in other situations non-comparability may be more subtle. For example, in some countries, public schools provide a representative sample of youth, but in other countries these same types of schools may represent a particular socio-economic class. One could therefore question the validity of a study sampling youth from public schools across a variety of contexts. Any seemingly apparent cultural differences may reflect socio-economic differences rather than real cultural differences.

Diminishing Audience

Another hazard emerges when cross-cultural research fails to consider previously studied cultural dimensions, limiting the relevance of findings to a relatively small audience. For example, a study of youth beliefs about resilience in Canada and Lithuania could be quite fascinating for people with prior concerns about both Canada and Lithuania. However, that potential audience may be relatively small. The audience can be greatly expanded with minimal effort by simultaneously examining not just cultural groups, but also previously studied cultural dimensions such as collectivism, power-distance (Hofstede, 1980), and self-expression (Inglehart, 2000).

Cultural Distrust

Some participants may not trust researchers. Distrust of researchers, especially researchers from cultural backgrounds different from those of participants, may produce results that suggest differences across cultures but that, in actuality, reflect differential non-disclosure from participants who view the researcher as foreign. Such participants may provide socially-acceptable answers, simply write down random responses without reading the questions, or even refuse to respond.

Threats to Scale Reliability and Validity

Developing psychometrically sound questionnaires can be challenging and brings with it the need to establish the validity of the scale. The use of measures with known reliability and validity can avoid many issues that may arise when using newly developed questionnaires. However, a researcher cannot assume that a scale that is valid in one cultural context will necessarily be so in another. The obvious inappropriateness of some commonly used scales for cross-cultural use may therefore lead researchers to construct new measures that may be less culturally biased. However, those who develop their own questionnaires may end up with instruments that fail to adequately measure the intended construct.

Even competent, experienced researchers can have difficulty designing appropriate questionnaires. Sternberg and Wagner (1991; see also Sternberg, 1997), for example, developed an eight-item scale to assess judicial thinking style (the extent to which people like to judge or rate ideas or objects). If all eight questionnaire items assess the same underlying construct, then there should be high internal consistency and a positive correlation among responses to all eight questions. In fact, scores on seven of the eight items have been found to be interrelated (Sternberg & Wagner, 1991); participants who expressed agreement with any one of the statements were more likely than other participants to agree with all seven (e.g., 'I enjoy work that involves analyzing, grading, or comparing things'; Sternberg, 1997, p. 37). This finding suggests that these seven items assess a common underlying construct. The eighth item in the scale, however, is likely investigating a different construct ('When discussing or writing down ideas, I like to criticize others' way of doing things.'). Sternberg and Wagner (1991) found that participants who agreed with this one statement were not much more likely than other participants to agree with the other seven questions. Thus, despite great efforts and familiarity with the construct under study, even an experienced research team can be humbled. In Sternberg and Wagner's work, the seven statements seemed to measure a thinking style, while the eighth assessed a different construct than that intended by the authors.

Minimizing Hazards

As suggested above, threats to validity often cannot be completely eliminated. They can, however, be minimized. Suggestions for minimizing threats to validity are discussed below.

Enhancing Translation Accuracy

A very common procedure for assuring adequate translation involves the use of back-translation (Brislin, 1970). In this procedure, the document is first translated from one language, for example English, into a second language, such as Mandarin. Subsequently, a translator who had not seen the original English document would translate the Mandarin document back into English. Consistency between the two English documents then indicates consistency of the translation. Inconsistency may require revision of the Mandarin document, the original English document, or both. The back-translation procedure catches many of the problems that are typically encountered when translating documents.

Avoiding Imposed Etic Research

In order to avoid imposed etic research, each questionnaire must be modified to make it relevant to all cultures being studied. This may mean revising the wording of some items and/or adding items because the original questionnaire fails to assess a variable of great importance in one of the cultures being studied. Cultural sensitivity requires effort; cultural blinders are difficult if not impossible to remove. Thus, members of each culture being studied should be involved in planning the research. These representatives can suggest revisions to the protocol to assure that relevant variables are assessed and culturally sensitive procedures are followed. The International Resilience Project is an example of how people from many different cultures can be involved in multisite research planning (Ungar & Liebenberg, 2005).

Recruiting Comparable Samples

Recruiting comparable samples from two cultures can be a challenge. In his classic cross-cultural study, Hofstede (1980) recruited somewhat comparable samples of adults from a wide variety of countries by involving employees from a single multinational corporation. Though some might still criticize this approach, his procedure assured that he compared groups of people who were all employed and whose work-place had a somewhat similar organizational culture. Likewise, Schwartz sought comparable samples by recruiting teachers from a variety of regions of the world (Smith & Schwartz, 1997). He argued that teachers in each country are particularly important because this group passes on culture to the young, and thus might actually reflect the direction that culture is moving. Also, teachers have similar jobs and are relatively educated compared to the general populace.

Studies of youth resilience cannot, of course, follow these strategies exactly, but researchers should nonetheless seek samples from each cultural group that are somewhat similar. The challenge is to find sources of relatively comparable participants in each cultural group. This task may sometimes be easier with youth than with adults because schools in some cultural groups provide a fairly representa-tive sample of youth and a convenient venue for recruitment.

Most cross-cultural studies use university students despite some obvious drawbacks. Many of those who face difficult childhoods never attend university, and so will be excluded from these studies. Also, Snibbe and Markus (2005) suggest that university students tend to have more of an internal locus of control than do other, less educated members of the population. Furthermore, use of university students may shrink effect sizes of cultural differences across regions because attendance at university exposes students to the influence of an elitist and possibly somewhat Westernized view of the world. Nonetheless, the use of post-secondary students may be justifiable, especially for studies seeking initial tests of hypotheses.

Expanding Audience

The potential audience of cross-cultural studies can be greatly increased by simultaneously studying cultural groups and previously studied cultural dimensions. Such studies not only assess group dif-ferences, but also assess which previously studied cultural dimensions best account for these differences. For those interested in this type of approach, some of the central cultural dimensions worthy of consider-ation can be found in research by Smith and Schwartz (1997), Bond (2004), Inglehart (2000; see also www.worldvaluessurvey.org), the

Chinese Culture Connection (1987), and Hofstede (1980). These studies include variables such as collectivism, power-distance (Hofstede, 1980), and self-expression (Inglehart, 2000), all factors possibly associated with resilience.

Consider the previously mentioned hypothetical study of beliefs about resilience among Lithuanian and Canadian youth. This study would be important, but might interest only a small audience because few researchers have a prior interest in comparisons of Lithuania and Canada. Researchers can expand their audience by designing the study to allow at least tentative conclusions about cultural dimensions (such as valuing self-expression [Inglehart, 2000]) that have been previously studied in other nations. One could construct, for example, an argument that those participants valuing self-expression may tend to believe that resilience depends more on relations with peers and less on relations with authority figures. Peers could be more likely than authority figures to provide opportunities for the self-expression so highly valued in these participants' culture.

The study could then test not only for differences between cultural groups, but also whether the hypothesized cultural factor accounts for the difference. The researcher may find, for example, that (1) Canadians tend to believe peer relations are especially important to resilience and (2) Canadians also tend to place more value on self-expression than do Lithuanians. The researcher may hypothesize that value placed on self-expression may account for the observed difference in beliefs about resilience. Then the researcher could assess whether separate analyses of the Canadian data and Lithuanian data both demonstrate a positive correlation between valuing self-expression and stronger affirmation of the role of peers. This finding would suggest that self-expression values seem to account at least in part for the cultural differences. The strength of the argument is increased if this pattern is not observed for other cultural variables. The study would then not only provide information about those two cultural groups, but also suggest hypotheses regarding many different cultural groups known to differ on the cultural dimensions included in the study.

Cultural Distrust

Some researchers might anticipate (possibly from pilot testing of the questionnaire) that distrust and resulting random responding will be a serious problem in a cross-cultural study. To address issues of trust and random responding, researchers could ask trusted figures in the community to conduct the research on their behalf. The researchers could also read the questionnaire to the participants and ask for oral responses in an effort to maintain motivation on the part of participants. Participants are more likely to remain engaged when involved in this type of oral communication than when completing a written questionnaire. This type of interview, however, takes more time than a questionnaire, allows for fewer participants, and is not always necessary.

Also, on written questionnaires, the researchers could include statements to highlight those participants who are randomly responding (Millon et al., 2006). One could include a statement such as 'I usually sleep less than seven hours per week.' Agreement with such a statement would be so infrequent that the researcher would be justified in excluding the data from any person agreeing with this statement. Likewise, the researcher could be justified in excluding anyone disagreeing with 'I am more than sixty centimetres tall.'

Minimizing the Effect of Idiosyncratic Rating Scale Statements

For highly objective variables such as age and birthplace, the following recommendations are not applicable, but for many other variables such as ratings of social support, exposure to violence, self-esteem, and many of the other variables of interest to resilience researchers, extreme care must be exercised to assure that scales measure what they are intended to measure.

USE PREVIOUSLY TESTED RATING SCALE STATEMENTS WHEN POSSIBLE
The threat of poorly worded rating scale statements can be minimized by choosing statements that have proved effective in prior studies and modifying them where necessary to make them culturally appropriate. Some such questionnaires are in the public domain (e.g., www.ipip.ori.org); others are available by mailing the authors of the questionnaire; and others must be purchased from test companies. Sadly, psychology has historically focused more on assessing pathology than on assessing human strengths and well-being. Some recent publications have begun to provide more guidance for assessing strengths (e.g., Lopez, 2003). Publication alone, however, does not guarantee that a particular questionnaire is valid. The publications should be examined to ensure that the measures have adequate relia-

bility (e.g., respectable Cronbach's alpha [Cronbach, 1951]) and construct validity (e.g., produce expected correlations with other variables). More detail will be provided below on how to assess the quality of rating scales.

Sometimes, however, no previously tested set of items exists for assessing a particular variable. As discussed earlier, designing questionnaire items can be difficult. Some suggestions for doing so follow.

Use simple, brief wording. Rating scale statements should use simple words and be brief. Ideally, the central content of the statement (especially the main verb) will come early in the statement. For example, it is more time consuming to read 'When I consider my relations with my friends, I think that I have at least one friend who could be described as a good friend ' than 'I have at least one good friend.' The main verb comes earlier in the second statement, and the second statement is brief.

Some word-processing programs will assess the reading grade level of a particular piece of text. Researchers should consider using these indicators to assess whether the wording of their questionnaire is too complex. Even better, youth at the targeted age can identify unnecessarily complex wording in the questionnaire.

Assess reliability. In order to assess whether particular questionnaire statements intended to measure any one variable are functioning as intended, reliability should be assessed. Reliability in this context refers to consistency. Reliability can be assessed by examining test-retest correlations if the questionnaire item(s) under consideration are assessing a variable that should be stable across time. In other words, participants could be tested on one day and then tested again at a later date to determine whether the test produces consistent scores.

More frequently, reliability is assessed by administering the questionnaire and then using the data to calculate a measure of internal consistency, usually Cronbach's alpha (Cronbach, 1951) for each set of statements intended to measure a single underlying factor. This coefficient can only be calculated for questionnaires with multiple items measuring each variable. For example, in order to assess positive peer relations, a researcher might include the following items in the questionnaire: 'I have a good friend,' 'I can tell my best friend about my worries,' 'I could ask my best friend for advice about my schoolwork,' and 'I am popular with many kids.' Participants would rate their agreement with each statement. Usually at least three statements and more frequently approximately eight statements will be used to assess each variable. Using a higher number of statements for each variable tends to produce more accurate measurement, but also tends to cause participant fatigue.

If the items all succeed in measuring the same variable, then internal consistency will be evident. In other words, once the data are collected, expected correlations will emerge between all three or more statements. Each participant who responds in a particular direction to one of the statements will also tend to respond in the expected way to the other statements assessing the same variable. If these correlations do not emerge, then at least one of the questions may be measuring a different factor than the others and should be excluded.

Cronbach's alpha provides a means of assessing this type of internal consistency and reliability among questionnaire items. It is difficult to suggest an appropriate level for alpha because alpha is influenced by the number of statements in the scale, but ideally an alpha should be above .80. Including more statements tends to increase the alpha and can increase the likelihood that the study will uncover statistically significant findings.

The researcher will also want to calculate Cronbach's alpha with each questionnaire item removed. Thus, the researcher will calculate alpha for the whole set of statements measuring one variable, then will recalculate alpha with only the first questionnaire item deleted, then with only the second questionnaire item deleted, and so on. If alpha increases when any item is deleted, then this suggests that the particular item is measuring a different variable than that measured by the other items. Consider the items suggested above as possible measures of social support. The first three items may assess social support, but the last item may assess self-esteem or extroversion. The data could show, for example, that the alpha is low (e.g., .60) when data from all four items are included in the calculation, but that if the researcher excludes the fourth item, Cronbach's alpha may be acceptable (e.g., .80). More in-depth analyses could be provided with exploratory or confirmatory factor analyses of the measures being implemented, but the details of these procedures deserve a chapter unto themselves.

In many situations, ratings come from observers (e.g., teachers, parents, social workers) rather than from the participants themselves. When two different types of raters (e.g., teachers and parents) each rate a child, one can assess the reliability of these ratings after the data are collected by examining correlations between the sets of ratings. A strong positive correlation would indicate that the two groups were, as instructed, rating the same variable. Low or negative correlations suggest that the two groups were considering different factors when making their ratings (even though they may have been given exactly the same instructions). For example, both groups may be asked to rate the child's well-being. Teachers, however, may rely more on the child's comfort with academic tasks when rating well-being. Parents may put more emphasis on signs of positive emotion during family activities. Low correlations in situations such as this don't necessarily invalidate the ratings, but do suggest that the observers are rating different dimensions; thus it may not make sense to combine the ratings into a single composite score if the correlation between them is low. If three or more different groups are making the ratings, one could conceivably calculate Cronbach's alpha using these data. If observers instead categorize each child into one category from a list of non-ordered categories (e.g., secure attachment, avoidant attachment, and ambivalent attachment [Muris, Mayer, & Meesters, 2000]), then a different statistic, kappa (Cohen, 1960), would be appropriate. Kappa indicates the extent to which raters using a non-ordered set of categories tend to agree beyond what would be expected by chance. An acceptable level of reliability suggests that one variable is being consistently measured. Reliability alone, however, is not enough. Researchers will also want evidence that statements assess the intended variable, that is, have construct validity. All of these procedures can become more complicated when raters are from different cultural backgrounds. Their own cultural baggage is likely to skew their perceptions.

Assess validity by including expected correlates in the study. Preliminary evidence of construct validity can be provided by demonstrating that the measure of the variable in question correlates in an expected direction with other related variables (Cook & Campbell, 1979). If that type of evidence for construct validity is not available from prior studies in all the cultures being studied, the researcher should consider gathering the data as part of his or her own study.

For example, imagine the researcher wants to use the following four rating scale statements to assess availability of social support: 'I have a good friend,' 'I can tell my best friend about my worries,' 'I could ask my best friend for advice about my schoolwork,' and 'I play with a friend after school at least twice a week.' The researcher could reasonably expect the average score for these items to be correlated with other variables such as agreeableness (e.g., www.ipip.ori.org), and possibly with size of social network. Thus, the researcher can include questions to assess these latter two dimensions in the questionnaire. Then, after the data are collected, the researcher can assess whether the mean score for the availability of social support items is positively associated as expected with being agreeable and having a large social network (as shown for example by positive Pearson *r* correlation coefficients). Such findings would provide at least some evidence for construct validity (Cook & Campbell, 1979).

Possibly assess validity by including expected non-correlates. Further evidence of construct validity can be collected by showing that the measure in question is not correlated with variables with which it should not have a relation (Cook & Campbell, 1979). For example, if one is assessing subjective well-being (i.e., happiness), one would hope that high scores on the subjective well-being scale actually assess happiness and not simply efforts by some participants to impress the researcher. Again, when working with youth across cultures one can reasonably expect participants to want to represent themselves somewhat how they think researchers want them to appear, or alternately to resist stereotypes. Either way, one must be careful to account for how participants perceived their experience of answering the questionnaire.

By way of illustration, with adults, studies of domestic violence are hampered because men who abuse their spouses frequently minimize and deny their abuse. Youth researchers face a similar problem of potential misreporting whenever they ask participants to report on socially desirable or socially undesirable aspects of the self. In one of our studies, we asked participants at a Canadian university to report their school grades. The Euro-Canadian students reported higher grades on average than did students who had been born in East Asia, even though prior evidence suggested that in reality students born in East Asia tended to achieve grades as high as those of Euro-Canadians. Thus, it seemed that the Euro-Canadians were exaggerating the socially desirable outcome of high grades and thereby invalidating the data.

Tools to assess socially desirable responding have been developed. In general, wording of these measures is usually designed for older youth or adults. Crowne and Marlowe (1960), for example, designed a questionnaire to assess the extent to which participants are influenced by a motivation towards a socially desirable impression. The length of this questionnaire has prompted shorter forms. Paulhus (1998) designed the Deception Scales for a similar purpose. Paulhus' scales have the advantage of differentiating impression management (efforts to make oneself look good to others) from self-deception (lying to oneself). The Crowne-Marlowe and the Deception Scales (also known as the Balanced Inventory of Desirable Responding, or BIDR) both ask participants to rate their agreement with a set of statements that are socially desirable, but that few if any respondents can honestly assert. For example, people may be asked to rate their agreement with the statement 'I have never wanted something bad to happen to someone else' and 'I have almost never broken the law.' The tests assume that people who strongly agree with many such statements are probably altering their responses to make themselves look better. One problem with these types of scales is the possibility that true exemplars of culturally esteemed behaviour will score high on impression management just because they affirm infrequent responses. In other words, people who strongly adhere to cultural norms may get scores on these scales that wrongly suggest they are lying. Thus, these measures of socially desirable responding will give erroneous scores to some individuals. Nonetheless, when considering the group as a whole, the scales can help researchers evaluate their findings.

We would expect most variables (e.g., self-report of exposure to violence) to be largely unrelated to impression management scores. If there is an unanticipated relation, the researcher must consider whether the questionnaire items are assessing what they are intended to assess. Researchers could consider redesigning their questionnaire to avoid this outcome in the future. Alternatively, researchers can alter their statistical analysis of the data by partialing the impression management score out of their statistical analyses. Another possibility is that the researcher can regress the affected variable on the impression management scale, and then use the residual scores in the remaining analyses (Saunders, 1991). These latter two procedures would remove the variance that can be accounted for by the impression management scale. Ideally, the researcher can merely confirm that the main variables of the study are unrelated to impression management unless one expects them to be related.

Impression management is merely provided as an example of the issues that will arise in resilience research using standardized measures across cultures. Researchers can generate their own list of variables they want to include in their studies in order to assure they are not assessing unintended variables with their questionnaire.

Evaluate previously tested measures. Often the task of designing a study can be made easier by using questionnaire items that have been used in previous studies. If the researcher chooses to use rating scales designed by others, he or she should also examine the results of the prior studies to gather evidence of reliability (e.g., test-retest correlations or Cronbach's alpha) and validity (expected patterns of correlations) in order to justify the use of these scales.

Pilot testing. When possible, researchers should attempt to conduct their study with a very small number of participants in order to uncover major problems before the study design is finalized. The pilot participants can be asked not only to answer the questions but also to comment on their perception of possible problems. This type of pilot testing will uncover problems with unclear wording, excessive length, and other potential problems likely to plague cross-cultural research with youth. Focus groups can be used for this purpose as well.

Minimizing the Hazard of the Reference Effect

The reference effect can be difficult to overcome. Some evidence suggests that the reference effect may be less problematic when participants are asked to choose from among alternative behaviours rather than to respond to statements about values (Peng, Nisbett, & Wong, 1997). For example, the researcher could ask not 'To what extent would you agree that you value your family' but rather 'If you were free tomorrow night, would you rather spend an evening with your immediate family members or going out with people from your school?' The second question doesn't require an implicit reference group, but merely a stated preference. This strategy, however, may not be appropriate for all types of variables.

A second strategy that we recommend involves conducting research both across and within regions. For example, one study of resilience beliefs could compare responses of youth in Egypt to youth in New York City. This study could have great value, but might be subject to the reference effect. A second follow-up study could exclusively examine participants in the New York public school system, but compare those born in Egypt to those born in New York. This approach reduces the reference effect and may produce larger differences across cultural groups because all participants could be asked to compare themselves to other students in the school. Thus all participants would have a common reference group. Findings are most believable if the same results emerge when the research is conducted both across and within regions.

Correcting for Nay-Saying

Corrections for nay-saying and extremism have been used in some of the most widely cited cross-cultural studies (e.g., Hofstede, 1980; Smith & Schwartz, 1997), but the procedure still remains somewhat controversial (Fischer, 2004). A thorough discussion of this correction is beyond the scope of this chapter, but correction for nay-saying has been helpful in our experience and has tended to make cross-cultural data more meaningful, at least when comparing North American and Chinese cultural groups (e.g., Tweed, 2000; Tweed, White, & Lehman, 2004).

One can design the rating scale portion of the questionnaire so that it is possible to use a subset of the questionnaire item responses to assess nay-saying. One could include, for example, a diverse collection of personality or attitude measures. The total score for all these questions may provide an acceptable indicator of nay-saying. In other words, participants who tend to disagree with all the items may be expressing a nay-saying bias. Preferably all questions in this section of the questionnaire will have the same response options (e.g., 'strongly disagree,' 'disagree,' 'disagree somewhat,' 'neutral,' 'agree somewhat,' 'agree,' 'strongly agree'). In order to provide an acceptable indicator of nay-saying, the total score across the questions cannot provide an indicator of any meaningful construct other than nay-saying. For example, a questionnaire assessing various forms of well-being would not provide an adequate indicator of nay-saying. If cultural groups differed on the total score for this measure of well-being, it would be unclear whether the difference indicated true differences in well-being or merely nay-saying by one cultural group.

One must carefully consider, however, whether the selected items provide an acceptable indicator of nay-saying. A questionnaire assessing a diverse mix of values, resilience resources, resilience threats, indicators of well-being, and indicators of psychopathology may provide a reasonable indicator of nay-saying if there is no reason to expect that the total true score of any cultural group should be higher than that of any other cultural group across the whole set of items.

Second, after the data have been collected, a total score for each participant across these items can be calculated.

Third, the total scores for each cultural group can be statistically compared. If cultural groups significantly differ on this total score, it may be reasonable to assume that this difference indicates not a true-score difference, but a different tendency towards nay-saying.

Fourth, the researcher can implement a transformation that converts the raw scores into a relative score. In particular, for each person, the transformation will subtract the person's average rating across the whole questionnaire from every one of their ratings. After the transformation, a positive score for a particular question for a particular participant will indicate that the participant provided a more positive rating for that statement than he or she did on average for the other statements. Vitaliano et al. (1987) described a related correction used in coping research. Their approach, however, corrects by means of mathematical division rather than by means of subtraction. The consequences of this difference will not be fully discussed here except to say that for cross-cultural research the method discussed here probably makes more sense.

The procedure described here is easier than this explanation might suggest. For those interested in using this transformation, the two required equations will be described. Other readers may want to skip this paragraph. First, the researcher can write a transformation command that calculates the mean across all items for each individual (e.g., meanrating = mean.70 (qn1 to qn99)). The 'mean.70' applies only to users of SPSS and indicates that the mean will be calculated for each participant who responded to at least seventy of the questionnaire statements. Next, for each statement, one writes a command calculating a corrected variable (e.g., trans_qn1= qn1-meanrating). These commands will work with SPSS, but will be similar to those used in other programs such as MSExcel. This procedure centres all scores around zero. In other words, each respondent will have an average score of zero on the ratings. A positive score for a particular item will indicate that the individual endorsed that item more than they tended to endorse the other items. A negative score will indicate that the individual endorsed that item less than they tended to endorse other items. Because negative scores make tables difficult to read, one can add a constant to all scores to raise the scores above zero.

Some caveats deserve mention here. If some of the rating scale items have different response options than do other items, the strategy for calculating an indicator of nay-saying becomes more complicated and possibly less reliable (Tweed et al., 2004). For example, some items may ask for a rating of agreement on a seven-point scale, while other questions may ask for a response on a four-point scale. Also, nay-saying may affect behavioural self-reports much less or at least quite differently from the way it affects reports of attitudinal agreement. Thus, corrections may not make sense for some types of behavioural self-reports and also for many other questions such as demographic questions.

Correcting for Extremism

Extremism can simultaneously be corrected by slightly modifying the transformations above to cause all participants to have the same mean and standard deviation across the questionnaire items [step 1: mean-rating = mean.70(qn1 to qn99), step 2: sdrating = sd(qn1 to qn99), step 3: trans_qn1 = (qn1-meanrating)/sdrating)]. Some evidence, however, suggests that extremism usually does not affect study results (Chen, Lee, & Stevenson, 1995), and so for this and other reasons we recommend usually not correcting for extremism (Tweed et al., 2004) even if working across cultures

An Alternative to Statistical Corrections for Nay-Saying and Extremism

An alternative procedure exists that avoids the controversy of the corrections described above, but requires more expensive and difficult research methods. This approach requires that researchers gather data from each participant at several time points. The data can then be analysed with multilevel modelling software such as HLM (Raudenbush et al., 2004).

The advantage of this procedure is that each person serves as their own control. In other words, the procedure can explore variables that predict changes within persons across time. This procedure could assess, for example, whether times during which children report particularly positive relations with peers tend to be followed by greater increases in well-being than do times when those same children report less positive relations with peers (Raudenbush & Bryk, 2002). This procedure has excellent potential to overcome many problems of cross-cultural response bias.

Conclusion

As suggested at the beginning of this chapter, all research has flaws. Threats to validity cannot be completely eliminated. These threats include nay-saying, extremism, the reference effect, translation problems, imposed etic research, non-comparable samples, reducing the audience (by studying cultural groups and not cultural dimensions), cultural distrust, and idiosyncratic questionnaire statements. Those planning resilience research across cultures are correct to fear they will never be able to design and run a perfect study. Nonetheless, the threats to validity can be minimized and, by minimizing these threats, the researcher can gather important information and thereby improve our understanding of and interventions for youth.

References

Berry, J.W. (1989). Imposed etics-emics-derived etics: The operationalization of a compelling idea. *International Journal of Psychology, 24*(6), 721–35.

Bond, M.H. (2004). Culture-level dimensions of social axioms and their correlates across 41 cultures. *Journal of Cross-Cultural Psychology, 35*(5), 548–70.

Brislin, R.W. (1970). Back-translation for cross-cultural research. *Journal of Cross-Cultural Psychology, 1*(3), 185–216.

Chen, C., Lee, S., & Stevenson, H.W. (1995). Response style and cross-cultural comparisons of rating scales among East Asian and North American students. *Psychological Science, 6*(3), 170–5.

Chesterton, G.K. (1994 [1908]). *Orthodoxy*. Salt Lake City, UT: Project Gutenberg Etext.

Chinese Culture Connection. (1987). Chinese values and the search for culture-free dimensions of culture. *Journal of Cross-Cultural Psychology, 18*(2), 143–64.

Cohen, J. (1960). A coefficient of agreement for nominal scales. *Educational and Psychological Measurement, 20*, 37–46.

Cook, T.D., & Campbell, D.T. (1979). *Quasi-experimentation: Design and analysis for field settings*. Boston: Houghton Mifflin.

Cronbach, L.J. (1951). Coefficient alpha and the internal structure of tests. *Psychometrika, 16*, 297–334.

Crowne, D.P., & Marlow, D. (1960). A new scale of social desirability independent of psychopathology. *Journal of Consulting Psychology, 24*(4), 349–54.

Fischer, R. (2004). Standardization to account for cross-cultural response bias. *Journal of Cross-Cultural Psychology, 35*(3), 263–82.

178   Roger G. Tweed and Anita DeLongis

Heine, S.J., Lehman, D.R., Peng, K., & Greenholtz, J. (2002). What's wrong with cross-cultural comparisons of subjective Likert scales? The reference-group effect. *Journal of Personality and Social Psychology, 82*(6), 903–18.

Hobfoll, S.E., Jackson, A., Hobfoll, I., Pierce, C.A., & Young, S. (2002). The impact of communal-mastery versus self-mastery on emotional outcomes during stressful conditions: A prospective study of Native American women. *American Journal of Community Psychology, 30*(6), 853–72.

Hofstede, G.H. (1980). *Culture's consequences: International differences in work-related values.* Beverly Hills, CA: Sage.

Inglehart, R. (2000). Globalization and postmodern values. *The Washington Quarterly, 23*(1), 215–28.

Lebra, T.S. (1984). Nonconfrontational strategies for management of interpersonal conflicts. In E.S. Kraus, T.P. Rohlen, & P.G. Steinhoff (Eds.), *Conflict in Japan* (pp. 41–60). Honolulu: University of Hawaii Press.

Lopez, S.J. (2003). *Positive psychological assessment: A handbook of models and measures.* Washington, DC: American Psychological Association.

Markus, H.R., & Kitayama, S. (1991). Culture and the self: Implications for cognition, emotion, and motivation. *Psychological Review, 98*(2), 224–53.

Millon, T., Millon, C., Davis, R., & Grossman, S. (2006). *Millon Clinical Multiaxial Inventory–III.* Minneapolis, MN: NCS Pearson.

Muris, P., Mayer, B., & Meesters, C. (2000). Self-reported attachment style, anxiety, and depression in children. *Social Behavior and Personality, 28*(2), 157–62.

Oyserman, D., Coon, H.M., & Kemmelmeier, M. (2002). Rethinking individualism and collectivism: Evaluation of theoretical assumptions and meta-analyses. *Psychological Bulletin, 128*(1), 3–72.

Paulhus, D.L. (1998). *The Paulhus Deception Scales: BIDR Version 7.* Toronto/Buffalo: Multi-Health Systems.

Peng, K., Nisbett, R.E., & Wong, N.Y.C. (1997). Validity problems comparing values across cultures and possible solutions. *Psychological Methods, 2*(4), 329–44.

Raudenbush, S.W., & Bryk, A.S. (2002). *Hierarchial linear models: Applications and data analysis methods.* Thousand Oaks, CA: Sage.

Raudenbush, S., Bryk, A., Cheong, Y.F., Congdon, R., & du Toit, M. (2004). *HLM 6 Hierarchical linear and nonlinear modeling.* Lincolnwood, IL: Scientific Software International.

Saunders, D.G. (1991). Procedures for adjusting self-reports of violence for social desirability bias. *Journal of Interpersonal Violence, 6*, 336–44.

Smith, P.B., & Schwartz, S. (1997). Values. In J.W. Berry, M.H. Segall, & C. Kagitcibasi (Eds.), *Handbook of cross-cultural psychology*, Vol. 3: *Social behavior and applications* (2nd ed., pp. 291–326). Boston: Allyn and Bacon.

Snibbe, A.C., & Markus, H.R. (2005). You can't always get what you want: Educational attainment, agency, and choice. *Journal of Personality and Social Psychology, 88*(4), 703–20.

Sternberg, R.J. (1997). *Thinking styles.* New York: Cambridge University Press.

Sternberg, R.J., & Wagner, R.K. (1991). *MSG Thinking Styles Inventory.* Unpublished manual.

Tweed, R.G. (2000). *Learning considered within a cultural context: Confucian and Socratic approaches.* Doctoral dissertation, University of British Columbia.

Tweed, R.G., Conway, L.G., Ryder, A.G., & Lehman, D.R. (2004). *Ipsatization: Reducing measurement error in cross-cultural research.* Unpublished manuscript.

Tweed, R.G., White, K., & Lehman, D.R. (2004). Culture, stress, and coping: Internally- and externally-targeted control strategies of European Canadians, East Asian-Canadians, and Japanese. *Journal of Cross-Cultural Psychology, 35*(6), 652–8.

Twenge, J. (2006). *Generation me: Why today's young Americans are more confident, assertive, entitled – and more miserable than ever before.* New York: Free Press.

Ungar, M., & Liebenberg, L. (2005). The International Resilience Project: A mixed methods approach to the study of resilience across cultures. In M. Ungar (Ed.), *Handbook for working with children and youth: Pathways to resilience across cultures and contexts* (pp. 211–26). Thousand Oaks, CA: Sage.

Vitaliano, P.B., Maiuro, R.D., Russo, J., & Becker, J. (1987). Raw versus relative scores in the assessment of coping strategies. *Journal of Behavioral Medicine, 10*(1), 1–18.

7 Use of Meta-Analysis to Study Resilience Factors: An Exemplar

ALEXA SMITH-OSBORNE

In this chapter, meta-analysis methodology is discussed in terms of its utility for resilience research and the development of resilience theory. As an exemplar, a meta-analysis studying resilience factors among students with psychiatric disorders is discussed. Prior theory-driven studies that use meta-analytic methods to test theoretical constructs are also examined. Particular attention is given to syntheses of contextual variables relevant to youth across cultures, such as exposure to familial and community violence, dimensions of cultural values, and institutional policies affecting young adults with psychiatric disorders. The strengths and limitations of meta-analysis methodology in the study of resilience are reviewed and recommendations for future meta-analyses of resilience literature presented.

Resilience research has relied on a number of quantitative and qualitative designs, especially longitudinal studies (Garmezy, 1991; Luthar, Cicchetti, & Becker, 2000; Masten & Coatsworth, 1998; McCubbin et al., 1976; Richardson, 2002; Rutter, 1999; Smith & Carson, 1997; Werner, 1992). However, systematic review of the literature, and particularly quantitative research synthesis, has been underutilized in this area of research. An electronic search of the EBSCO database aggregator, which includes approximately two hundred full text and secondary databases across multiple disciplines, indexing over 16,000 journals (EBSCO, n.d.), shows a paucity of such analyses. Keywords for the search were selected from the EBSCO comprehensive thesaurus of terms. A search of all fields (abstracts, titles, keywords, and full text) in journals published from 1988 to 2005 disclosed 18,698 publications using the keyword 'meta-analysis,' but only 814 using the keywords 'meta-analysis' and 'risk factors,' and only nine using the keywords 'meta-analysis' and 'protective factors.' Furthermore, the majority of risk factor publications were medical studies. These studies therefore applied the term 'risk factor' to physical disease referents, rather than as the term is used in the study of resilience with its broader psychosocial understanding of risk determinants. No publications were found using the keywords 'meta-analysis' and 'resiliency theory.' Only one publication was found with the keywords 'meta-analysis' and 'resilience': the exemplar study referenced in this paper (Smith-Osborne, 2005).

Introduction to Quantitative Research Synthesis

Research synthesis is a quantitative review of literature in a specific research area, addressing a specific research question. A quantitative review may stand alone as an initial review of an area; build on existing qualitative, narrative reviews of the literature; or be part of a systematic narrative review when it provides quantitative analysis of a subset of suitable studies (Cooper & Hedges, 1994). Meta-analysis is the statistical analysis of an integrative research synthesis, which is intended to be exhaustive in coverage of the research base. It can synthesize data across multiple replication studies to disclose the overall strength and direction of associations among two or more variables, such as the association between specific risk and protective factors or among chains of variables that create a protective mechanism. Meta-analysis techniques can be applied to data integration of multivariate and non-independent data sets as well as data sets with missing data. They can be used to assess models and to perform sensitivity analyses (i.e., systematically addressing alternatives, such as whether research findings in an area are influenced by methodological quality) and subgroup analyses.

Meta-analysis offers the advantages of being more systematic, explicit, and statistically powerful than primary studies and narrative literature reviews. A major strength of meta-analysis, as compared to narrative literature reviews, is its replicable and transparent inclusion criteria, and selection of studies by agreement of more than one reviewer according to these criteria. Study characteristics of interest are then coded (that is, extracted from each study for the purpose of calculation of effect sizes and other statistical analyses) according to a pre-established coding system (set forth in a uniform codebook), and each coding is independently verified by another reviewer. Inter-rater reliability can then be established both for study inclusion and for study coding. Reliably coded items are statistically analysed in subsequent phases of the meta-analysis, and variations in effect sizes accounted for by examining the influence of study quality, control group characteristics, sample size, measurement issues, and other potential confounders. In this way, study variables associated with significant, meaningful effects that may move us closer to evidence-based practices of benefit to society are isolated.

The purpose of the study that is to be reviewed here was to use meta-analytic statistical techniques to create generalizations about the literature from a neutral position, rather than to find support for a particular intervention or model. The step-by-step performance of an exemplar meta-analysis is reviewed to provide a practical application of a resilience theory–driven quantitative systematic literature synthesis. This exemplar shows the basic phases of a meta-analysis within a narrow field of inquiry. The initial phase includes electronic, manual, and personal inquiry searches to identify all published and unpublished research literature in the field of inquiry (i.e., addressing the meta-analysis research question). Next, all identified literature is reviewed by more than one reader, initially through review of abstracts, followed by review of full-text articles and manuscripts, to determine whether the studies meet the inclusion criteria of the meta-analysis. Inclusion criteria must be transparent and specified in advance, and should be developed so as to avoid selection of a biased sample of published studies.

Bringing Substantive Theory into a Meta-analysis

In order to be of maximum utility in resilience research, a meta-analytic research design must be informed by extant resilience theory (Masten & Powell, 2003). Many meta-analyses in the medical field are performed without being grounded in a theoretical framework. However, it is feasible to perform this type of research within a specific framework by using inclusion criteria to select primary studies that are theory driven and include the theory or theories of interest. According to Becker and Schram (1994), approaches to such a theory-driven research synthesis may include:

- emphasis on complete specification of an explanatory or predictive chain of events;

- emphasis on predicting variation in explanatory outcomes; or
- a combination of the two using multivariate analyses for the synthesis.

Meta-analysis can also be used to assess a theory-based relationship among variables to account for outcome variance among studies or subgroups, to assess the nature of the relationship among theoretical constructs, and to specify mediating processes and moderator variables such as protective and risk mechanisms. Primary studies can also be synthesized to test new theoretical constructs/hypotheses that were not addressed in the original research. Miller and Pollock (1994, following Judd & Kenny, 1981; Baron & Kenny, 1986) suggest that groups of studies on hypothesized mediating variables could be tested using three separate meta-analyses: on the link between the independent and dependent variable; on the link between the independent variable and the mediators; and on the link between the mediators and the dependent variable.

In the following sections studies are presented that have used substantive theories in concert with meta-analytic methods, including an exemplar of a resilience theory-driven meta-analysis.

Meta-analysis Using Theory-Driven Inclusion Criteria and Unit of Analysis

Theory-driven inclusion criteria for studies in a quantitative synthesis can implement a mezzo- or macro-level research focus, or unit of analysis, in order to examine contextual variables crucial to the elucidation of resilience in the face of adversity (Gerard & Buehler, 2004; Rutter, 2001; Ungar, 2004) and to contextually valid research in general (Margolin & Gordis, 2000). That is, a meta-analysis can include a group of studies that took a micro-level research focus, such as the levels of self-efficacy of individual research participants, and synthesize their findings according to a mezzo- or macro-level unit of analysis when a relevant contextual variable, such as community rates of residential instability, is available across those studies.

For example, Bergeron and Schneider (2005) used extant theory on dimensions of national cultural-level values to establish inclusion criteria for their quantitative synthesis of studies on youth aggression towards peers. As national culture groups were their unit of analysis, the authors included in their meta-analysis only studies that contained data from at least two cultures, and in which the participants were residing within the authors' country of origin. Three theory-based classification systems of national values were used to operationalize the contextual moderator variable of cross-national cultural-level values. These systems were Hofstede's dimensions of Power Distance, Uncertainty Avoidance, Individualism, and Masculinity (Bergeron & Schneider, 2005, p.117); Schwartz's dimensions of Conservation, Affective Autonomy, Intellectual Autonomy, Hierarchy, Mastery, Egalitarian Commitment, and Harmony (p.119); and the Chinese Culture Connection dimensions of Integration, Confucian Work Dynamism, Human Heartedness, and Moral Discipline (p. 118). This synthesis of thirty-six studies found that each of the three macro-contextual classification systems was able to predict cross-national variations in levels of peer-to-peer aggression, thus advancing theory useful to cross-cultural work on youth aggression.

Meta-analysis Using Theory-Driven Subgroup Analyses

Wolfe et al.'s (2003) meta-analysis of forty-one studies on children's exposure to domestic violence provides an example of the use of meta-analysis to test a developmental psychopathology theoretical framework (Rutter & Sroufe, 2000). The authors specified that they had chosen not to perform an exhaustive synthesis of all available studies in this research area, but rather to conduct a more targeted, theory-driven approach to allow subgroup analyses of specific moderators and levels of exposure (witness only and combined witness/direct abuse victims). They noted that this approach to research synthesis, using more stringent, theory-based inclusion criteria, is in contrast to the historical approach of including all appropriate and valid published and unpublished studies from a research literature that is too large to lend itself readily to a clear conceptual overview via systematic literature reviews.

Their choice of theory was made to allow simultaneous examination of multiple dimensions, specifically subgroups such as age, gender, and victim-versus-witness-only status. However, the dearth of studies that examined more than one of the dimensions of interest limited the utility of applying the theoretical framework in this way to this research area. For example, although examination of the dimensions of age, sex, and type of study outcome as possible moderators was of primary interest in this study, only nineteen of the studies provided usable data on two dimensions (seven of the studies in the synthesis provided information on both gender-specific results and child developmental stage, and twelve included data on both internalizing and externalizing behaviors as types of outcome), and only three provided data on three of the dimensions, out of the forty-one studies analysed (Wolfe et al., 2003).

This synthesis illustrates that examination of how protective and risk mechanisms differ by subgroups, such as age/developmental stage, gender, and type of outcome, may be hampered by the limited number of appropriate studies available when a single meta-analysis identifies multiple outcomes in tandem with other moderator variables. Consequently, narrowly focused, theory-driven syntheses that calculate one outcome effect size per study and control for one or more important variables (e.g., life stage) through inclusion criteria are more likely to yield insight into which specific protective mechanisms benefit specific subgroups for specific outcomes – a current focus in developing the body of knowledge on resilience (Gerard & Buehler, 2004; Masten & Coatsworth, 1998; Resnick, 2000). The use of only one effect size per study also has the advantage of avoiding potential bias by ensuring independence of samples in the aggregated studies (Chambers, 2004; Glass, McGaw, & Smith, 1981).

Meta-analysis Using Theory-Driven Sensitivity Analysis

An important function of research synthesis is sensitivity analysis. This is the consideration of whether differences in findings across the literature may be due to methodological characteristics of the primary studies (as alternative explanations of findings), rather than due to the posited associations among independent, moderating, and dependent variables. Methodological characteristics could relate to differences in study quality, differences in operationalization of key constructs, or sample heterogeneity. A meta-analysis of intervention studies based on attachment theory, by Bakermans-Kranenburg, Van IJzendoorn, and Juffer (2005), utilized this approach to examine differences in study control groups as an alternative explanation for findings, a form of sensitivity analysis. They found that studies using samples with a higher proportion of control group participants with disorganized attachment showed larger effect sizes (appeared to be significantly more successful in prevention, the outcome of interest).

Similarly, Sawatzky, Ratner, and Chiu (2005) performed a meta-analysis to examine the relationship between spirituality and quality of life, defining spirituality as a theoretical construct that was subjective and relational to the transcendent, and not overlapping with the construct of quality of life. They utilized this definition to conduct a sensitivity analysis of the impact of different operationalizations of the construct in instrumentation used by the individual studies. Differences in how the concepts were operationalized did account for a statistically significant amount of the variance in primary effect sizes.

In their cross-cultural synthesis of youth studies utilizing cultural values theories, Bergeron and Schneider's (2005) sensitivity analyses also found that differing definitions and methods (i.e., observation/interview versus questionnaire/vignette) of measuring their dependent variable, youth peer-to-peer aggression, accounted for significant variance in findings. These findings lead them to suggest that cross-cultural research may demand particular attention to methodological issues regarding definitions and measurement methods. As has been found in primary cross-cultural research on externalizing behaviours (Bergeron & Schneider, 2005), rating scales, questionnaires, and vignettes are more likely to be interpreted differently across cultures than other measurement strategies such as direct observation. Similarly, aggression may be manifested differently across cultures, so that differing definitions of the construct by country could confound findings of cross-national research syntheses.

Resilience Theory-Driven Meta-analysis: An Exemplar

To study resilience factors among students with psychiatric disorders, I performed a meta-analysis of nine studies examining the relationship between several variables and post-secondary educational attainment for this population (Smith-Osborne, 2005). Unlike some resilience research, this meta-analysis considered psychiatric disorder as the adversity to be overcome rather than as a non-resilient outcome, with the outcome of interest being level of post-secondary educational attainment.

This synthesis was driven by resilience theory, specifying variables of interest on the basis of risk and protective mechanisms. Primary studies were synthesized in order to test these theoretical concepts and relationships among them in ways that were not addressed in the primary studies. Resilience theory informed the choice of variables in several ways. In keeping with theoretical interest in contextual variables involved in protective mechanisms, the study focused exclusively on individual attributes and risk factors. The study was, however, also structured around three variable domains beyond the individual level: interpersonal, transpersonal, and organizational. In addition, study inclusion criteria and preset data extraction criteria gave preference to contextual variables and protective variables identified in the theoretical literature, such as extended support networks, supportive organizational policies and procedures, and targeted service delivery context (Luthar & Zelazo, 2003; Masten & Coatsworth, 1998; Masten & Garmezy, 1985; McCubbin et al., 1976; Richardson, 2002; Rutter, 1987, 2001).

Based on resilience theory and literature, I hypothesized that these variables, which had been found to be protective for other populations at risk, may also be protective for students with psychiatric disorders with reference to the specific resilient outcome of increased postsecondary educational attainment. The use of educational attainment as a resilient outcome is consistent with resilience theory and the literature (Fraser, 1997; Garmezy, 1991; Werner, 1992; Werner & Smith, 2001). Similarly, it was hypothesized that the risk factors of specific types and higher severity of disorder would be associated with the non-resilient outcome of decreased postsecondary educational attainment. For example, the National Comorbidity Study of psychiatric disorders found that a diagnosis of conduct disorder for males and anxiety disorder for females was associated with the least postsecondary educational attainment (Kessler et al., 1995).

A single operationalization of educational attainment, the outcome variable, was selected from each study included in the analysis; when more than one operationalization was available in a study, preference was given to measures associated with protective factors and contextual variables as guided by resilience theory. Outcome measures included level of educational attainment by age fifty-four, educational attainment at the five-year follow-up, grade point average, number of courses completed, and number of semesters completed. Thus, following resilience theory, the synthesis was conducted by:

- identifying variables as risk or protective factors *a priori* based on literature and resilience theory;
- examining use of theory in each primary study *a priori*;
- including primary studies with variables in both individual and environmental/contextual domains;

- testing hypotheses based on resilience theory and literature that were not tested in all the primary studies; and
- examining outcomes related to resilient adaptation.

In this meta-analysis, 178 potentially relevant studies were identified using accepted electronic and manual search techniques; correspondence with relevant researchers, program staff, and presenters at two research conferences to identify unpublished literature, footnote, and reference list searches; and forward citation searches for key studies using the Social Science Citation Index (e.g., finding studies published from 1980 to 2004 that had cited an earlier key longitudinal resilience study reported by Werner in 1992).

Electronic databases searched included Academic Search Premier (ERIC), CINAHL, MEDLINE, and PsycINFO from 1980 to 2004. Search terms used were 'mental disorder,' 'mental illness,' 'students,' 'college students,' 'prediction of occupational success,' academic achievement,' 'mental disorders/rehabilitation,' 'education,' 'special education,' 'recurrence,' 'treatment outcome,' 'risk factors,' 'student health services,' 'mental health services,' 'adolescent psychology,' 'adolescent psychiatry,' 'reentry students,' and 'college academic achievement.' Manual searches of *College Student Journal* issues from 1990 to 2003 and *Journal of College Student Psychotherapy* issues from 1990 to 2004 were conducted using the same key terms.

Single-diagnosis studies were excluded due to insufficient breadth for the purpose of this research synthesis, as were dissertations and non-English language articles due to time constraints. Single-diagnosis studies were those that examined only one psychiatric disorder, whereas this meta-analysis focused on synthesizing data on the more broadly defined population of college students with any type of psychiatric disorder, and the range of contextual variables included in studies on this larger population.

The resulting 123 studies were retrieved, and 83 of those excluded due to insufficient quantitative analysis as required for this quantitative synthesis. That is, the excluded studies were either conceptual, descriptive, or qualitative studies or contained insufficient quantitative data on the selected predictor (i.e., risk and protective factors) and outcome variables to allow calculation of effect sizes.

The remaining forty studies were then rated on theory-driven, predefined inclusion criteria by two independent raters. Inclusion criteria included factors of study quality and quantitative data sufficiency that are of concern to both theory-driven and non-theory-driven meta-analysis studies. Specifically, studies were rated for inclusion if they were empirical studies examining antecedents to college educational attainment, were published between 1980 and 2004, did not utilize single-subject or one-group pre/post quasi-experimental designs, had a relevant outcome measure, had sufficient statistical information to allow calculation of an effect size, and had a study report available in English. Additional, resilience theory–driven criteria particular to this meta-analysis were that studies:

- examined the resilient outcome of post-secondary educational attainment;
- defined a study population facing a type of adversity representing a barrier to the resilient outcome of interest (for this meta-analysis, the population in adversity was college students with psychiatric symptoms/disorders or a history of the same); and
- addressed at least two of the four domains of risk and protective variables, to permit a research focus that goes beyond the individual.

The application of inclusion criteria resulted in selection of fifteen studies, for which data were extracted using a codebook developed on the basis of the literature on risk and protective factors (see Appendix A).

Psychopathology and maladaptation are often conceptualized as outcomes in resilience studies, with risk factors defined as personal and contextual variables that increase the risk of these non-resilient or negative developmental outcomes for individuals in adverse circumstances (Gerard & Buehler, 2004). The present meta-analysis focused on psychopathology as the adversity condition, and the negative range of attributes of the psychopathology (e.g., higher severity, type of disorder associated with lowered educational attainment), as well as contextual variables (e.g., special education student status in high school, punitive college withdrawal policies), as risk factors. Protective factors were conceptualized as personal and contextual variables that interact with risk to promote resilient outcomes for high-risk populations by moderating the impact of risk factors, minimizing negative chain reactions, providing opportunities for optimal development, or enacting positive chain reactions (Gerard & Buehler, 2004; Rutter, 1987).

Coding and data extraction procedures yielded nine studies with sufficient information for the calculation of effect sizes for predictor and outcome variables of interest. The hypothesized risk and protective variables found in the nine useable studies included disability status in high school, type of psychiatric disorder during college, number of psychopathology factors during the first post-secondary year of education, use of mental health services during college, type of withdrawal policy in the college, and type of supported education program utilized.

The strongest predictors of educational attainment found in this meta-analysis in terms of statistical significance were personal domain characteristics of type and severity of the disorder (risk factors) and productive leave/re-entry procedures utilized (protective factor), while contextual (interpersonal and organizational domain) variables approached statistical significance. These contextual variables were participation in a supported education program and use of mental health services upon re-entry to college after medical leave (protective factors).

Statistical Considerations in the Use of Meta-analysis to Study Resilience

The literature suggests that effect sizes for each of the component variables that comprise resilience tend to be small (Luthar, Cicchetti, & Becker, 2000; Rutter, 2001; Rutter & Sroufe, 2000), thus offering a further rationale for the use of meta-analytic methods to permit analysis of aggregated samples that provide sufficient size to detect resilience effects. Nevertheless, in syntheses of studies with small sample sizes, it may still be necessary to keep the number of predictors, and levels of predictors, reduced as much as possible to preserve the power to detect statistically significant, small effect sizes.

In the exemplar study the quality, as well as sample sizes, of studies with risk factor predictors was higher than those of studies with protective factor predictors (Smith-Osborne, 2005), suggesting that statistical subgroup analyses by type of predictor (risk vs. protective) may be important in syntheses of resilience research, particularly in research areas dominated by risk factor studies. Use of this type of subgroup analysis may be preferable to the common approach of weighting higher quality studies statistically, prior to combining studies (Cooper & Hedges, 1994), since the latter approach may be problematic in resilience meta-analyses in statistically privileging risk factor studies. Alternatively, in research areas with sufficient studies suitable for quantitative synthesis, risk predictor studies could be synthesized separately from protective predictor studies in the same research area, utilizing a common outcome construct(s), and the two meta-analyses then compared.

Statistical correction for random error of measurement of the independent and dependent variables, as a source of artificial variation across studies, should be considered when synthesizing resilience studies, particularly given the variability in operationalizing risk, protective, and resilience constructs found in the literature (Luthar, Cicchetti, & Becker, 2000; Richardson, 2002; Rutter, 2001). Inclusion criteria could specify selection of studies that report reliability coefficients for the measures used in the study, and those coefficients included in the coding of each study for the meta-analysis. These data can then be used in statistical corrections of the effects of measurement error on the synthesized effects sizes. Applicable procedures are discussed at length in Hunter and Schmidt (1990) and Cooper and Hedges (1994).

Strengths and Limitations of Meta-analysis Methodology in the Study of Resilience

As with any research design, research synthesis has both strengths and weaknesses. Beginning with the weaknesses, research synthesis experiences threats to validity. An excellent summary and discussion of these may be found in Shadish, Cook, and Campbell (2002) as well as Cooper and Hedges (1994).

There are several limitations of particular pertinence to theory-driven resilience research synthesis. Most importantly, the nature of the primary studies' designs constrains meta-analytic findings. For example, a meta-analysis examining mediating variables of interest in resilience theory (that is, potential protective or risk mechanisms) may require aggregating studies that experimentally manipulated the mediator at two levels (such as different levels of quantity or severity) of the independent variable. This type of synthesis would require a larger number of such studies (i.e., primary studies that examined both levels of the independent variable) to permit analyses of each level or amount of the independent variable. An example of this limitation is seen in the discussion of child exposure to domestic violence by Wolfe et al. (2003), in which the original aim to compare witnesses (first, lower level of exposure) with witness/victims (second, higher level of exposure), had to be curtailed due to the small number of studies providing data on both levels of domestic violence exposure.

Also, some bodies of literature relevant to resilience theory offer few quantitative studies with sufficient information to allow calculation of effect sizes of a type useable in meta-analysis (Miller & Pollock, 1994). The limited number of cross-cultural studies that focus both on contextual variables or a given potential mediator and examine the same outcomes, for example, poses a challenge to synthesizing research on youth across cultures at this time (Bergeron & Schneider, 2005).

Publication bias is a second limitation confronting research synthesis. Fryers et al. (2004), for example, performed a cross-cultural synthesis of multinational psychiatric prevalence studies. This group of researchers concluded that certain fields may be more susceptible to publication bias (Rosenthal, 1979; Torgerson, 2006) in meta-analysis than others. These publications may therefore not be as suited to search by electronic literature databases, even those that include grey literature (i.e., unpublished or administratively published studies). Fryers et al. emphasized using personal networks and personal knowledge of local experts to identify the larger pool of studies (particularly surveys) that had been unpublished or published in sources not captured by the major electronic databases. In line with meta-analyses' heavy reliance on electronic literature searches, Holden and Barker (1990) pointed out that CD-ROM disks used in certain search procedures can be corrupted and yield differing search results at different times.

Another possible limitation of meta-analysis in the study of resilience is the use of moderator analysis to identify protective mechanisms and examine multiple outcomes. This may require the calculation of multiple effect sizes for the same population, thus increasing statistical dependencies (Chambers, 2004). However, this limitation can be avoided. In the exemplar meta-analysis highlighted in this paper, statistical dependencies were reduced by calculating only one effect size for each group of participants (i.e., each primary study). Another approach would be to calculate multiple effect sizes only for independent samples within studies.

By contrast, research synthesis also offers the researcher certain strengths. For example, using meta-analysis methodology for the study of resilience offers the capacity to test theoretical frameworks by examining the importance and roles of potential moderators for a single condition across studies. Thus, research synthesis has the potential to include consideration of contextual variables of interest to resilience researchers from numerous studies that were not conducted within this theoretical framework. The exemplar meta-analysis discussed here again demonstrated how protective mechanisms in the presence of a common adverse condition, with attributes of the condition considered risk factors, could be examined across all studies. In the same way, research synthesis can be used to explore the operation of a single protective mechanism at different life stages or trajectories for the same adverse condition or the same target outcome.

Another strength of meta-analysis is that it permits investigation of how the existing research addresses entire theoretical models of resilience or parts thereof (e.g., application of path analysis procedures to meta-analytic data). It has the advantage of aggregation of study populations to increase statistical power and partially overcome low reliability and validity as sources of variation among the primary studies. It expands examination of temporal effects and avoids some constraints of individual studies (e.g., logistical and institutional, as in aggression research). Through sensitivity analysis, quantitative synthesis can help to explain contradictory or disparate findings of a body of primary studies that may be due to methodological differences. Thus, as demonstrated here, increased utilization of quantitative research synthesis in resilience research holds promise for advancing understanding of the underlying mechanisms of known protective and risk factors.

APPENDIX A

CODEBOOK Resiliency Factors
Data Extraction Record

Coding date _____
Coder initial _____
  1. Study ID number _____
  2. Authors _____
  3. Publication year _____

Demographics
  4. Percentage female _____
  5. Mean education level or proxy _____
  6. Mean age; standard dev.; range of age _____

7. Mean SES or proxy _____
8. Mean IQ or proxy (SAT percentile; GPA) _____

Other Antecedent Factors
 9. College GPA (1st entry; 2nd entry; other) _____
10. Age of onset of psyc sx _____
11. Primary diagnosis; severity _____
12. Dual dx (Yes; No; %) _____
13. Age at start of tx. _____
14. Social support level (peer and non-peer) _____
15. Religious affiliation _____
16. Frequency of religious attendance (on- vs. off-campus) _____
17. Religious orientation (intrinsic/extrinsic) _____
18. Engagement in individual spiritual observances/practices
    _____
19. College leave status (medical vs. drop-out vs. termination)
    _____
20. Voluntary nature of withdrawal _____
21. Use of support services (Disability Office, etc.)
    _____
22. Use of mental health services (on- vs. off-campus) _____
    (If yes) Type of mental health service used _____
23. Mental health option in health insurance?
    _____
    (If yes) Level of benefits _____
24. Availability of community college/trade school? _____
    (If yes) Attendance at comm. college? _____

CODEBOOK/Data Record: Resiliency A2
Methodology

25. Study design _____
    (If survey) Response rate _____
26. Sampling method _____
27. Sample size Total:_____ Group 1:_____Group 2:_____
    Group 3:_____
28. Theory basis _____

Effect Size Data

29. Test statistics; specify
    T statistic _____

Degrees of freedom _____
Chi squared _____
Correlation coefficient (r) _____
P value _____

30. Analysis of variance/covariance; specify
Sum of squares _____
F statistic _____
Degrees of freedom _____
Includes SS due covariate? _____
P value _____

31. Multiple regression/logistic regression: specify
Coefficients _____
Odds ratios _____
R squared _____
P value _____

32. Time series analysis: specify
Hazard ratio _____
Repeated measures data _____
P value _____

33. Descriptive statistics; specify
Mean _____
Standard deviation _____
Degrees of freedom _____
N of college students _____

DRAFT CODEBOOK/Data Record A3

Criterion Measure

34. Type of criterion measure _____
35. Reliability reported _____
36. Number of times outcome measured _____
37. Time period for outcome measurement _____
38. Unit of analysis _____

References

Bakermans-Kranenburg, M.J., Van IJzendoorn, M.H., & Juffer, F. (2005). Dis-organized infant attachment and preventive interventions: A review and meta-analysis. *Infant Mental Health Journal, 26,* 191–216.

Baron, R.M., & Kenny, D.A. (1986). The moderator-mediator variable distinc-tion in social psychological research: Conceptual, strategic and statistical considerations. *Journal of Personality and Social Psychology, 51,* 1173–82.

Becker, B.J., & Schram, C.M. (1994). Examining explanatory models through research synthesis. In H. Cooper & L.V. Hedges (Eds.), *The handbook of research synthesis* (pp. 357–81). New York: Russell Sage Foundation.

Bergeron, N., & Schneider, B.H. (2005). Explaining cross-national differences in peer-directed aggression: A quantitative synthesis. *Aggressive Behavior, 31,* 116–37.

Chambers, E.A. (2004). An introduction to meta-analysis with articles from *The Journal of Educational Research* (1992–2002). *Journal of Educational Research, 98,* 35–44.

Cooper, H., & Hedges, L.V. (Eds.). (1994). *The handbook of research synthesis.* New York: Russell Sage Foundation.

EBSCO. (n.d.). *Title lists: September/October.* Retrieved 23 October 2006 from http://www.epnet.com/titleLists.php.

Fraser, M. (Ed.). (1997). *Risk and resilience in childhood: An ecological perspective.* Washington, DC: NASW Press.

Fryers, T., Brugha, T., Morgan, Z., Smith, J., Hill, T., Carta, M., et al. (2004). Prevalence of psychiatric disorder in Europe: The potential and reality of meta-analysis. *Social Psychiatry & Psychiatric Epidemiology, 39,* 899–905.

Garmezy, N. (1991). Resiliency and vulnerability to adverse developmental outcomes associated with poverty. *American Behavioral Scientist, 34,* 416–30.

Gerard, J.M., & Buehler, C. (2004). Cumulative environmental risk and youth maladjustment: The role of youth attributes. *Child Development, 75,* 1832–49.

Glass, G.V., McGaw, B., & Smith, M.L. (1981). *Meta-analysis in social research.* Beverly Hills: Sage.

Holden, G., & Barker, K.M. (1990). Potential for technological dependency: An example. *Social Work Research and Abstracts, 26,* 35–6.

Hunter, J.E., & Schmidt, F.L. (1990). *Methods of meta-analysis: Correcting error and bias in research findings.* Beverly Hills, CA: Sage.

Judd, C.M., & Kenny, D.A. (1981). Process analysis: Estimating mediation in treatment evaluations. *Evaluation Review, 5,* 602–19.

Kessler, R.C., Foster, C.L., Saunders, W. B., & Stang, P.E. (1995). Social consequences of psychiatric disorders, 1: Educational attainment. *The American Journal of Psychiatry, 152,* 1026–32.

Luthar, S., Cicchetti, D., & Becker, B. (2000). The construct of resilience: A critical evaluation and guidelines for future work. *Child Development, 71,* 543–62.

Luthar, S.S., & Zelazo, L.B. (2003). Research on resilience: An integrative review. In S.S. Luthar (Ed.), *Resilience and vulnerability: Adaptation in the context of childhood adversities* (pp. 510–49). Cambridge: Cambridge University Press.

Margolin, G., & Gordis, E. (2000). The effects of family and community violence on children. *Annual Reviews Psychology, 51,* 445–79.

Masten, A.S., & Coatsworth, J.D. (1998). The development of competence in favorable and unfavorable environments: Lessons from research on successful children. *American Psychologist, 53,* 205–20.

Masten, A.S., & Garmezy, N. (1985). Risk, vulnerability, and protective factors in developmental psychopathology. In B.B. Lahey & A.E. Kazdin (Eds.), *Advances in clinical child psychology,* Vol. 8 (pp. 1–52). New York: Plenum.

Masten, A.S., & Powell, J.L. (2003). A resilience framework for research, policy and practice. In S.S. Luthar (Ed.), *Resilience and vulnerability: Adaptation in the context of childhood adversities* (pp. 1–25). Cambridge: Cambridge University Press.

McCubbin, H.I., Dahl, B.B., Lester, G.R., Benson, D., & Robertson, M.L. (1976). Coping repertoires of families adapting to prolonged war-induced separations. *Journal of Marriage and the Family, 38,* 461–71.

Miller, N., & Pollock, V.E. (1994). Meta-analytic synthesis for theory development. In H. Cooper & L.V. Hedges (Eds.), *The handbook of research synthesis* (pp. 457–83). New York: Russell Sage Foundation.

Resnick, M.D. (2000). Protective factors, resiliency, and healthy youth development. *Adolescent Medicine, 11,* 157–64.

Richardson, G.E. (2002). The metatheory of resilience and resiliency. *Journal of Clinical Psychology, 58,* 307–21.

Rosenthal, R. (1979). The 'file drawer problem' and tolerance for null results. *Psychological Bulletin, 86,* 638–41.

Rutter, M. (1987). Psychosocial resilience and protective mechanisms. *American Journal of Orthopsychiatry, 57,* 316–31.

Rutter, M. (1999). Psychosocial adversity and child psychopathology. *British Journal of Psychiatry, 174,* 480–93.

Rutter, M. (2001). Psychosocial adversity: Risk, resilience and recovery. In J.M. Richman & M.W. Fraser (Eds.), *The context of youth violence: Resilience, risk and protection* (pp. 13–41). Westport, CT: Praeger.

Rutter, M., & Sroufe, L.A. (2000). Developmental psychopathology: Concepts and challenges. *Development and Psychopathology, 12,* 265–96.

Sawatzky, R., Ratner, P.A., & Chiu, L. (2005). A meta-analysis of the relationship between spirituality and quality of life. *Social Indicators Research, 72,* 153–88.

Shadish, W.R., Cook, T.D., & Campbell, D.T. (2002). *Experimental and quasi-experimental designs for generalized causal inference.* New York: Houghton Mifflin.

Smith, C., & Carson, B.E. (1997). Stress, coping, and resilience in children and youth. *Social Service Review, 6,* 231–56.

Smith-Osborne, A. (2005). Antecedents to post-secondary educational attainment for individuals with psychiatric disorders: A meta-analysis. *Best Practices in Mental Health: An International Journal, 1,* 15–30.

Torgerson, C.J. (2006). Publication bias: The Achilles' heel of systematic reviews? *British Journal of Educational Studies, 54,* 89–102.

Ungar, M. (2004). A constructionist discourse on resilience: Multiple contexts, multiple realities among at-risk children and youth. *Youth and Society, 35,* 341–65.

Werner, E.E. (1992). The children of Kauai: Resiliency and recovery in adolescence and adulthood. *Journal of Adolescent Health, 13,* 262–8.

Werner, E.E., & Smith, R.S. (2001). *Journeys from childhood to midlife: Risk, resilience, and recovery.* Ithaca: Cornell University Press.

Wolfe, D.A., Crooks, C.V., Lee, V., McIntyre-Smith, A., & Jaffe, P.G. (2003). The effects of children's exposure to domestic violence: A meta-analysis and critique. *Clinical Child and Family Psychology Review, 6,* 174–87.

MIXED METHODS

8 Using Mixed Methods to Understand Youth Resilience

DAVID ESTE, KATHLEEN SITTER, AND BRUCE MACLAURIN

Until recently, quantitative research has been the dominant approach to the study of resilience in both the social and health sciences, with a variety of methods, including cross-sectional and longitudinal surveys, being preferred. In commenting on this dominant mode of conducting resilience research, Ungar and Liebenberg (2005) remarked, 'Typically, studies of resilience have employed designs that integrate established test instruments with demonstrated reliability and validity from studies of mental and social functioning' (p. 211). However, these same researchers assert that quantitative studies possess two types of shortcomings: '[The first is] arbitrariness in the selection of outcome variables and [the second] the challenge of accounting for the social and cultural context in which resilience occurs' (2005, pp. 211–12; see also Ungar, 2003, and Ungar & Teram, 2005). Therefore, Ungar (2003) maintains that qualitative research can contribute to enhancing our understanding of youth resilience. Reflecting on the value of qualitative resilience studies, Barton (2005) argues that the results of these types of investigations reinforce and strengthen the findings generated by quantitative studies. As he states, 'There is converging evidence regarding the key protective factors that appear to promote resilience in the presence of a variety of risks and across several distinct population groups, mostly in the United States and Europe' (p. 141).

During the past decade several writers (Bryman, 2007; Creswell, 2003; Johnson, Onwuegbuzie, & Turner, 2007; Mason, 2006; Onwuegbuzie & Leech, 2005) have advocated the use of mixed methods, combining qualitative and quantitative approaches in studies of social and health phenomena. Commenting on this development, Mason (2006) argues that 'mixing qualitative and quantitative methods has come to be seen in some quarters as intrinsically a "good thing" to do although the reasoning or logic behind such assumptions is not always as readily expressed as is the sentiment itself' (p. 9). In describing the current status of mixed-methods research, Johnson, Onwuegbuzie, and Turner (2007) write that 'mixed methods research ... is becoming increasingly articulated to research practice, and recognized as the third major research approach or research paradigm, along with qualitative and quantitative research' (p. 112).

In this chapter we will show that understanding youth resilience across different contexts and cultures is enhanced by the use of mixed methods. The chapter is organized as follows: In the first section we provide an overview of resilience as both a concept and process. This is followed by a discussion of quantitative research methods and resilience research. Various approaches to quantitative research, as well as the strengths and limitations of this approach in the study of youth resilience, comprise the salient component of this discussion. A similar discussion is then presented on qualitative research methods. The balance of the chapter is focused on mixed methods as a means of increasing our understanding of youth resilience. Here, factors that have contributed to the emergence of mixed methods as a research approach are set out, followed by some recent definitions of mixed methods. The benefits and challenges of mixed methods in relation to the study of resilience are then presented.

Resilience: What Is It?

There is a rich body of literature that deals with different aspects of resilience. The past decade has witnessed what Ungar (2005) describes as a 'burgeoning interest in the study of resilience.' Ungar notes that the pioneering work of researchers such as Werner and Smith (1982), Rutter and colleagues (1979), Garmezy (1976), and Murphy and Moriarty (1976) established the foundation for this growth in resilience research. Within the literature, a number of definitions are associated with the term. There seems to be a general consensus that at a basic level, the ability to bounce back, recover, or successfully adapt in the face of obstacles and adversity is the common theme.

Concisely, Luthar, Cicchetti, and Becker (2000) define resilience as 'a dynamic process encompassing positive adaptation within the context of a significant adversity' (p. 543). They contend that there are two critical notions associated with resilience. The first point they raise is that individuals need to be exposed to a significant threat or severe adversity to demonstrate resilience. The second attribute is that resilience is the achievement of positive adaptation despite major assaults on the developmental process. Turner (2001) expressed similar sentiments in her definition of the construct, stating that 'resilience is the remarkable capacity of individuals to withstand considerable hardship, to bounce back in the face of adversity, and to go on to have functional lives with a sense of well-being (p. 441).

Two concepts that are key to understanding resilience are protective and risk factors. Wright and Masten (2006) define the two terms in the following manner: '[A protective factor] is a quality of a person or context of their interaction that predicts better outcomes, particularly in situations of adversity' (p. 19). Good cognitive skills, having effective parents, and attending good schools are examples of protective factors. Conversly, risk factors are considered 'a measurable characteristic in a group of individuals or their situation that predicts negative outcome on a specific outcome criteria' (p. 19). Examples of risk factors include premature birth, parental divorce, poverty, and parental mental illness.

Not surprisingly, most of the resilience literature is focused on child resilience. In defining child resilience Goldstein and Brooks (2005) remarked:

> Resilience can be understood as the capacity of a child to deal effectively with stress and pressure, to cope with everyday challenges, to rebound from disappointment, mistake, trauma and adversity, to develop clear and realistic goals, to solve problems, to interact comfortably with others and to treat oneself and others with respect and dignity. (p. 3)

However, it is important to stress that children do not develop these competencies on their own. Wright and Masten (2006) contend that there may be some negative consequences of viewing resilience from an individual perspective. They believe that this perpetuates the 'blaming the individual syndrome' whereby children who are not successful are deemed not to have the abilities to make it in society. Secondly, the perspective negates the existence of stressors manifested by other systems within the society with which children interact.

A prevailing theme in the literature stresses that child resilience should be viewed as a process that may involve a number of different systems. The implications of this perspective to research are profound. Assessing resilience is likely to require a multilevel approach that looks beyond individuals. As Wright and Masten (2006) remark, 'Because adaptation is embedded with a content of multiple systems of interactions, including the family, school, neighbourhood, community and culture, a child's resilience is very dependent upon other people and systems of influence' (p. 29).

Though gaining an understanding of multiple levels of interaction is important, the most well-studied set of interrelationships are those found at the level of family. Researchers such as McCubbin and McCubbin (1988) and Hill (1998) clearly stress how vital families can be in fostering child and youth resilience. For example, in his conceptual framework of resilience focused on African American families, Hill contends that the following protective mechanisms can be facilitated: instilling positive family values, promoting positive communications and social interactions, maintaining flexible family roles, exercising control over children, and providing academic support to children. These types of supports are extremely important for African American children and youth, for example, who most likely encounter what Essed (1991) described as 'everyday racism.'

Writers such as Weiner (1984) and Rutter (1990) contend, however, that there are various other individuals, such as teachers, school counsellors, coaches, mental health workers, clergy, and good neighbours in the environment, who may contribute to positive outcomes in children. Such persons are well situated to work with children and to convey the message that these children will succeed in life.

Quantitative Research

The quantitative approach to knowledge building is described in a systematic manner in most graduate research method texts (Grinnell & Unrau, 2005; Rubin & Babbie, 2001). This process includes a well-identified problem statement, a clearly articulated and formulated research question, a clear study design to address the question in hand, a systematic approach to data collection, a plan for data analysis that utilizes the level of data collected, and an objective interpretation of findings followed by presentation and dissemination of findings (Unrau, Grinnell, & Williams, 2005). Unrau, Grinnell, and Williams (2005) argue that conducting quantitative research highlights the need to study phenomena that can be objectively measured, reducing uncertainty; to design research that can be duplicated by other researchers; and to use standardized procedures. The success of the researcher in meeting these criteria will determine the rigour of the study and the ability to generalize findings from the sample to the population in question. Two common approaches to quantitative research include cross-sectional surveys to examine a phenomenon at a single point in time and longitudinal studies that track causal influences on specific outcomes over an extended time period (Grinnell & Unrau, 2005). Both approaches have contributed significantly to the foundation of youth resilience literature over the past few decades.

Contributions to Youth Resilience Research

An increasing level of attention has been paid to the construct of resilience for children and youth in the professional literature over the last fifty years. As Luthar (2006) highlights, 'there is broad consensus that in working with at-risk groups, it is far more prudent to promote the development of resilient functioning early in the course of development rather than to implement treatments to repair disorders once they have already crystallized' (p. 739). Much of this literature has relied heavily on cross-sectional or retrospective designs (Luthar, 2006; Luthar & Zigler, 1991). These study designs have been valuable in providing clarity on the factors that affect resilience. In addition, the relatively large sample sizes of cross-sectional surveys support a wide range of multivariate analyses that can address initial research questions and later secondary-data analyses. Cross-sectional studies do not, however, support the examination of causal relationships between risk factors or stressors and outcomes over time.

A number of prospective longitudinal studies conducted over the past forty years have contributed significantly to the foundation for current resilience research in the twenty-first century (Garmezy, Masten, & Tellegen, 1984; Moffatt et al., 1996; Werner & Smith, 1982). Werner's longitudinal study of infants at risk in Kauai is frequently described as a landmark study for resilience. This study developed a cohort of all known pregnancies on the island of Kauai in 1954 and assessed current status at regular intervals continuing to adulthood (W erner, 1989). Initial findings of the early contact with this cohort clarified that the children involved in this study experienced significant challenges when experiencing poverty in addition to perinatal risk. Furthermore, the relationship between poverty and family stability was clearly demonstrated through follow-up contact over time (Werner & Smith, 1982; Werner, 1989). Such longitudinal quantitative studies have demonstrated considerable worth, and specific benefits are related to the assessment of reliability and to the predictive validity of short-term and longer-term outcomes.

Considerations and Limitations of Quantitative Research Methods

A number of issues should be considered when examining the contributions and the limitations of quantitative research in the field of resilience (Ahern et al., 2006; Heller et al., 1999; Jew, Green, & Kroger, 1999; LeBlanc, Talbot, & Craig, 2005; Olsson et al., 2003; Reininger et al., 2003; Ungar, 2007; Windle, 1998). These issues are related to definitions of risk and resilience, the measurement of resilience, research methods, and the context of resilience.

There has been significant variation between studies of outcomes representing adolescent resilience (Olsson et al., 2003). Researchers have tended to define resilience in ways that address the unique focus, purpose, and perspective of the research question. In this regard it has been suggested that there are as many definitions of resilience as there are studies. In a review of literature on outcomes, Blum (1998) found that outcome measures of resilience can include 'mental health and psychopathology, functional capacity (the ability to carry out social roles such as school, work and marriage), social competence (the success of a person in achieving his or her aspirations), behaviour problems, pregnancy, drug abuse, and school failure' (p. 371). A critical concern is that these multiple definitions will reflect the values of the researcher or the social setting of the research, and will determine what protective factors or risk factors may be included. Recent mixed-methods studies examining resilience from multiple points of view support this concern (Lietz, 2007, 2006; Ungar & Liebenberg, 2005).

There has been a longstanding belief that in order to fully understand the dynamic process of child and youth resilience, it is necessary to develop standardized psychometrically sound instruments with the capacity to measure youth resilience within the individual, the family, and the larger environment (Olsson et al., 2003). A review of measurement tools utilized in resilience research indicates that not all measures have been psychometrically validated, nor do they always measure resilience in a manner that allows clear comparisons between studies

(Ahern et al., 2006; Jew, Green, & Kroger, 1999; Windle, 1998). Further questions have been raised about how all phenomena can be consistently studied in a manner emphasizing objectivity, precision, and generalizability. Researchers are beginning to appreciate the benefits of examining complex issues such as resilience from multiple points of views and using multiple methods.

The literature identifies a number of methodological issues with the potential to affect quantitative resilience research findings. These issues include sources of data, point of data collection, and research design. While some studies utilize a single reporter to report on behaviour to gain information on issues related to risk or resilience, other have used multiple reporters (school teacher, parent, child) to contrast how resilience is perceived (Heller et al., 1999; Kinard, 1998). The time at which data are collected may also have an impact upon research findings, as current or retrospective reports on externalizing or internalizing behaviours may differ greatly from the results of tracking behaviours in a prospective manner (Heller et al., 1999). The final consideration is related to whether the study utilizes a cross-sectional or longitudinal design, as children may appear resilient to risk at a single point in time but that status may change over an extended period (Cicchetti & Toth, 1995).

Finally, context is an important consideration when utilizing quantitative research in youth resilience, specifically as it relates to comparisons between counties and cultures (LeBlanc, Talbot, & Craig, 2005; Ungar, 2007). Quantitative researchers are challenged to examine the differences that may exist in different cultures regarding constructs such as depression, externalizing behaviours, and social supports, and to examine their own assumptions about these constructs. Ungar (2007), for example, highlights the risks in assuming there are universal truths in how children or adults view health, mental health, or stress when using only Western perspectives.

Qualitative Research

With the explosion of literature on qualitative research, there are numerous definitions describing this particular approach. Denzin and Lincoln (1994) define qualitative research as 'multimethod in focus involving an interpretive naturalistic approach to its subject matter. This means qualitative researchers study things in their own natural settings attempting to make sense of or interpret phenomena in terms of the meanings people bring them' (p. 2). Creswell (1994) describes qualitative research 'as an inquiry process of understanding a social or human problem based on building a complex, holistic picture, formed with words, reporting detailed views of informants, and conducted in a natural setting' (p. 2). Essentially, qualitative research is focused on understanding how people think, feel, and behave in the world.

A salient feature of this type of research is the centrality of the researcher as the human instrument and key determinant in the quality of research when using qualitative methods. The researcher's personal experience and insights are deemed to be vital aspects of any qualitative inquiry. Increasingly the term 'reflexivity' is being used to highlight the salient roles of the individual who conducts qualitative research. Throughout the entire process, the researcher influences and affects the study. It is important that the research reflect on how he/she shapes and is shaped by the world being investigated. As Ungar (2003) notes, 'When using qualitative methods the researcher … must deconstruct his or her relationship with participants and their data' (p. 96).

The majority of qualitative studies involve the personal engagement of the researcher with those individual and/or communities involved in the research process. Patton (2002) stresses that this type of research involves direct contact and interaction with people. Hence, qualitative researchers engage in fieldwork that positions these individuals to gain a thorough understanding of the world as experienced by the research participants.

Another attribute of this type of research is that researchers study what writers such as Patton (2002) and Lincoln and Guba (1985) describe as real-world situations as they naturally unfold. Hence, this approach is characterized as being non-manipulative, unobstrusive, and non-controlling.

Closely related is the characteristic of design flexibility. The researcher must be open in adapting his/her inquiry as understanding of the phenomenon under study increases or situations change that affect the flow of the research. Hence a qualitative researcher needs to be pragmatic.

Contributions and Limitations of Qualitative Research

In recent years, the use of qualitative research in understanding youth resilience has gained greater prominence. Ungar (2003, 2007), Ungar and Teram (2005), and Ungar and Liebenberg (2005) contend that qualitative research can contribute to resilience by highlighting unnamed processes, amplifying marginalized voices, and accounting for cultural context.

With regard to identifying unnamed process, it is believed that the researcher, because of his or her prolonged engagement with participants or institutions, is well positioned to identify processes that facilitate resilience – processes that may not be detected through the use of quantitative methods. The engagement process provides opportunities for researchers to collect thick, rich descriptions from participants. Such descriptions from youth serve as evidence in the researcher's presentation of the salient themes that emerge in qualitative research.

The second benefit of using qualitative research methods is that they provide opportunities for the voices of marginalized youth to be heard. These individuals are well positioned to contribute to the literature as to what indeed are the salient protective and risk factors. As Ungar and Teram (2005) argue, 'seeing the world through the eyes of youth can help us gain an understanding of what we consider signs of disordered behaviour' (p. 153). As such, the use of qualitative methods may assist in determining of the strengths of youth involved in resilience research. Utilizing the strengths approach is a critical component of the resilience process. Weick et al. (1989) maintain that this perspective serves 'as a corrective for the imbalance caused by the preoccupation with people's deficits and liabilities. A strengths perspective rests on an appreciation of positive attributes and capabilities that people express and on the ways in which individual and social resources can be developed and sustained' (p. 352).

In the introduction to *Handbook for Working with Children and Youth: Pathways to Resilience across Cultures and Contexts*, Ungar (2005) makes a passionate argument that in order to better understand youth resilience, it is vital that researchers pay attention to and understand the context and culture of their research participants. In the conclusion of the introductory chapter, Ungar remarks:

> It is an appropriate place to conclude the book, with the argument for a more contextual understanding of resiliency, one that acknowledges the structural as well as the personal factors that foster resilience demonstrated on a large scale in a context far beyond that normally discussed in the resilience literature. (p. xxxvi)

The culture and context within which a study on youth resilience is conducted may then influence the particular type of research design that will be used.

Historically, the debate surrounding the utilization of qualitative research has concerned the question of rigour. More specifically, the salient query has been 'How can rigour be ensured or enhanced?' It is incumbent on researchers using this research paradigm to ensure that their design is clearly presented along with the rationale for the methodology chosen.

A strategy for enhancing the quality of qualitative research is to use conceptual frameworks that deal with the issue of trustworthiness. The typology developed by Lincoln and Guba (1985) is useful in this regard: (a) creditability: prolonged, engaged, member checking; (b) transferability: use of thick description as evidence for salient themes; (c) dependability: use of different data collection techniques, different data sources; and (d) confirmability: different data collection techniques, different group of respondents. All are important elements of a rigorous qualitative inquiry into the phenomenon of resilience.

Currently, the focus on qualitative limitations concerns the specificity of context and findings. Stated differently, the most pressing limitation of qualitative research may be the question of how transferable findings are across cultures and contexts – clearly an important issue in the study of youth resilience. However, again drawing on Lincoln and Guba's (1985) typology, the use of thick description in research may facilitate a consideration of use of findings across sites.

As shown above, both qualitative and quantitative research approaches have strengths and limitations when it comes to researching youth resilience. The emergence of mixed methods as a research approach is viewed as one mechanism that can take advantage of the benefits as well as address the limitations of quantitative and qualitative research.

What Are Mixed Methods?

As mixed-methods research continues to develop and gain attention across various academic disciplines, it becomes a challenging endeavour to identify an agreed-upon definition of what exactly constitutes 'mixed-methods' research. There appears to be general consensus among scholars that at the rudimentary level, mixed-methods research includes aspects of both quantitative and qualitative approaches in a study or program of inquiry (Creswell 2003; Johnson, Onwuegbuzie, & Turner, 2007; Morse, 2003; Tashakkori & Creswell, 2007; Tashakkori & Teddlie, 2003). When Tashakkori and Creswell (2007) conducted a search for mixed-method studies in the behavioural, social, and health sciences, they identified the following characteristics related to the mixing of qualitative and quantitative approaches:

- two types of research questions (with qualitative and quantitative approaches);
- the manner in which the research questions are developed;
- two types of sampling procedures (e.g., probability and purposive);
- two types of data collection procedures (e.g., focus groups and surveys);
- two types of data (e.g., numerical and textual);
- two types of data analysis (e.g., statistical and thematic); and
- two types of conclusions (emic and etic representations) (p. 4).

With reference to the above criteria, mixed methods is research 'in which the investigator collects and analyses data, integrates the findings, and draws inferences using both qualitative and quantitative approaches or methods in a single study or program of inquiry' (Tashakkori & Creswell, 2007, p. 4). Hence, the level at which convergence and corroboration occur throughout the research process is the distinguishing feature between viewing mixed methods as a straightforward exercise of collecting and analysing two forms of data as opposed to that of *integrating* both quantitative and qualitative approaches to research.

Benefits of Mixed-Methods Research

Mixed-methods research provides researchers with the opportunity to leverage the strengths of both qualitative and quantitative approaches from the problem identification through to the data collection, analysis, and interpretation phases of inquiry. The underlying logic of applying mixed-methods research is that the strengths from each respective method can offset the disadvantages or limitations of the other (Barton, 2005; Creswell, Fetters, & Ivankova, 2004; Creswell et al., 2003). And its efficacy is exemplified in the triangulation of data, where researchers can combine the reliability, validity, and generalizability of quantitative methods with the trustworthiness and authenticity of qualitative methods (Barton, 2005).

As noted by Johnson and Onwuegbuzie (2004), other benefits associated with mixed-methods research include the opportunity to answer research questions more holistically than by solely applying a quantitative or qualitative methodology, and the provision of stronger evidence for conclusions, where researchers can use the findings from one method to help inform the other and ultimately produce the rich insights and more complete knowledge necessary to inform theory and practice. For a field like resilience, where new perspectives are needed to advance thinking, such richness is not only desirable but necessary. An example of this can be seen in the case description of the Calgary Youth, Health and the Street study.

Case Study 8.1: The Calgary Youth, Health and the Street Study

The *Calgary Youth, Health and the Street* study is a community-based research initiative funded by the Canadian Institutes of Health Research (CIHR), HIV Community-Based Research Program. The study used a mixed-method approach designed to: 1) describe the spectrum of street-involved youth in Calgary and explore variations among these groups in terms of HIV and health risks, coping mechanisms, and service needs, and 2) use this information for collaborative service planning. An important principle of community-based research is that communities participate in a meaningful research collaboration that should enhance their research capacity while contributing to the quality of research. The research capacity of community partners, street-involved youth advisors, and street outreach workers was built through direct participation in each critical phase of the research. In this research, agency partners collaborated on the development of research question formulation and design, the development of survey and interview instruments, data collection, data analysis, and dissemination of the results. Street outreach workers were hired as research assistants while street-involved youth acted as advisors to the research process. The experience of the research assistants facilitated contact and engagement with street-involved youth but required specific training in research methods.

Data collection occurred over a 16-month period. The survey instrument was a self-administered questionnaire in booklet format composed of 70 closed- and open-ended questions. The questions were designed to collect basic demographic characteristics and explore participants' experiences of neglect and abuse; contact with the child welfare system; perceived physical, mental, and emotional health; perceived HIV and health risks; current social support, employment, and education activities; coping strategies; personal strengths; opinions of current services for street-involved youth in Calgary; and future goals. Surveys were completed by 370 street-involved youth who reflected a wide spectrum of street involvement. In-depth qualitative interviews were completed with 44 youth and were started when approximately half of the surveys had been completed. The interview schedule was developed from an initial list of questions prepared by the research team and reflected observations of the research assistants and the preliminary analysis of survey findings. In-depth interviews provided further context and clarification on data from the completed surveys and focused on specific aspects of the street-involved youths' strengths, coping mechanisms, and view of existing services.

Quantitative data were entered into SPSS and univariate and bivariate analyses were conducted to provide an initial description of the spectrum of street involvement for the final report. Multi-variate analyses were conducted to examine factors predictive of select outcome variables. All data from in-depth qualitative interviews were recorded on tape and then transcribed. ATLAS Ti was used to conduct the preliminary thematic coding for these data. Qualitative data were categorized to describe demographic information and then analyzed thematically to better understand youths' perspectives on street experiences and services. The final report reflects findings based on both quantitative and qualitative data and dissemination efforts will focus on both forms of data. Publications that are being prepared will utilize qualitative data, quantitative data or structured analyses of both data types depending on the focus and intent of the research questions. (Worthington et al., [2007]).

For this study, researchers conducted in-depth interviews in order to gain further insight into data collected from the questionnaire, thus allowing a plethora of details to be gathered on youth perspectives and experiences. Johnson and Turner (2003) refer to this as the *fundamental principle of mixed methods research*: 'methods should be mixed in a way that has complementary strengths and nonoverlapping weaknesses' (as cited in Teddlie & Tashakkori, 2003, p. 16), thus concomitantly leveraging the breadth and depth of both qualitative and quantitative approaches.

A mixed-method approach also possesses the capabilities of transcending cultural limitations while creating dynamic insights into a program of inquiry (Barton, 2005). One such example is the International Resilience Project (IRP). With a multidisciplinary research team from around the world, the objective of the project is to develop the 'tools to conduct research sensitively across many different cultures' in order to recognize variances in how health among youth is understood (Ungar & Liebenberg, 2005, p. 215). More details of the project are as follows:

> The purpose of the IRP is to develop a better, more culturally sensitive understanding of how youth around the world effectively cope with the adversities that they face in life. The IRP uses a unique cross-cultural approach that employs both quantitative and qualitative research methods to examine individual, interpersonal, family, community and cultural factors associated with building resilience in youth around the world. (International Resilience Project, 2007, para. 1)

Qualitative methods were applied to contextualize the Child and Youth Resilience Measure (CYRM), and a variety of qualitative methods occurred alongside the quantitative data collection. The IRP project collected data from over 1500 children world wide over a three-year period of the first phase of their research. During the second phase, researchers will continue 'to investigate the culturally and contextually varied ways resilience is understood and good outcomes achieved by children faced with adversities such as poverty, war, violence, drugs, the illness of a parent, family or community dislocation and cultural disintegration' (International Resilience Project, 2007, para. 2). Ungar and Liebenberg (2005) explain the rationale for using mixed methods when studying resilience:

> In combining the quantitative tradition in resilience research with a qualitative component, the IRP's investigation of the phenomenon of resilience is necessarily broad and multidisciplinary. Employing a number of different methods has created a dovetailed design rather than a stepwise progression in which, as is typically the case, qualitative techniques are considered exploratory, and quantitative techniques are used to confirm hypothesis. Within a relational research context that is attentive to how different groups define their worlds and successful growth in them (more routinely the type of data that qualitative methods generate),

one can see the need for a mixed methods approach to the study of resilience. (p. 212)

Ungar and Liebenberg (2005) contend that cultural context is a fundamental element in understanding child resilience, and that mixed methods can help address arbitrariness and contextual problems through data triangulation and integration. Barton (2005) further supports the application of mixed methods in the study of child resilience, noting that multiple factors at the micro, mezzo, and macro level influence resilience, and that these components should not be explored separately, but holistically.

Considerations of and Limitations to Mixed-Methods Research

Although mixed-method studies are frequently more advanced and complex in their application than each of the constitutive approaches on its own, this method is still young in comparison to more dominant methods. As this approach is still evolving, so are discussions surrounding structured guidelines on the stages of research; the formatting of questions for mixed methods; the effective application of sampling; and overall definitions, typology, nomenclature, design, and analysis that transcends qualitative and quantitative language (Creswell, 2003; Tashakkori & Creswell, 2007). These challenges are further heightened when applied to researching youth resilience across cultures, as strengths, social support, and health, for example, are constructed with consideration to various cultural contexts. These mixed-methods issues must be taken into account before designing the overall mixed-methods approach in order to be relevant outside of Western perspectives.

Another principle challenge with this form of research is the extensive data collection and analysis required, which translates into a demanding, costly, and time-intensive praxis (Creswell, 2003, Johnson & Onwuegbuzie, 2004). As mentioned in previous sections, time lapses and points of data collection are important considerations when conducting resilience research, as these factors can affect the overall research findings. When we consider that these significant aspects are further layered by the complexity of mixed methods, ensuring rigour becomes even more demanding. Thus the capabilities and skills of the researcher(s) must also be considered, as well as the cost and time commitments needed to effectively implement this approach.

Mixed Methods Research Process:
Sequential and Concurrent Research Designs

The following metaphor described by Johnson, Onwuegbuzie, and Turner (2007) postulates potential designs found within mixed methods research:

> If one were to view mixed methods research, metaphorically, as the trunk of a tree, then what are its branches? ... should the major branches be labelled QUAL + quan, QUAN + qual and QUAN + QUAL? What other branches or specialized types might develop over time (e.g. transformative mixed methods, collaborative mixed methods, reflective mixed methods)? (p.128)

Mixed methods can employ a number of research designs that include varying degrees of mixing in different stages of research, though not necessarily throughout the entire program of inquiry. Thus, mixing can occur at any point, or at multiple points within a research project. In the case of the Calgary Youth, Health, and the Street study, mixing occurred at the data analysis phase, whereas in the case study the Chinese Youth of Parental Divorce (see Case Study 8.2) mixing also took place during both data collection and analysis phases. However, the findings from both studies plan to mutually integrate analysis from the qualitative and quantitative data.

Case Study 8.2: The Chinese Youth of Parental Divorce

The Chinese Youth of Parental Divorce is a five-year Vancouver-based longitudinal study designed to understand Chinese youth experiences surrounding parental separation and divorce. Sixty-two children were recruited (30 girls and 32 boys) at the beginning of the study, with ages ranging between 12 and 14. All had experienced parental separation or divorce within a 12-month period from the beginning of the study. The study included gathering both quantitative and qualitative data simultaneously, with self-administered questionnaires at various timeframes during the 5-year period in order to measure changes in a youth's well-being. The survey included 89 closed and open-ended questions, and collected information on the participant's experience since the divorce, specifically focusing on parental and peer relationships, cultural aspects, economic changes, coping strategies, personal strengths, and support mechanisms within the Chinese community. In-depth, semi-structured interviews were also conducted every 12 months in order to gather further insight into the participant's experiences surrounding life post-divorce or parental separation. These interviews lasted 45 minutes to an hour in length, and were guided by the same areas of focus as previously mentioned. Quantitative and qualitative data were analysed separately and concurrently throughout the process, and findings reflected a blending of both data.

Although strategies of convergence can occur at multiple points within a study, there are different research designs that fall under the canopy of mixed-methods research that ultimately affect how and when mixing occurs. Within mixed-method designs, both quantitative and qualitative approaches may be used concurrently or sequentially, where each method may be given equal or dominant status within the design process (Creswell, 2003; Johnson & Onwuegbuzie, 2004; Sandelowski, 2000). The Calgary, Youth, Health and the Street case study is an example in which data collection occurred sequentially; first quantitative data were gathered via surveys from 370 street-involved youth, which included a plethora of perspectives, experiences, and demographic information. This stage was followed by in-depth interviews from a subset of the sample frame who participated in the first phase of inquiry. The interviews contributed to the first phase by providing more context to the findings from the quantitative data collection, as well as giving the youth an opportunity to share their experiences in a narrative format.

Concurrent strategies involve collecting qualitative and quantitative data simultaneously. There are two distinguishing approaches under this strategy: concurrent triangulation and concurrent nesting strategies. The former gives equal priority to both methods, whereas the ladder gives less priority to the data collection embedded in the predominant method (Creswell, 2003). An example of a concurrent triangulation mixed-methods design is the Chinese Youth of Parental Divorce case study, where data from in-depth interviews and questionnaires were gathered simultaneously in order to understand what the participants were going through over the course of the five years after parental divorce.

A researcher's paradigm position may also influence how mixed-methods techniques are employed (Sandelowski, 2000). In the mixed-methods literature, a number of scholars have written about the paradigm challenges associated with synthesizing qualitative and quantitative research (Brannen, 2005; Creswell & Plano Clark, 2007; Green & Preston, 2005; Greene & Caracelli, 1997; Morgan, 2007; Onwuegbuzie & Leech, 2005; Sandelowski, 2000; Tashakkori & Teddlie, 2003). Historically, specific methods have been attributed to certain paradigms, with quantitative methods associated with post-positivism and qualitative methods linked to constructivism (Creswell & Plano Clark, 2007; Sandelowski, 2003). Purists from either stance support what Howe (1988) refers to as 'the incompatibility thesis,' according to which combining quantitative and qualitative methods is impossible, as each distinctive approach represents the philosophical underpinnings of a separate paradigm (Brannen, 2005; Creswell & Plano Clark, 2007; Morgan, 2007; Teddlie & Tashakkori, 2003).

However, a number of mixed-methods researchers would argue that linking qualitative and quantitative techniques to a specific paradigm or method is a false dichotomy (Green & Preston, 2005; Greene & Caracelli, 1997; Sandelowski, 2000). A growing number of scholars have also advocated for pragmatism as the best philosophical foundation for mixed-methods research (Creswell & Plano Clark, 2007; Greene & Caracelli, 1997; Johnson & Onwuegbuzie, 2004; Onwuegbuzie & Johnson, 2006; Tashakkori & Teddlie, 2003). As explained by Creswell (2003), 'pragmatism is not committed to one system of philosophy and reality ... thus, for the mixed methods researcher, pragmatism opens the door to multiple methods, different worldviews, and different assumptions, as well as different forms of data collection and analysis in the mixed methods study' (p.12).

Sandelowski (2000) asserts that it is possible for researchers from different paradigm positions to apply mixed methods, as their philosophical views will ultimately guide how data collection and analysis techniques are implemented:

> Both the researcher in a positivist viewing position and the researcher in a critical theory viewing position may use interviews and even the very same standardized measures to answer their questions, but they will employ these techniques, and more importantly, analytically, treat their

results differently … although techniques can be mixed, the resulting mix will reveal the researcher's viewing position. (p.247)

Within the context of mixed-methods design, Creswell (2003) refers to this as a transformative procedure, where the theoretical lens guides how data are collected. Transformative approaches can take the form of both sequential and concurrent designs, sharing similar strengths and weaknesses in the implementation. We can also refer to the Calgary Youth, Health and the Street case study as an example of a transformative sequential mixed-methods design. The case clearly outlines the motivations behind adopting a pragmatic approach to research, where findings will be used towards collaborative service planning. The research also takes on a strengths perspective, where in-depth interviews focused on the strengths and coping of street youth.

Although concurrent designs include a relatively short data collection time, these approaches require expertise adequately to study a phenomenon while integrating separate methods. In contrast, sequential designs are easier to implement, describe, and report than concurrent designs, yet one of the foremost challenges is the length of time required to complete sequential mixed methods (Creswell, 2003).

Conclusion

We believe that mixed methods presents an opportunity of the greatest magnitude for studying resilience. As Ungar and Liebenberg (2005) assert, 'a mixed methods approach may provide a better balance between the quality and quantity of our findings' (p. 214). They further explain their rationale for investigators researching child resilience to employ mixed-method research:

> Within a relational research context that is attentive to how different groups define their worlds and successful growth in them (more routinely the type of data that qualitative methods generate), one can see the need for a mixed-methods approach to the study of resilience. Only then are we likely to weave a rich tapestry of detail that is able to capture a person's pattern of growth and survival. (p. 214)

Within the context of resilience, mixed methods can provide a forum to uncover a range of insights surrounding the numerous macro and micro elements at play when understanding the capacities associated with resilience. As youth resilience involves various risks and protective factors, with further consideration to cultural context, environment, and relationships amongst family, peers, schools, community members, and mentors, a mixed-methods approach has the potential to address the dynamic interplay associated with resilience research. It does this by gathering robust qualitative and quantitative data. It uncovers a broader understanding of the strengths associated with positive outcomes for children who successfully overcome various risk factors and adversity.

References

Ahern, N.R., Kiehl, E.M., Sole, M.L., & Byers, J. (2006). A review of instruments measuring resilience. *Issues in Comprehensive Pediatric Nursing, 29,* 103–25.

Barton, W.H. (2005). Methodological challenges in the study of resilience. In M. Ungar (Ed.), *Handbook for working with children and youth: Pathways to resilience across cultures and contexts* (pp. 135–47). Thousand Oaks, CA: Sage.

Blum, R.W. (1998). Healthy youth development as a model for youth health promotion. *Journal of Adolescent Health, 22*(5), 368–75.

Brannen, J. (2005). Mixing methods: The entry of qualitative and quantitative approaches into the research process. *International Journal of Social Research Methodology, 8*(3), 173–84.

Bryman, A. (2007). Barriers to integrating quantitative and qualitative research. *Journal of Mixed Methods, 1*(1), 8–22.

Cicchetti, D., & Toth, S.L. (1995). A developmental psychopathology perspective on child abuse and neglect. *Journal of the American Academy of Child Adolescent Psychiatry, 34,* 541–65

Creswell, J.W. (1994). *Research design: Qualitative and quantitative approaches.* Thousand Oaks, CA: Sage.

Creswell, J.W. (2003). *Research design: Qualitative, quantitative and mixed methods approaches* (2nd ed.). Thousand Oaks, CA: Sage.

Creswell, J.W., Fetters, M.D., & Ivankova, N.V. (2004). Designing a mixed methods study in primary care. *Annals of Family Medicine, 2*(1), 7–12.

Creswell, J.W., & Plano Clark, V.L. (2007). *Designing and conducting mixed methods research.* Thousand Oaks, CA.: Sage.

Creswell, J.W., Plano Clark, V.L., Gutmann, M.L., & Hanson, W.E. (2003). Advanced mixed methods research designs. In A. Tashakkori & C. Teddlie

(Eds.), *Handbook of mixed methods in social and behavioral research* (pp. 209–40). Thousand Oaks, CA: Sage.

Denzin,, N. & Lincoln, Y. (1994). Introduction: Entering the field of qualitative research. In N. Denzin & Y. Lincoln (Eds.), *Handbook of qualitative research* (1st ed., pp. 1–17). Thousand Oaks, CA: Sage.

Essed, P. (1991). *Understanding everyday racism: An interdisciplinary theory.* Newbury Park, CA: Sage.

Garmezy, N. (1976). Vulnerable and invulnerable children: Theory, research and intervention. Journal Supplement Abstract Service, APA.

Garmezy, N., Masten, A.S., & Tellegen, A. (1984). The study of stress and competence in children: A building block for developmental psychopathology. *Child Development, 55,* 97–111.

Goldstein, S., & Brooks, R. (2005). Why study resilience? In S. Goldstein and R. Brooks (Eds.), *Handbook of child resilience* (pp. 3–16). New York: Springer.

Green, A. & Preston, J. (2005). Speaking in tongues – Diversity in mixed methods research (Editorial). *International Journal of Social Research Methodology, 8*(3), 167–71.

Greene, J.C., & Caracelli, VJ. (1997). (Eds.). *Advances in mixed-methods evaluation: The challenges and benefits of integrating diverse paradigms.* San Francisco, CA: Jossey-Bass.

Grinnell, R.M., & Unrau, Y.A. (2005). Social work research and evaluation: Quantitative and qualitative approaches (7th ed.). New York: Oxford University Press.

Heller, S.S., Larrieu, J. A., D'Imperio, R., & Boris, N.W. (1999). Research on resilience to child maltreatment: Empirical considerations. *Child Abuse and Neglect, 23*(4), 321–38.

Hill, R. (1998). Enhancing the resilience of African American families. *Journal of Human Behaviour in the Social Environment, 1,* 49–61.

Howe, K.R. (1988). Against the quantitative-qualitative incompatibility thesis, or, dogmas die hard. *Educational researcher, 17*(8), 10–16.

The International Resilience Project. (2007). Retrieved 27 May 2007 from http://www.resilienceproject.org/cmp_text/.

Jew, C.L., Green, K.E., & Kroger, J. (1999). Development and validation of a measure of resiliency. *Measurement and Evaluation in Counseling and Development, 32*(2), 75–90.

Johnson, R.B., & Turner, L.A. (2003). Data collection strategies in mixed methods research. In A. Tashakori and C. Teddlie (Eds.), Handbook of mixed methods in social and behavioral research (pp. 297–319). Thousand Oaks, CA: Sage.

Johnson, R.B., & Onwuegbuzie, A.J. (2004). Mixed methods research: a research paradigm whose time has come. *Educational Researcher, 33*(7), 14–26.

Johnson, R.B., Onwuegbuzie, A.J., & Turner, L.A. (2007). Toward a definition of mixed methods research. *Journal of Mixed Methods Research, 1*(2), 112–33.

Kinard, E.M. (1998). Methodological issues in assessing resilience in maltreated children. *Child Abuse and Neglect, 22*(7), 669–80.

LeBlanc, J.C., Talbot, P.J., & Craig, W.M. (2005). Psychosocial health in youth: An international perspective. In M. Ungar (Ed.), *Handbook for working with children and youth: Pathways to resilience across cultures and contexts* (pp. 165–88). Thousand Oaks: Sage.

Lietz, C. (2006). Uncovering stories of family resilience: A mixed methods study of resilient families – Part I. *Families in Society, 87*(4), 575–582.

Lietz, C. (2007). Uncovering stories of family resilience: A mixed methods study of resilient families – Part II. *Families in Society, 88*(1), 147–155.

Lincoln, Y.S., & Guba, E.G. (1985). *Naturalistic inquiry*. Beverly Hills, CA: Sage.

Luthar, S.S. (2006). Resilience in development: A synthesis of research across five decades. In D. Cicchetti & D.J. Cohen (Eds.), *Developmental psychopathology, Vol. 3: Risk, disorder and adaptation* (pp. 739–95). Hoboken, NJ: John Wiley and Sons.

Luthar, S.S., Cicchetti, D., & Becker, B. (2000). The construct of resilience: A critical evaluation and guidelines for future work. *Child Development, 72* (3), 543–62.

Luthar, S.S., & Zigler, E. (1991). Vulnerability and competence: A review of research on resilience in childhood. *American Journal of Orthopsychiatry, 61*(1), 6–22.

Mason, J. (2006). Mixing methods in a qualitatively driven way. *Qualitative Research, 6*(1), 9–25.

McCubbin, H.I., & McCubbin, M.A. (1998). Typologies of resilient families: Emergency roles of social class and ethnicity. *Family Relations, 37*, 247–54.

Moffatt, T.E., Caspi, A., Dickson, N., Siilva, P., & Stanton, W. (1996). Child-onset versus adolescent-onset antisocial conduct problems in males: Natural history from ages 3 to 18 years. *Development and Psychopathology, 8*(2), 399–424.

Morgan, D.L. (2007). Paradigms lost and pragmatism regained: Methodological implications of combining qualitative and quantitative methods. *Journal of Mixed Methods Research, 1*(1), 48–76.

Morse, J.M. (2003). Principles of mixed methods and multimethods research design. In A. Tashakkori & C. Teddlie (Eds.), *Handbook of mixed methods in social and behavioural research* (pp.189–208). Thousand Oaks, CA: Sage.

Murphy, L.B. & Moriarty, A.E. (1976). *Vulnerability, coping and growth from infancy to adolescence*. New Haven: Yale University Press.

Olsson, C.A., Bond, L., Burns, J.M., Vella-Brodrick, D.A., & Sawyer, S.M. (2003). Adolescent resilience: A concept analysis. *Journal of Adolescence, 26*(1), 1–11.

Onweugbuzie, A.J., & Johnson, R.B. (2006). The validity issue in mixed research. *Research in the Schools, 13*(1), 48–63.

Onwuegbuzie, A.J., & Leech, N.J. (2005). On becoming a pragmatic researcher: The importance of combining quantitative and qualitative methodologies. *International Journal of Social Research Methodology, 8*, 375–87.

Patton, M. (2002). Qualitative research and evaluation methods. Thousand Oaks, CA: Sage.

Reininger, B., Evans, A.E., Griffin, S.F., Valois, R.F., Vincent, M.L., Parra-Medina, D., et al. (2003). Development of a youth survey to measure risk behaviours, attitudes and assets: Examining multiple influences. *Health Education Research Theory and Practice, 18*(4), 461–76.

Rubin, A., & Babbie, E. (2001). Research methods for social work (4th ed). Belmont, CA: Wadsworth/Thomson Learning.

Rutter, M. (1990). Psychosocial resilience and protective mechanisms. In J. Rolf, A.S. Masten, D. Cicchetti, K.H. Nvechterlein, & S. Weintraub (Eds.), *Risk and development of psychopathology* (pp. 181–214). New York: Cambridge University Press.

Rutter, M., Maughan, B., Mortimore, P., & Oustor, J. (1979). *Fifteen thousand hours: Secondary schools and their effects on children*. Cambridge, MA: Harvard University Press.

Sandelowski, M. (2000). Focus on research methods: Combining qualitative and quantitative sampling, data collection, and analysis techniques in mixed-method studies. *Research in Nursing and Health, 23*(3), 246–55.

Sandelowski, M. (2003). Tables or tableaux? The challenges of writing and reading mixed methods studies. In A.Tashakkori & C. Teddlie (Eds.), *Handbook of mixed methods in social and behavioral research* (pp. 321–50). Thousand Oaks, CA: Sage.

Tashakkori, A., & Creswell, J.W. (2007). The new era of mixed methods (Editorial). *Journal of Mixed Methods Research, 1*(1), 3–7.

Tashakkori, A., & Teddlie, C. (Eds.). (2003). *Handbook of mixed methods in social and behavioral research*. Thousand Oaks, CA: Sage.

Teddlie, C., & Tashakkori, A. (2003). Major issues and controversies in the use of mixed methods in the social and behavioral sciences. In A. Tashakkori & C. Teddlie (Eds.), *Handbook of mixed methods in social and behavioural research* (pp. 3–50). Thousand Oaks, CA: Sage.

Turner, S. (2001). Resilience and social work practice: Three case studies. *Families in Society: The Journal of Contemporary Human Services, 82*(5), 441–48.

Ungar, M. (2003). Qualitative contributions to resilience research. *Qualitative Social Work. 2*(1), 85–102.

Ungar, M. (2005). Introduction: Resilience across cultures and contexts. In M. Ungar (Ed.), *Handbook for working with children and youth: Pathways to resilience across cultures and contexts* (pp. xv–xxxix). Thousand Oaks, CA: Sage.

Ungar, M. (2007). Grow 'em strong: Conceptual challenges in researching childhood resilience. In A.L. Best (Ed.), *Representing youth: Methodological issues in critical youth studies* (pp. 84–109). New York: New York University Press

Ungar, M., & Liebenberg, L. (2005). The international resilience project: A mixed methods approach to the study of resilience across cultures. In M. Ungar (Ed.), *Handbook for working with children and youth: Pathways to resilience across cultures and contexts* (pp. 211–26). Thousand Oaks, CA: Sage.

Ungar, M. & Teram, E. (2005). Qualitative resilience research: Contributions and risks. In M. Ungar (Ed.), *Handbook for working with children and youth: Pathways to resilience across cultures and contexts* (pp. 149–64). Thousand Oaks, CA: Sage.

Unrau, Y.A., Grinnell, R.M., & Williams, M. (2005). The quantitative research approach. In R.M. Grinnell & Y.A. Unrau (Eds.), *Social work research and evaluation: Quantitative and qualitative approaches* (7th ed., pp. 61–74). New York: Oxford University Press.

Weick, A., Rapp, C., Sullivan, W., & Kisthardt, W. (1989). A strengths perspective for social work practice. *Social Work, 34*(4), 350–54.

Weiner, E.E. (1984). Resilient children. *Young Children, 40*(1), 68–72.

Werner, E.E. (1989). High-risk children in young adulthood: A longitudinal study from birth to 32 years. *American Journal of Orthopsychiatry, 59*, 72–81.

Werner, E.E., & Smith, R.S. (1982). *Vulnerable but invincible: A longitudinal study of resilient children and youth.* Ithaca: Cornell University Press.

Windle, M. (1998). Critical conceptual and measurement issues in the study of resilience. In M.D. Glaus (Ed.), *Resilience and development: Positive life adaptations* (pp. 161–76). Hingham, MA: Kluwer.

Worthington, C., MacLaurin, B., Huffey, N., Dittmann, D., Kitt, O., & Patten, S. (2007). *The Calgary youth, health and the street study: Final report.* Calgary: AIDS Calgary.

Wright, M., & Masten, A. (2006). Resilience processes in development. In S. Goldstein & R. Brooks (Eds.), *Handbook of resilience in children* (pp. 17–28). New York: Springer.

9 Constructing Syntheses: Striving for Convergent Methods for Investigating Youth in Diverse Cultures

CATHERINE ANN CAMERON

'What is the answer?'.... 'I was silent'.... 'In that case, what is the question?'

            – Alice B. Toklas, *What Is Remembered*

Historically, investigations of social-psychological phenomena have addressed research questions that lent themselves *either* to experimental inquiry, usually involving quantitative approaches, or to qualitative approaches. Traditionally, quantitative studies have sought to assess causal associations between specific factors in an effort to identify antecedents, whilst qualitative studies have striven for a deeper understanding of a phenomenon by observing or querying individuals regarding their experiences. The more recent, salutary trend, of combining both qualitative and quantitative methods within either a single study or a series of studies iterating between qualitative and quantitative approaches, promises to deepen as well as broaden understanding of many social phenomena (Ercikan & Roth, 2006; Johnson & Christensen, 2004; Tashakkori & Creswell, 2007; Todd et al., 2004).

In this chapter, I examine several efforts to bring under the same roof qualitative and quantitative approaches to the study of childhood and youth resilience, not simply as mixed-method approaches, however, but as integrated syntheses of a disparate range of methodologies. I suggest that such integrated syntheses can both enhance construction of multidimensional models of child and youth well-being and at the same time forecast effective intervention mechanisms that can support children and youth in overcoming adverse situations that pose threats to their living safely and well.

Current social-scientific research methodologies are notoriously inadequate for such an ambitious agenda. Each and every method embodies threats to empirical validity or trustworthiness. Furthermore, undertaking multiple initiatives with a single methodological approach, that is, simple replication, can result in *either* depth *or* breadth in understanding a phenomenon, but leave the investigator without both aspects fully examined, legitimately creating concern about investigative errors being compounded rather than compensated for. In consequence, it is advisable to use more than one method to explore a phenomenon. But loosely coordinated application of different methods that are not securely integrated can have little combinatorial power. This concern can be stated more generally to include not simply specific methods (be they questionnaires, focus groups, or interviews), but also broader methodologies (such as ecological, experimental training interventions, grounded theoretical, or discourse-analytic approaches). Such limits posed by the use of only one method result in threats to the required trustworthiness, validity, and reliability that would serve as a firm theoretical foundation for the practical application of findings.

Until recently, political rather than scientific claims of incommensurability between qualitative and quantitative approaches have been a significant factor in preventing necessary triangulations in perspectives that would advance social-scientific understanding (Lincoln & Guba, 2000). This incommensurability barrier appears to be dissolving due to helpful advances in a number of recent mixed-methods research initiatives. Not being satisfied with this heartening advance, however, I wish to argue for more integrally synchronized approaches. These call for careful planning.

As we have been taught, the first step of any empirical investigation involves posing clear, researchable questions. These questions will determine the choice of methodologies and methods that are best suited to answering those questions. Gertrude Stein's deathbed aphorism, as reported by Alice B. Toklas (1963), can remind those in search of pertinent answers to ask fundamental questions. Appropriate methodologies should naturally emanate if we frame our questions to seek answers with both theoretical and practical import. We then seek not a single perfect method (for such do not exist), but the most fitting suite of methods available under the circumstances. For this reason, this chapter is about better, not best, research designs and practices.

I posit that a dialogic orientation, a 'pragmatism of the middle,' one that recognizes and embraces pluralism in the choice of research approaches and designs (many true things can be said about the same entity, and human entities can be understood in many different ways), as methodologic combinations yield untold benefits (Morgan, 2007; Overton, 1998). Such benefits include the possibility of describing *and* explaining: the researcher can focus on the processes *as well as* the products of the inquiry. Through this pragmatic eclecticism, a construction of meaning becomes possible, as well as an understanding of causality.

While it is recommended that methodological selection commence immediately and only *after* initial questions have been posed, it is frequently the case in mixed-methods research that different approaches are deployed recursively, and convergent analyses are only introduced at later data analysis stages, if at all. Bryman interviewed twenty social scientists concerned with combining quantitative and qualitative research approaches and reported that barriers to timely and effective integration included the divergent research structures in place for many mixed-methods studies, disjunctive timelines of the different orientations, and challenges of bridging ontological divides. Commonly, the integration of multiple methods seems to occur no sooner than at the interpretation and reporting stage of a research initiative (Bryman, 2007). However, the earlier and more completely that integration occurs, the more benefits accrue for synthesizing theoretical and practical research solutions. We will see this in the examples discussed below.

What follows is a sampling of several efforts that demonstrate varying degrees of success in integrating divergent qualitative and quantitative methodologies to enhance theoretical and practical understanding of positive development in children and youth, as well as affording us direction in how to apply new knowledge to benefit participants in such research and the populations they represent.

Cultural Differences in Youths' Sexual Scripts

Our first illustration involves an exemplary exploration of cultural differences in Mexican American and African American youths' sexual scripts through the administration and analysis of an innovative vernacular interviewing technique developed to identify mental models of intimate relationships.

The *Vernacular Term Interview* (Eyre, 1997), which can also be used to investigate focused discussion sessions (Milbrath, Ohlson, & Eyre, 2009), is a methodology incorporating both qualitative and quantitative approaches to the same data set. The vernacular interview technique focuses on youths' thoughts and perceptions, as opposed to their personal experiences. Milbrath, Ohlson, and Eyre distinguish it from grounded theoretical approaches in that analyses exploit participants' verbal or vernacular expressions to represent cultural models, rather than employing researcher-generated interpretive categories. Vernacular terms are expressions with particular meaning to a particular cultural group. For example, with the teenagers interviewed in that study, 'gold digger', 'punk,' and *'machista'* were such referential terms. During an interview, participants are prompted to share their understanding of the use of these commonly used words or phrases so that investigators may extract the youths' relational models. The Glaser (1998) method of constant comparison was used for the initial stages of data analysis, using participants' own concepts to represent their mental models.

Milbrath, Ohlson, and Eyre (2009) reported that transcripts of 127 interviews were indexed and categorized into superordinate and subordinate topics of twenty-four conceptual models. Independent raters using a coding manual developed by the initial raters identified eleven major and thirteen subordinate models. These models give a comprehensive cross-cultural picture of the participants' intimate relational conceptualizations. Once the models were developed, key vernacular words were indexed for linguistic, quantitative analysis, which were then amenable to a factor-analytic approach. When the models were grouped in a factor analysis, certain aspects or clusters of relationship models clearly represented major differences between cultural groups. The first factor, cultural mores, related to views of the Mexican American students, including the morality of sex and its focus on the regulation of female sexuality. Romantic care, the second derived factor, reflected a Mexican American concept of idealized male behaviour, while the third factor, involving serious exchanges, reflected African American youths' contractual conceptions of intimate relationships. The fourth factor, involving multiple partners, was associated with both ethnic groups of participants and was a complex construct concerning gender and group approaches to goals surrounding sex and chastity within and outside an intimate partnership. The fifth factor of gaming represents forms of social mastery to represent difficult social positioning, including persuasive discourses, during a courtship, for instance. It is more associated with the African American than the Mexican American youths' models. These mental models confirm and enhance understanding of data on sexual practices of these subcultures of youth, and appreciating them can enhance efforts to intervene in protecting such adolescents from risky sexual practices, thereby enhancing their resilience.

This study moves beyond mixed methods, as it integrates approaches into a convergent methodology that allows for both description and explanation of issues arising from resilience findings. This 'pragmatism of the middle' that I attribute to Overton (1998) embraces pluralism of methodological selection. By carefully asking apposite questions, Milbrath, Ohlson, and Eyre (2009) allowed a methodology to emerge that provides better opportunities for both rich interpretations of youth cognitions and behaviours and openings for practical solutions. They scrutinized their data qualitatively, as well as situating these same findings within a quantitative factor analytic process. Designed to identify culturally divergent conceptual intimacy models, the analyses can thus confidently afford suggestions for differential, culturally sensitive, strategies for intervening on teenage sexual health issues whether with African or Mexican American youths. The findings inform these prevention efforts whether the target of intervention is sexually transmitted diseases or birth control strategies.

This salutary integration of qualitative and quantitative approaches to the same data set generates a firm foundation upon which to build cultural understandings of intimate relations. This is the kind of cultural sensitivity we feel is required in studies of resilience. Incorporating opportunities for synthesizing qualitative data into forms that allow for quantitative analysis and vice versa extends an opportunity for theoretical breakthroughs that one or another approach alone cannot provide. Attitudes revealed in questionnaire research findings that have been established to be replicable can be enriched by the exploration of the conceptual sources underlying participants' mental models. This deeper understanding of the processes at work in determining risky sexual behaviours in concert with stable quantitative findings can assist in determining ecologically valid, culturally targeted, health-promoting interventions.

Creating Peaceful Learning Environments:
Primary Interventions for Positive Learning Environments

Our own evaluations of community-based violence prevention initiatives (Cameron & Team, 2002a; Cameron, 2004) employ both qualitative and quantitative techniques. For fifteen years, school personnel in anglophone community schools in the Canadian Atlantic provinces have been invited by the Creating Peaceful Learning Environments (CPLE) team of the Muriel McQueen Fergusson Centre for Family Violence Research at the University of New Brunswick, Fredericton, to request help in monitoring violence prevention initiatives. The goal of these research projects is to justify program sustainability. In collaboration with Status of Women Canada, a government agency focusing on facilitating community initiatives promoting women's equality, CPLE team members have evaluated various gender-segregated and gender-integrated violence prevention programs for adolescents.

Our questions explored critical factors in the development of effective community-based, participant-action-oriented approaches to creating safe environments for teenagers who too frequently experience violence in their lives. A major focus was on determining appropriate violence prevention interventions for both girls and boys. Our participants were community samples of students in five rural Atlantic Canadian high schools that wished to develop sustainable, effective primary violence prevention initiatives. All students in the schools participated in the programs. Though participation in the evaluations was voluntary, over 90% of students participated. While close to 50% of both females and males self-identified as never experiencing violence in their relationships, about 25% of them reported being victims of verbal abuse on a daily basis, and 17% claimed they were verbally abusive daily. However, males' and females' experiences of physical violence differed dramatically. Whereas almost 10% of girls reported being victims of physical abuse on a daily basis, 20% of boys experienced physical violence daily. Only 6% of girls said they were physical victimizers, while 14% of boys reported physically victimizing others (Cameron & Team, 2002b). It is perhaps this significant minority of a community sample that had potentially the most to gain from community violence prevention initiatives.

In keeping with our ecological perspective, and as recommended by Bronfenbrenner (1979), we employed diverse methods to explore on many levels participants' experiences and responses to violence and its prevention. In addition to inquiring about their experiences of violence, we queried their readiness for change in respect to these experiences. We administered pre- and post-intervention questionnaires, including self-report measures of their current attachment relationships with parents and peers. These self-reports were analysed quantitatively. We also taped and qualitatively analysed interviews with students as they experienced the day-long programs (details of our indices are available in Cameron & Team, 2002a, and Cameron, 2004). We monitored all interventions and held focused discussions with participants. Members of the research team also encouraged participants to produce poetry, videos, and graphic arts to represent their experiences. Only one aspect of our findings as reflected in both qualitative and quantitative data will be summarized here.

Our mixed-method approach was guided by our primary research questions, both those generated by the community, which sought better methods for primary violence prevention intervention; the investigators, who had theoretical issues to explore with respect to gendered developmental influences in the experience and alleviation of violence; and the funder's advocacy priorities regarding protection of the Canadian girl child. A number of separate but associated student research projects and theses were coordinated so the questions on all levels could be inspected from several perspectives, and ultimately conjoined. All sub-projects had both qualitative and quantitative components, so all addressed questions from more than one perspective. Evidence from interview data were inspected in concert with the questionnaire data for boys and girls and younger and older students at first separately and then were compared and contrasted. The free artistic expressions of the student participants were used to highlight or in some cases to modify generalizations from the more systematic data set.

The mixed-method participatory research model we employed was effective in answering several questions regarding gender and development in experiences of violence in a community context. The data converged with several compelling messages. Many of the youths emerged as change agents in their communities. They took ownership of the parts they might play in creating more peaceful learning environments. The process of the research was of value in training them for community leadership roles. A major product of the research, a youth-spearheaded video and handbook reflecting the empirical results in a youth-transformed form, ensured that the process could be replicated at very low to no community cost and to enormous community gain (Cameron & Team, 2002b). The multiple approaches iterating throughout the evaluation paid off in a multiperspectival, but unified, set of findings. For instance, the high-priority needs of girls, due to their risk status for intimate abuse, called at first for separate, intensive consideration that potentially marginalized boys in the research process. This was in conflict with the schools' need to work with all students. Specifically, the inclusion of boys placed them at risk either of engaging in workshops that were not entirely appropriate to their needs or of being left out of some of the proceedings; or, alternatively, necessitated recruitment from the start of an intervention of a comparable number of youth-friendly pro-feminist male facilitators at the community and student participant levels. This final resolution yielded highly efficacious, inclusive interventions that even those who advocated for a focus on the girls found appropriate.

The potential of using such participant action research processes to enable youth participants to articulate and disseminate their own vital messages was key to the project's success. Youth identified conditions important for them to live in their diverse communities safely. Their efforts enriched the many communities involved with youth development and resilience-enhancing initiatives, as well as contributed to theoretical knowledge generation regarding both the general as well as more localized factors related to violence and violence prevention. The greatest successes identified by CPLE research on *primary* prevention initiatives may have been the enhancement of already present student strengths in community building. In other words, those students most ready for change with regard to violence were the ones most positively affected. Unfortunately, and presumably, those students who were hardest to reach, especially some boys, and those with a need for *secondary or even tertiary* intervention, may not only have been left somewhat untouched, but also have been negatively affected by the interventions. That is, they reacted to violence prevention messages with either agnosticism or hostility. Some might even have pre-empted messages and abandoned skills they were using prior to intervention to enhance their negative social influences. The negative reactions of that significant minority of students in the community sample led us to hypothesize that youths with negative early affective experiences might advisedly be unresponsive to changes in orientations to abuse. Their responses could be justifiable (and certainly from their perspectives, they were seen as justified) given that some of the youths' adaptive protective mechanisms were generated as a consequence of their exposure to violence.

Adolescent Psychosocial Stress Reactivity

To answer questions arising from the primary intervention study just discussed, we embarked upon a series of experimental studies that examined many individual difference variables. Attachment relations, anger, externalizing behaviours, and coping strategies in association with hypothalamic-adrenal-pituitary axis (the stress hormone cortisol) and sympathetic nervous system (heart rate) reactions to stress were examined. We manipulated the stressors and tested our hypothesis that positive early attachment experiences and coping strategies, associated with minimal anger and aggression, would be associated with reactivity facilitative of positive adaptation to stress. The converse would be associated with adverse stress reactivity, calling for more intensive therapeutic interventions before community-based violence prevention initiatives might be efficacious. Thus, we shifted our focus from a more participatory model of research with direct application to intervention, to a more theory-driven approach dependent upon analyses of biological and well as verbal and behavioural responses among youth.

Mixed methods were determined to be an effective strategy for getting at basic processes of physiological and psychological reactivity. We first subjected participants to challenging stress protocols, stimulating anxiety reactions. Youths then remained with us individually for one hour so we could monitor their return to baseline physiologic reactivity. We sampled salivary cortisol and heart rates throughout the ninety-minute laboratory procedure. During this time we also had the opportunity to request self-reports from participants, which they willingly provided, mostly in questionnaire and psychometric test formats. We also collected behavioural data and obtained subjective interview data. Parents and teachers provided us with further insights about the youth (Cameron, Wright, & Susman, 2009). The application of an experimental manipulative intervention allows us to discuss precursor or causal factors in reactivity; that is, to know what conditions affect which sorts of reactions (Campbell & Stanley, 1963). Asking the students how they felt at various points during the protocols allowed us to represent both their subjective and physiological stress experiences.

This research regarding adolescents' self-reported attachment relationships, emotional status, coping styles, and behavioural profiles of internalizing and externalizing propensities in relationship to stress reactivity yielded numerous interesting findings that have both theoretical and clinical implications related to helping young people overcome adversity. Our first study showed that girls who reported rather negative attachment relations with their mothers, being relatively angry much of the time, and whose teachers reported them to be quite aggressive, were atypically under-reactive physiologically to the psychosocial stressor. Had these girls learned from earlier aversive experiences to be very wary of the threat of psychosocial stress, and in consequence not respond, or suppress responsivity? Was their reaction a reflection of self-preservative vigilance? Further, although boys' responsivity was similar to the girls', the association between boys' attachment, anger and aggression, and stress reactivity was not confirmed in the same study (Cameron, Wright, & Susman, 2009). Even this integration of methods did not yield a cohesive answer to our original question.

Consequently, we conducted another intervention study in which we focused our preparations of the stressor for the boys. In the first study, we had used an anxiety-provoking intervention, which did, as expected, elicit more cohesive reactions from girls than boys. In the second study, we devised a protocol that elicited more frustration or anger than anxiety. We were successful in eliminating gender differences in reactivity, and were in a better position then to observe gender differences in coping strategies as they relate to stress reactivity. In addition to examining attachment, emotional status, and externalizing behaviours, we also questioned students about their coping strategies both in general and in our psychosocial stress situation.

Results confirmed that the new, specially designed *Frustration Social Stressor for Adolescents* was a reliable and valid psychosocial stress procedure and that it is comparably effective for both boys and girls, eliciting primarily anger/frustration and secondarily anxiety. Results also show that the measure was perceived by participants as having both intra-and inter-personal effects (McKay, Nanayakkara, et al., 2006). Cortisol and heart rate changes under stress were associated with trait anger, externalizing behaviour problems, and paternal attachment reports. This time the relationship was not moderated by gender. Coping responses were associated with maternal attachment, trait anger, and externalizing behaviour problems. Gender moderated the relationship between coping responses and individual differences. Theoretical and clinical implications are now being explored in relation to developing a multidimensional, biopsychosocial conceptual model of youth stress reactivity.

Such an experimental paradigm can discover causal linkages unattainable by any other means. Importantly, the self-reports of participants modulated our understanding of their subjective experiences (McKay, Jackson, et al., 2005). Developers of secondary and tertiary violence prevention interventions would be well advised to take into account not only individual differences in participants' attachment relations, their state and trait emotions, their specific behavioural challenges, and their accustomed coping strategies, but also their psychological and physiological stress reactivity patterns.

Such basic process manipulation could be a necessary component of research truly geared to understanding causal factors in resilience. Smaller-scale microgenetic experiments that yield information on psychophysiological processes, as revealed in other components of the study, could be iterated throughout the duration of multidimensional research programs to enhance knowledge at the personal, familial, community, and cultural levels of youth ecologies as they relate to thriving in the face of adversity. This suite of studies tells us a good deal about both adaptive and maladaptive responses to stress and violence in youths' lives. Because investigating adaptation and risk in separate iterations of a common research initiative leaves some of the findings gathered from different cohorts quite disconnected, the value of asking the initial research questions in a more inclusive manner opens doors for cross-reference between subsets of groups of participants. Next steps can involve clinically identified youth.

A Day in the Life of Strong Children

An international ecological study of toddlers in seven cultures provided a way to interrogate the broad term 'strong child' and an opportunity for participants, parents, caregivers, and researchers alike, in each location, to self-define child strength according to their own culture and context. We chose this open term 'strong child' to provide broad scope for inspecting the foundations families are helping their children establish for the most advantageous outcomes they can envision for their offspring.

This methodological innovation was developed specifically to facilitate the ecological investigation of childhood as lived and enacted in very divergent cultures and contexts (Gillen et al., 2007). We sought to correct a paucity of research that focuses on strength-based analysis of female resilience. Our *'Day in the Life'* study was designed to interfere minimally with the ongoing ecology of children in their home situations. We explored familial supports for the nurturance of seven 'strong' two-and-a-half-year-old participants, their families, and their shared engagement with available cultural tools. Days in the lives of these seven toddlers were observed in Asia, North and South America, Europe, and the Middle East. What the team of investigators observed were the personal and environmental foundations for resilience.

During the first phase of the research, the local research partners recruited an appropriate family, with an apparently thriving two-and-a-half-year-old girl, willing to engage in the project. Parenting-practices interviews were conducted, followed by the filming of a day in the child's life during a single home visit. The children, living in Thailand, Canada, Peru, Italy, the United Kingdom, the United States, and Turkey, spent a full day in the company of our researchers (at least one of whom was culturally indigenous to the context). These researchers videotaped the children's activities and interactions with their caregivers, recorded field notes, and drew environmental plans to enhance the international team's understanding of the interchanges. Particularly notable in cataloguing instances of soothing mutual care-giving and -receiving was the ubiquity of swinging and rocking, singing and dancing, quietly poring over pictures and texts, and of the very great care taken to ensure well-balanced nutritional intake (Cameron, Tapanya, & Gillen, 2006).

The primary investigators (Cameron and Gillen) viewed the videotapes and conjointly derived separate half-hour composites that were reviewed with the local investigators in each research site. The second phase of the research involved showing these selected video clips of the *day* to the caregivers and asking for their reflections. Transcripts of the interactions in the situations were made and translated into English, and interpreted by individuals indigenous to the context. Tapes were digitized and shared among research sites.

After a careful viewing of all days in the lives of our two-year-old children, we explored contextually the soothing resources toddlers and their caregivers enlist that appear to support and promote autonomy and social maturity. We identified instances of the establishment of respites from the 'busy give-and-take' of ongoing activities that seemed to us to be establishing the child's 'secure base' for confident exploration (Bowlby, 1988; Kaye, 1982). We then identified the contexts in which respites occurred, the interlocutors associated with those respites, and associated artefacts. We inferred the goals of the caregiver and child within the contexts. Notable was the aplomb with which these seven children engaged in their daily rounds. Identifying sources of this ease with engagement made sense, when we separated proaction from respite opportunities. Self-efficacy seemed to come from exploratory, agentive activity alternating with withdrawal and nurturing activities. Management of transitions and emotional regulation also seemed associated with the soothing we documented (Main, 1990).

Our findings included: in Thailand, mother, grandmother, and aunts offered comfortable hammock-swinging interludes; in Canada, the toddler, at home with mother and infant sibling, depended on her parent for comfort (most notably when companionably swinging side-by-side); in Italy, on awakening from a nap, the child spent a comforting period of time on her mother's lap, preparing to venture back to explore independently her home play environment; in Peru, aunt, grandfather, and parents each afforded opportunities for the child to engage in quiet opportunities to regroup in the face of more challenging interpersonal interactions; in the United Kingdom, both grandparents and parents were available to monitor the proclivities of the very young children in their care, striving for the interactional synchronies that the children and their caregivers mutually achieved; in the United States and Turkey, our most recent cases for investigation, we have commenced to look at pats and gentle touches that were exchanged between carers and the children. These ethnographic investigations of healthy toddlers in seven cultures show impressive similarities and intriguing differences in the provision of a secure base from which the children venture to explore their primary familial worlds, whether they reside within a nuclear or an extended family structure, as has been documented in other cultural and cross-cultural attachment investigations (Van IJzendoorn & Sagi, 1999).

This innovative methodology is now being applied in several research initiatives where strength-based analyses are sought. Sample sizes are necessarily small, but the depth of analysis seems almost limitless. We have examined the video footage to explore beyond resilience: children's geographies, emergent literacy and musicality experiences, eating artefacts, use of humour to negotiate relationships, and so forth. In several of these latter investigations we have also quantified information on the children's and their carers' discourse and psycholinguistics characteristics in order to identify developmental levels of skill development and interactivity such that we will be able to make more general statements regarding the functioning of the children in context, as in work by Khan et al. (2004). With resilient adolescents, ownership of the process affords many other benefits and a deeper understanding of their perspectives on their quotidian experiences. With both qualitative and quantitatively derived observations, it is hoped that such intense engagement with children across many different cultures and contexts can help us to expand our theory of the cornerstones of resilience, both the common links and the unique aspects of healthy development under stress.

Constructing Syntheses with the International Resilience Project

This volume is an outcome of the International Resilience Project (IRP) (www.resilienceproject.org) (Ungar, Brown, et al., 2007; Ungar, Clark, et al., 2005; Ungar & Liebenberg, 2005), launched to investigate commonalities and divergences in the many faces of youth resilience around the globe. It was very early decided that mixed methods would be most efficacious in approaching this work. With a participant action philosophy and a keen interest in making contributions in the challenges and challenging locations where the research was being conducted, the principal investigators were open to developing a broad base for information gathering. Similar to the studies just discussed, the IRP also sought innovation in its research design in order to investigate resilience with methods congruent with the topics under study.

Fourteen sites volunteered to participate in this pilot study. A total of 1451 youth worldwide were administered a standardized questionnaire, the *Child and Youth Resilience Measure* (CYRM) (Ungar & Liebenberg, 2005), and 89 youth representing each location were queried in an individual interview. Typically, the researchers had a background in either qualitative methodologies or quantitative research. All were familiar with Western notions of mental health and social science research. While the project has produced numerous publications describing its questionnaire, the CYRM, and its interview and focus group work (Ungar, Brown, et al., 2007), the integration of these two strands of the research has yet to be fully realized for reasons common to many mixed-method studies.

Bringing those with qualitative expertise together with those specializing in quantitative methodologies is daunting. Each has her/his skill set on offer, and the language and techniques of the other tend to be foreign, if not alienating. In consequence, cross-dialogues are slow in coming, as is the differential pace of data collection. Publication outlets for work integrating both qualitative and quantitative approaches are rare, and even when editors are open to such integration, reviewers can often be intolerant of varying perspectives.

On the one (qualitative) hand, seven tensions regarding resilience have been carefully abstracted from the interviews and focus groups conducted by IRP collaborators globally. These tensions are: access to material resources, relationships, identity, cohesion, power and control, social justice, and cultural adherence. They have not been inspected in direct relation to the findings from administration of the CYRM. On the other (quantitative) hand, analyses of the results from piloting the CYRM have yielded some interesting preliminary findings regarding its factor structures that vary between Western and non-Western world youth (including aboriginal populations), between non-Western girls and boys, and further, between non-Western boys in socially cohesive as opposed to less socially cohesive contexts. Questions regarding contextual variations verge on tentative answers and have produced a growing list of topics for further inquiry, not the least of which is how to reconcile results from both the qualitative and quantitative aspects of the IRP work.

Suggestions for Integration of Methods

Although each of the research examples described above demonstrates the use of integrated qualitative and quantitative research designs, they also highlight the need to continue development of innovative ways to integrate qualitative and quantitative research in the study of resilience. Continued review of the IRP in particular, then, presents the opportunity to reflect on some of the potential ways this integration can occur.

The questions we might first ask involve the commonalities and differences between sources of positive youth development, or resilience, in diverse global contexts in light of the data already gathered. Our interest is in discovering at many ecological levels (personal, familial, community, and cultural levels) the necessary and sufficient conditions for surviving and thriving across diverse contexts. The purposeful selection of a restricted set of sites based upon previous research would focus the investigation for a second phase of the study. A revised and shortened version of CYRM, now available, would be administered to all participants from the nominated sites. The purposeful selection of sites could include ones best representing the seven tensions already identified. Based on the evidence already accumulated, care would be taken to ensure adequate representations of youth from Western and non-Western settings, inclusion of indigenous and aboriginal youth, equal representation of girls and boys, and youth sample selection from communities with more or less social cohesion.

Proceeding qualitatively with a sub-sample of the youth who complete the CYRM, focused discussions could include adaptations of the vernacular interview techniques discussed earlier. Results would be analysed both quantitatively and qualitatively as explained by Milbrath, Ohlsen, and Eyre (2009), capitalizing on the results from the local administrations of the CYRM and its resulting factor structure. Vernacular interviews with resilient youth participants in their indigenous contexts could provide valuable information about cross-cultural similarities and differences in mental models of well-being as well as help to explore perceptions of the prevailing risks faced. Furthermore, cultural models of both risk and protective factors could then be tested qualitatively and quantitatively for cultural similarities and differences across sites.

Grounded theoretical analyses of the focused discussions can be used to help inform the theoretical analyses of the rest of the data. Discourse analyses and psycholinguistic analyses (Clark, 1996) accounting for both affective and cognitive factors in discourse (Cameron, Kennedy, & Cameron, 2008) could also be integrated into the analysis, enhancing the depth and well as comparative breadth of understanding of the youth views as investigated within the same data set. Digging down even deeper, a sub-sample of these same youth would become active partners in creating video records of one day in their own lives. A recursive process could be employed to examine iterations from different locations, with youth active in the analysis of tapes shared between sites. The ownership of these artefacts would necessarily be a delicate but not irresolvable ethical matter in most contexts, but the potential outcomes for informing social change and engaging youth actively as spokespersons for their experiences of resilience are enormous.

Multiple approaches in such research yield the potential for meaningful and timely triangulation, improve confidence in results, stimulate creative ways of collecting data, and afford richer data that integrate theories and uncover contradictions. The logic of inquiry for such an enterprise engages continual and dialectical use of induction (e.g., discovery of patterns from past experience or from data and development of probabilistic generalizations); abduction (e.g., making an inference to the best explanation for understanding the meaning of a complex situation); and deduction (e.g., empirical testing of theories and hypotheses).

An integrated mixed-methods approach to research enriches the entire research process. Questionnaires may be used to document normative perceptions and test hypotheses. Specifically, contextually relevant questionnaires may be used to help focus discussions on outcomes nominated through qualitative investigations, and thus, in reverse order, to generate questions and test hypotheses. Focus groups and action research approaches to engaging with participants can be used to enhance and enrich understanding of youths' models of resilience as derived from their questionnaire responses. Ecologically valid techniques for documenting selected resilient youths in context, such as that achieved through a *day in their life* documentary, could be both a product and a process for a deeper understanding of the universal tensions previously identified. Proceeding further, brief controlled interventions may be crucial for confirming causal associations. Microgenetic intervention studies can, when well designed, produce generalizable understanding of underlying developmental processes (Fischer & Granott, 1995), be they attachment relations, stress reactivity, coping style, or the many faces of resiliency.

The potential of such integrated methods includes the fact that they provide separate but equal outlooks on particular research questions. They may stimulate thinking about creative possibilities for the means of responding to a range of different questions. They can uncover and handle threats to validity *and* verifiability if designed to iterate amongst them. They represent good investigative practice and rigour while producing more comprehensive, internally consistent outcomes. Early integration has the potential to validate and explicate findings from various approaches, affording deeper understanding, a fuller picture, and richer, more meaningful, and more useful answers. Perhaps best of all, integrated methods can move towards valid applications that have more potential to promote social transformation and social justice and to avoid oppression than do single approaches. We have moved to a methodological stage in our development as resilience researchers that begs for the creation of hybrid methods. A complex construct like resilience needs integrated investigative research approaches that bridge theoretical gaps and that focus our attention as a research community on generating both knowledge of and advocacy for positive development (see, for example, International Society for the Study of Behavioural Development Newsletter, 2006).

One unfortunate weakness of the process, which is often a challenge to those conducting community-based research that seeks to inform programs and policies directly, is the reality that academic dissemination of such research is difficult. The potential contributions to theory building can be compromised by time and financial constraints imposed by funders, and by the challenges of finding sympathetic scholarly venues for research that merges both qualitative and quantitative methods and captures many ecological domains. These impediments make new venues for such integrative reports, like the *Journal of Mixed Methods Research*, especially welcome (Bryman, 2007; Ercikan & Roth, 2006; Morgan, 2007; Tashakkori & Cresswell, 2007).

References

Bowlby, J. (1988). *A secure base*. New York; Basic.

Bronfenbrenner, U. (1979). *Ecology of human development*. Cambridge, MA: Harvard University Press.

Bryman, A. (2007). Barriers to integrative quantitative and qualitative research. *Journal of Mixed Methods Research, 1*(1), 8–22.

Cameron, C.A. (2004). Schools are not enough: It takes a whole community. In M.L. Stirling, C.A. Cameron, N. Nason-Clark, & B. Mediema (Eds.), *Understanding abuse: Partnering for change* (pp. 269–94). Toronto: University of Toronto Press.

Cameron, C.A., Tapanya, S., & Gillen, J. (2006). Swings, hammocks, and rocking chairs as secure bases during *A Day in the Life* in diverse cultures. *Child and Youth Care Forum, 35*(3), 231–47.

Cameron, C.A., & Team. (2002a). Worlds apart ... coming together: Gender segregated and integrated primary prevention implementations for adolescents in Atlantic rural communities. In H. Berman & Y. Jiwani (Eds.), *In the best interests of the girl child: Phase II Report* (pp. 143–69). London, ON: Alliance of Five Research Centres on Violence.

Cameron, C.A., & Team. (2002b). *Worlds apart ... coming together: Part 1, 'She said, he said'; Part 2, Together we can*. Evaluation research findings leading to community facilitator training video (32 minutes) and accompanying handbook (16 pages). Fredericton, NB: Muriel McQueen Fergusson Centre for Family Violence Research.

Cameron, C.A., Wright, J.M., & Susman, E.J. (2009). Cortisol social-stress responses of angry adolescent girls and boys. Manuscript under revision.

Cameron, E.L., Kennedy, K., & Cameron, C.A. (2008). 'Let me show you a trick!': A toddler's use of humor to explore, interpret, and negotiate her familial environment during *A Day in the Life*. *Journal of Research in Childhood Education, 23*, 5–18.

Clark, H.H. (1996). *Using language*. Cambridge: University of Cambridge Press.

Campbell, D.T., & Stanley, J.C. (1963). *Experimental and quasi-experimental designs for research*. Chicago: Rand McNally.

Ercikan, K., & Roth, W.-M. (2006). What good is polarizing research into qualitative and quantitative? *Educational Researcher, 35* (5), 14–23.

Eyre, S. (1997). The vernacular term interview: Eliciting social knowledge related to sex among adolescents. *Journal of Adolescence, 20*, 9–27.

Fischer, K.W., & Granott, N. (1995). Beyond one-dimensional change: Parallel, concurrent, socially distributed processes in learning and development. *Human Development, 38*, 302–14.

Gillen, J., Cameron, C.A., Tapanya, S., Pinto, G., Hancock, R., Young, S., & Accorti Gamannossi, B. (2007). 'A Day in the Life': Advancing a methodology for the cultural study of development and learning in early childhood. *Early Childhood Development and Care, 177*(2), 207–18.

Glaser, B.G. (1998). *Doing grounded theory: Issues and discussions*. Mill Valley, CA: Sociology Press.

International Society for the Study of Behavioural Development Newsletter. (2006, November). ISSBD Special Section: Research on interventions targeting the promotion of positive development. (Supplement of *International Journal of Behavioral Development, 30*(6), No. 2, Ser. No. 50.

Johnson, R.B., & Christensen, L.B. (2004). *Educational research: Quantitative, qualitative, and mixed approaches*. Boston: Allyn & Bacon.

Kaye, K. (1982). *The mental and social lives of babies*. Chicago: University of Chicago Press.

Khan, S., Jackson, L, Hodge, B., Kendrick, K., & Cameron, C.A. (2004, June). Methods for analyzing cognitive intentions and affect in parent/child telephone discourse. Poster presented at 34th Annual Meeting of Jean Piaget Society, Toronto.

Lincoln, Y.S., & Guba, E.G. (2000). Paradigmatic controversies, contradictions, and emerging confluences. In N.K. Denzin & Y.S. Lincoln (Eds.), *Handbook of qualitative research* (pp. 163–88). Thousand Oaks, CA: Sage.

Main, M. (1990). Cross-cultural studies of attachment organization: Recent studies, changing methodologies, and the concept of conditional strategies. *Human Development*, *33*, 48–61.

McKay, S.L., Jackson, L., Ruttle, P., Flett, R., Nanayakkara, D., & Cameron, C.A. (2005, March). The Frustration Social Stressor for Adolescent (FSS-A): A new experimental stress procedure. Poster presented at Biennial Meetings of Society for Research in Child Development, Atlanta.

McKay, S.L., Nanayakkara, D., Ruttle, P., Flett, R., & Cameron, C.A. (2006, March). Adolescent coping responses to psychosocial stress. Poster presented at Society for Research on Adolescence Biennial Meeting, San Francisco.

Milbrath, C., & Eyre, S. (2005, June). Analyzing cultural models in adolescent accounts of relationships. Paper presented at 35th Annual Meeting of Jean Piaget Society, Vancouver.

Milbrath, C., Ohlson, B., & Eyre, S.L. (2009). Analyzing cultural models in adolescent accounts of romantic relationships. *Journal of Research in Adolescence*, *19*(2), 313–51.

Morgan, D.L. (2007). Paradigms lost and pragmatism regained: Methodological implications of combining qualitative and quantitative methods. *Journal of Mixed Methods Research*, *1*(1), 48–79.

Overton, W.F. (1998). Developmental psychology: Philosophy, concepts, and methodology. In R.M. Learner (Ed.), *Theoretical models of human development*, Vol. 1: *Handbook of child psychology* (5th ed., pp.107–88). New York: Wiley.

Tashakkori, A., & Creswell, J.W. (2007). The new era of mixed methods (Editorial). *Journal of Mixed Methods Research*, *1*(1), 3–7.

Todd, Z., Nerlick, B., McKeown, S., & Clark, D.D. (2004). *Mixing methods in psychology: The integration of qualitative and quantitative methods in theory and practice.* Hove: Psychology Press.

Toklas, A.B. (1963). *What Is Remembered.* New York: Hold Rinehart & Winston.

Ungar, M., Brown, M., Liebenberg, L., Othman, R., Kwong, W.M., Armstrong, M. & Gilgun, J. (2007). Unique pathways to resilience across cultures. *Adolescence*, *42*(166), 287–310.

Ungar, M., Clark, S., Kwong, W.M., Cameron, A., & Makhnach, A. (2005). Researching resilience across cultures. *Journal of Cultural and Ethnic Social Work*, *14*(3/4), 1–20.

Ungar, M. & Liebenberg, L. (2005). The International Resilience Project: A mixed methods approach to the study of resilience across cultures. In M. Ungar (Ed.), *Handbook for working with children and youth: Pathways to resilience across cultures and contexts* (pp. 211–26). Thousand Oaks, CA: Sage.

Van IJzendoorn, M.H., & Sagi, A. (1999). Cross-cultural patterns of attachment. In J. Cassidy & P.R. Shaver (Eds.), *Handbook of attachment* (pp. 713–34). New York: Guilford.

APPLICATION OF METHODS

10 Playing Catch-Up: Evaluating a Mathematics Intervention for Disadvantaged Learners in South Africa

JOHANN MOUTON AND LAUREN WILDSCHUT

Programs, and their effectiveness, are integral to the resources available to youth living in adversity, and as such are an important part of researching and understanding healthy youth outcomes. In South Africa, many services and programs continue to be provided by non-governmental organizations[1] (NGOs). Indeed, the South African government's Reconstruction and Development Programme (RDP) articulated a central role for NGOs in all spheres of development.

With regard to youth resilience, then, it would appear that NGOs have an important role to play in contributing to and developing health outcomes amongst marginalized youth. There are a number of reasons for this. NGOs in South Africa are particularly well represented in areas such as community development, literacy, and public health that often require interventions by small agencies located in proximity to those most heavily and negatively affected by poverty, illiteracy, HIV/AIDS, and so on. The activist experience gained during the apartheid years still stands these agencies in good stead: networks are still in place, legitimacy in many areas has been gained and sustained, and the philosophy of making a difference is as strong as it used to be. In addition, most NGOs receive funding from overseas donor and philanthropic agencies, which means that they can act swiftly when implementing interventions. They are not, like their counterparts in government departments, constrained and sometimes even demotivated by the bureaucratic machinery. Although NGOs are seen as playing a significant role in dealing with social issues they are not without their problems, having had 'erratic success,' and have therefore been called upon to be 'transparent' and to respond 'with accountability and democracy to the communities they serve' (Stober, 1994). In the last decade, the call for clear evidence of effectiveness of programs has become much more salient. This call has come from various sectors – public, private, funding organizations – and has resulted in a growing demand that organizations evaluate their programs.

But the demand to evaluate the social and educational interventions of NGOs does not come without its own problems and challenges. The vast majority of NGOs operating in the social, health, and educational sectors are small organizations with no specialized expertise in program evaluation or even formal training in project management. In fact, many NGOs in South Africa have their origins in a more activist and populist culture that goes back to the struggle years. The rigours of monitoring and evaluation are typically not part of this 'developmental' and 'action-orientated' culture, with the consequence that demands for monitoring and evaluation are often met with suspicion, resistance, or outright rejection. Having said this, we have more recently also seen a growing appreciation of and interest in the value of (especially) formative evaluations. Where NGOs recognize the value of rigorous and appropriate evaluations that are useful to their own internal planning, there is a receptivity and willingness to learn about program evaluations.

This chapter is an account of an engagement with such an NGO working in the field of school education in the Western Cape province of South Africa. What makes this evaluation particularly interesting is its positioning across cultures: more 'traditional,' Western evaluation methods (i.e., with a predominance of quantitative methods) were retained in the design, being considered most appropriate given the demands on both staff and youth, allowing the evaluation to be less taxing on already strained groups.

The State of School Mathematics in Post-Apartheid South Africa

One of the more lasting legacies of the apartheid system has been its devastating effects on the schooling system in South Africa (Kahn, 2004, 2006; Reddy, 2006a, 2006b; Taylor, Vinjevold, & Muller, 2003). Many public schools remain under-resourced with poorly qualified teachers, while learners tend to come from poor socio-economic backgrounds with little or no access to learning resources.

These conditions apply particularly in the case of mathematics and science, where there is a national shortage of experienced and well-qualified teachers. The importance of mathematical and scientific knowledge and competence for the development of the country has been central to much of the education policy and curriculum reform introduced in South Africa in the last decade (Department of Education, 2004; Department of Science and Technology, 2002). The challenge facing educators in improving the quality of learners' performance in mathematics and science is brought home quite forcefully when the performance of South African learners is compared with that of other countries. Findings from the Third International Mathematics and Science Study (TIMMS) program, conducted under the auspices of the International Association for the Evaluation of Educational Achievement, rank South African learners well below the international average of 487 points (Reddy, 2006b). Specifically, South Africa's average score is 275 out of 800 points. These results are also significantly below the average scores of all other participating countries, such as Morocco, Tunisia, Malaysia, the Philippines, Indonesia, and Chile.

Against this background, it should come as no surprise that in addition to government initiatives to improve the quality of mathematics and science education in all public schools, many universities and NGOs have also established programs to address this problem. Improved educational outcomes are important not only for the redevelopment of the South African labour force and economy, but also for resilient outcomes in youth (Giligan, 2000; Krovetz, 1999; Murray Nettles, Mucherah, & Jones, 2000).

SAILI and Its Interventions in Mathematics and Science

The Scientific and Industrial Leadership Initiative (SAILI) is a Cape Town–based NGO that was established 'to promote improvement in mathematics and science education for learners and educators in schools servicing disadvantaged communities in the Western Cape' (SAILI mission statement, ERA Evaluation Report 2004: 8).

Officially started in January 1996, SAILI[2] operated at all levels of the school system and had targeted interventions at each level. In general terms the SAILI model consisted of four components that were envisaged to have an additive and cumulative effect over time. These components included:

- The General Education and Training (GET) program, at primary school level, focused on improving science and mathematics teaching of all educators in the selected nine schools. There was also a subprogram (the Catch-up program – the focus of this chapter) that targeted grade 6 learners in these nine schools.

- The Further Education and Training (FET) school program was primarily aimed at improving the science and mathematics knowledge and competencies of grade 8 to 12 educators.
- The School Management Program aimed at improving school management practices in general as well as improving curriculum management.
- The Post-school Program exposed students to a range of science and technology career options as well as tracking students after they left school.

The authors were commissioned by SAILI at the end of 2002 to undertake regular formative and summative evaluations of its work. Our initial work focused on issues related to clarificatory evaluation and the aim of producing – together with the SAILI staff – a theory-based understanding of the basic logic and structure of each of the SAILI program components.

Another major component of our evaluation approach was its emphasis on building the capacity of key staff at SAILI. This was important because the learner-focused model requires SAILI staff to be involved in:

- the development or modification of available learner materials;
- co-ordination of learner programs to ensure the SAILI ethic/ philosophical approach is implemented;
- facilitation of appropriate needs-based learner sessions; and
- assessment of learner knowledge and skills.

Capacity building was done in various ways: through formal training sessions in clarificatory evaluation (the use of the logic model) and observation techniques; by accompanying SAILI staff during observations sessions in class rooms; and through regular feedback and in-depth discussions with staff of evaluation results. In addition, the SAILI Board of Trustees required answers to new and different questions as annual evaluation reports came in.

Much of the SAILI primary school intervention focused on the GET program, which was aimed at improving the science and mathematics teaching of all educators in nine schools in the Greater Cape Town area. Four of the schools are predominantly Xhosa speaking and five are predominantly Afrikaans speaking. SAILI kept a detailed profile of learners, which was continually updated. This was used as the basis for tracking learners and their changing home circumstances (e.g., death of a parent, change in employment status, and so forth). It was also used for counselling purposes, as SAILI found itself engaging with many of the socio-economic issues that schools often ignore.

The Context of the Evaluation

An in-depth analysis of one of the primary schools (School A) was conducted in 2005 in order to establish more clarity on the home backgrounds of learners in these schools. This specific school was chosen because, although it seemed to be more functional than other schools in the area (it had key policies in place, a functioning governing body, well-maintained grounds, and so forth), the learners at the school were doing a lot worse than learners from other schools in the area.

Questionnaires were sent to parents or guardians of all learners in the school. From this survey of 179 learners, we found that the typical learner does not live with both parents, but more likely with mothers only (42%). Only one-third of learners live in a household where both parents are present. Educational levels of learners' parents are generally low. Half of fathers and 60% of mothers either have no schooling or have completed only part of primary school. Only about 10% of all parents have completed high school.

As far as employment is concerned, between 60% and 70% of parents are typically employed, that is, employed in either the informal sector or in casual employment. Not surprisingly, household incomes are very low, with nearly one-third of all households reporting that they have no formal income. Households are also very crowded, with an average of 7 people living in each house. Of these, an average of 2.7 members of the household are in school and only 1.5 have formal employment.

The typical learner has little access to learning resources. Only 30% have a personal desk at which to study at home, 27% have a computer, and 18% have their own bedroom. Half of learners never or very seldom go to a library, and the majority of households (55%) never or seldom buy any newspapers or magazines.

These statistics highlight the adversity in which youth targeted by SAILI live. Such constrained home environments increase the likelihood of youth leaving school early and becoming either street youth or involved in crime (Johnson, Crosnoe & Elder, 2001; Kramer, 2000; Lee, 2001; Maguin & Loeber, 1996). Importantly, the school that was selected typically caters to so-called coloured[3] students. African learners who attend some of the other 'historically African' schools live in much worse circumstances. Many of them would typically live in informal settlements or 'shacks' that are much more crowded, have no electricity or running water, and are often far away from the closest school.

Adding to the strain of learners' home environments is the reality of teacher capacity in their schools. In 2004 we tested the mathematics content knowledge of teachers in participating schools. Teachers were given the same tests as were administered to their own learners. That is, grade 6 teachers were asked to complete the standard grade 6 mathematics tests that would as a matter of course have been administered to their own learners. Of the 42 teachers who completed these tests, only 8 passed. In 4 of the 8 schools not a single teacher passed.

The results confirmed what classroom observations had suggested and previous studies hypothesized: the single biggest problem in many historically black schools, especially in subjects such as mathematics and science, is lack of knowledge of the teachers themselves.

The extremely poor results of high school learners in mathematics and science in South Africa are linked to home and the reality of poor elementary schooling, which are evidently not only not conducive to learning but in fact work against a culture of learning. Such findings support the need for interventions that attempt to reverse these adverse conditions.

Many interventions, however, are best described as 'remedial' in that they are aimed at redressing disadvantages that are recurring. They are often also 'experimental' in nature in that there are few best-practice examples or textbook solutions available. This meant that our approach to evaluating SAILI's interventions had to be equally open ended and adaptive. Over the three years of our engagement with the NGO we revised our evaluation design, instruments used, and analyses conducted on an annual basis. Learnings generated from past evaluation studies were incorporated into revised designs and instrumentation.

The main learnings from past evaluations that informed this study are threefold:

- Within the NGO domain it is essential that an evaluation design be properly aligned with the resourcing and skills levels of the staff. Our design could therefore not be overly complex or 'academic.' We had to design the study in such a way that the staff of the NGO could associate with it and assist in its execution.
- This also meant that we could not design an overly elaborate and intrusive design that would take up inordinate amounts of staff time. The staff in this NGO were already overly stretched, and it would have been unwise to burden them with excessive demands.
- On the positive side, we deemed it essential from the outset to incorporate a capacity-building component into this design. This meant involving staff in all stages of the study: approving the design, co-production of the logic models of the intervention, training in interviewing techniques and monitoring data collection as well as commenting on the final analysis and reporting.

The Catch-up Program

The main purpose of the Catch-up program was to address the deficit in grade 6 and 7 learners' conceptual understanding and content knowledge of mathematics. The program starts at grade 6 level with the identification of sixty disadvantaged learners from selected schools who show potential in mathematics. These learners remain on the program for two years (grades 6 and 7), attending classes on alternate Saturdays during the school term. At the end of grade 7 all learners are tested and up to forty of the top achievers advance to the following stage in SAILI's school program. We have focused on the Catch-up program because it is the only component in the SAILI program where learners are directly taught by substitute teachers. Given the poor performance of the teachers themselves, it seemed reasonable to focus on an intervention that bypasses these teachers and assess the results thereof. Within the broader context of this chapter, it is worth pointing out that this decision was made because it highlights and reaffirms the seriously adverse conditions under which these learners have to survive. The learners themselves are already disadvantaged at various levels: many come from broken homes, live in poor socio-economic conditions, and have few learning resources and a complete lack of a learning culture at home. The schools that they attend, the schools in our sample, are under-resourced and have been historically so for many decades. But in a very real sense, this adversity is deepened and

Figure 10.1: GET Theory of Change

Implementation Theory (Program activities)	Program Theory (Mechanisms of change) 8 schools are selected to be part of the SAILI program based on set criteria
GET team delivers 8 workshops to address needs of all mathematics and science teachers in 8 selected schools	Mathematic and science teachers from 8 schools **attend** workshops and their understanding of mathematics and science concepts and content is **improved**
GET team provides 12 work and 12 classroom support sessions per teacher in 8 selected schools	Teachers' teaching methodology improves
GET team supplies equipment and resource books for mathematics and science teachers in 8 selected schools	**Learner performance in mathematics and science in all 8 schools is improved**
GET team provides Catch-up classes for 60 learners from 8 selected schools (8 Saturdays per year and 2 days during holidays)	
Science Centre staff provide additional training and enrichment through Saturday sessions	

exacerbated by the fact that the majority of the teachers who teach in these schools are themselves woefully underprepared and poorly equipped to help the learners. The catch-up program could thus in a very important sense be understood as one of the few opportunities or spaces where they are given the chance to overcome this 'double' adversity.

In order to understand the place and purpose of the Catch-up program within SAILI's broader primary school program, we needed to develop the GET's 'program theory' (see Figure 10.1). This allowed us to better understand the Catch-up program and how its classes form an integral part of the overall intervention in the primary schools.

Figure 10.2: Logic Model

Problem	Causes	Objectives	Program Activities	Outcomes	Indicators	Sources of Evidence
Poor learner performance in mathematics	Lack of conceptual understanding and content knowledge Poor maths teaching in ex DET* and HOR* schools	To improve the maths results of group of learners from ex DET and HOR schools	1. 60 selected learners receive maths instruction: 14 sessions × 3.5h = 49h 2 classes × 30 learners 2. Learners receive quality instruction on specific topics 3. Learners are assessed on an ongoing basis 4. Test and select top 40 learners for Learner Placement Program	1. Learners' maths knowledge and skills are improved 2. Learners' needs are assessed and addressed in Catch-up sessions 3. Learners receive remedial work based on perceived weaknesses 4. 40 out of 60 learners are selected on relevant criteria for the LPP	1. Improved learner performance 2. Learners express that their needs are being met 3. Ongoing improved learner performance 4. At least 40 learners meet criteria	1. Test results 2.1. Test results 2.2. Student interviews 3. Test results 4. Test results

* DET – Department of Education and Training
HOR – House of Representatives
[former schools of coloured and black learners]

Table 10.1   Catch-up 'Conditions for Success' Listing

Conditions for Success	Outcomes
• Catch-up sessions are based on actual learner needs	1) Learners' mathematics knowledge and skills are improved
• There are sufficient workshops to allow for a positive impact on learners' knowledge and skills	
• Attendance levels at workshops are high	2) Learners' needs are addressed
• Facilitators are able to transfer necessary knowledge and skills to learners	
• Assessment of learners' knowledge and skills occurs on an ongoing basis and is used for teaching purposes	3) Learners receive remedial work
• The test given to learners to assess their potential for the LPP is appropriate	4) 40 out of 60 learners are selected for the LPP
• Selection processes (Catch-up) carried out by SAILI result in appropriate learners to feed the learner placement program (LPP)	

In addition to the special attention that learners in these classes receive, SAILI also targets their teachers (with additional Saturday workshops) as well as supplying these classes with additional resource books.

We next developed a logic model (see Figure 10.2), using the expected outcomes of this program as our starting point and identifying the underlying conditions for success. The resulting list of 'conditions of success' (see Table 10.1) provided us with a useful framework for analysing and interpreting the empirical evidence.

There are three crucial 'phases' that make up the Catch-up program:

- the selection of learners into the catch-up classes;
- the performance of learners on mathematics and science tests; and
- the progression of learners within the catch-up phase and on to the next stages.

In our discussion of our evaluation of the program in 2005, we presented our findings under these three headings. The reasons for focusing on these three components are twofold: (1) the conditions for success (outlined in Table 1) demonstrate, as it were, the implicit causal theory that drives this program, and these components capture – at a different level – these conditions; and (2) the three crucial phases identified above should also be seen as necessary conditions that needed to be met in order for us as evaluators to be able to make credible judgments about the success of the overall program. By disaggregating the program into these three phases we were better able to pinpoint areas of concern warranting further intervention as well as to show how these components work together to the overall achievement of program success.

The Selection Process

Robbie Gow-Kleinschmidt, director of SAILI, explains how learners were selected for the Catch-up classes in 2005 as follows:

[Prior to 2005] the selection of learners for Catch-up was restricted to schools … which [had historically catered to] either black or coloured youth in township areas with the majority being Xhosa or Afrikaans [speaking]. From a language perspective, the. [black] Xhosa-speaking learners on the Catch-up Programme were at a distinct disadvantage as the lessons and, most importantly, the selection test was in English. This, coupled with poor mathematical skills, contributed largely to the black learners' slow rate or lack of progress.

In order to increase the pool of black learners, a different approach was adopted [in] 2005... As the selection was no longer restricted to specific schools we were able to look further a field and identified 8 schools … They were approached and asked to select their top Grade 7 black learners … we deliberately targeted English-medium schools with a fairly large Xhosa-speaking population. Our reasoning was that learners from these schools would be more proficient in English which would help to address the language problem.

Here we see the reality of different 'degrees of disadvantagement' in historically African and 'coloured' schools. SAILI had traditionally aimed at improving the mathematics and science performance of both African and coloured learners. However, the reality is that the initial selection processes favoured 'coloured' learners and led to the under-

Table 10.2 Interval Distribution of Percentage Scores

Intervals	Frequency	Percentage
80%–100%	2	3.3
70%–79%	3	5.0
60%–69%	17	28.3
50%–59%	22	36.7
40%–49%	6	10.0
30%–39%	9	15.0
20%–29%	1	1.7
Total	60	100.0

representation of African black learners in the Catch-up classes. This quote illustrates how SAILI's selection process had to be changed in order to get a sufficient number of black, predominantly Xhosa-speaking, learners into the program.

Sixty candidates were eventually selected for the grade 7 Catch-up classes. This number was made up of two selections: a group of thirty-eight learners selected from the grade 6 Catch-up classes who were tested in September 2004 and a second group of twenty-two learners selected through the process described above. One of the consequences of broadening entrance into the Catch-up program was that 27% of learners who were ultimately selected for inclusion did not in fact pass (achieve more than 50%) on the initial 'selection' test (see Table 10.2).

It is important to keep this fact in mind when we present the learner performance results below, as it illustrates that even in a dedicated program such as this, the politics of selection dictated that learners had to be accepted in order to ensure that the right balance between African and coloured students was obtained, even if it meant that not all students passed the initial selection test.

Learner Performance

The sixty learners were assigned to two classes (B and M below). Learners were required to attend six teaching sessions during the course of 2005. The teaching schedule and attendance rates by class group are presented in Table 10.3.

We will comment on the attendance rates and their possible effect on

Table 10.3 Workshop Attendance, by Group

	Class B		Class M	
Workshop Date	Learners Attended	%	Learners Attended	%
9 April 2005	29	96.7%	28	93.3%
23 April 2005	29	96.7%	28	93.3%
7 May 2005 (progress test 1)	29	96.7%	28	93.3%
21 May 2005 (progress test 2)	27	90.0%	26	86.7%
4 June 2005 (progress test 3)	27	90.0%	26	86.7%
11 June 2005 (progress test 4)	27	90.0%	30	100.0%

Table 10.4 Progress Test Scores by Baseline Performance

Baseline	Statistics	Progress 1 (% score)	Progress 2 (% score)	Progress 3 (% score)	Progress 4 (% score)
Pass	Mean	72.0	73.6	75.8	65.4
	N	44	39	38	43
	Std. Deviation	14.8	14.6	11.3	14.8
Fail	Mean	59.5	61.3	64.7	51.6
	N	13	14	15	14
	Std. Deviation	17.7	16.7	15.5	14.9
Total	Mean	69.2	70.3	72.7	62.0
	N	57	53	53	57
	Std. Deviation	16.2	16.0	13.5	15.9

Note: For each progress test, the difference in mean scores ('baseline: pass' versus 'baseline: fail') is statistically significant, according to Mann-Whitney test. For 'baseline: pass' learners, the change from progress 1 to progress 2 is statistically non-significant, as well as the change from progress 2 to progress 3. Only the decline between progress 3 and progress 4 is statistically significant, according to the Wilcoxon Signed Ranks Test. The same is true for 'baseline: fail' learners.

learner performance below. Table 10.4 presents an overview of learner performance on each of the four progress tests (developed by SAILI) cross-tabulated by their baseline performance on the initial selection test.

The most striking trend evident in Table 10.4 is the fact that learners

Figure 10.3 Trends in Catch-up Progress Tests (Baseline Pass or Fail)

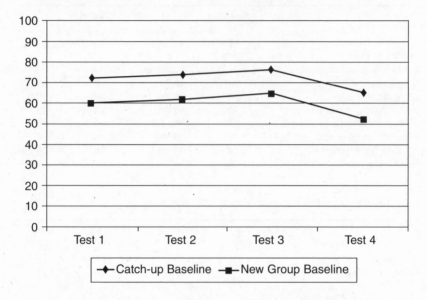

generally improved over the course of the year with the exception of their results on test 4. A more simplified graph of the performance profiles for each of the two groups is presented in Figure 10.3. Incidentally, the discrepancy in numbers between the initial group of 60 and the numbers of learners tested in each test (57 for Test 1; 53 in Test 2, and so on) is explained by changes in attendance rates.

Finally, we looked at the relationship between workshops or classes attended and performance. All learners were required to attend six classes. As Table 10.5 reveals, a statistically significant relationship between class attendance and mean performance on all test scores was found, with those attending fewest performing poorest, supporting the need for learners to attend the program regularly.

In an attempt to gain a better understanding of this result, we looked more closely at the five learners who attended only three or four of the six classes. One learner (male Xhosa learner) attended only three classes, and four learners (three female and one male; two Xhosa-, one Afrikaans-, and one English-speaking) attended only four of the classes. Interestingly enough, the two Xhosa-speaking learners from the 2004 Catch-up class who were selected ahead of other, better, learners in order to improve the representation of Xhosa-learners (Learners

Table 10.5 Average Progress Scores by Number of Classes Attended

Number Attended	Mean	N	Std. Deviation
3	28.0	1	–
4	54.5	4	11.6
5	68.5	15	10.5
6	70.4	40	12.4
Total	68.2	60	13.4

Note: Difference statistically significant, according to Kruskal-Wallis test.

Table 10.6 Interval Distribution of Baseline Test Performance with Average Performance on Progress Tests

	Average of Progress Tests					
	80–100%	70–79%	60–69%	50–59%	49% or less	Total
80–100%	2 100.0%	0 0.0%	0 0.0%	0 0.0%	0 0.0%	2 100.0%
70–79%	1 33.3%	2 66.7%	0 0.0%	0 0.0%	0 0.0%	3 100.0%
60–69%	4 23.5%	10 58.8%	2 11.8%	1 5.9%	0 0.0%	17 100.0%
50–59%	3 13.6%	8 36.4%	5 22.7%	3 13.6%	3 13.6%	22 100.0%
49% or less	1 6.3%	2 12.5%	4 25.0%	7 43.8%	2 12.5%	16 100.0%
Total	11 18.3%	22 36.7%	11 18.3%	11 18.3%	5 8.3%	60 100.0%

B and D) both attended fewer classes and were amongst the poorer performers.

Overall these results should, however, be seen in a positive light as they demonstrate that there is a strong and statistically significant relationship between class attendance and performance. The average performance of those forty learners who attended all six classes and even those fifteen who attended only five classes is significantly higher than those who attended only three or four classes.

We were next interested in the extent to which good performance on the baseline test paves the way for good performance on subsequent tests, and how learners group accordingly. To do this, we produced a cross-tabulation between the learners' baseline test performance and their average performance in the progress tests, where both sets of performance scores are grouped in terms of intervals (see Table 10.6). We have shaded and used different patterns to highlight the most interesting subgroups of learners:

- The cells with a fine grid refer to those four learners who generally did worse as the year went on. One learner got a score of between 60% and 69% on his baseline but his average score for the year fell to between 50% and 59%. The other three learners also moved one interval down.
- The 'darkly shaded' cell learners maintained their performance levels.
- The 'lightly shaded' cell learners on averaged improved their performance by one interval level.
- The 'left diagonal' cell learners are the star performers and improved their performance between 20% and 40%.

From a resilience perspective, it is important to better understand these twenty-two star performance learners (see Table 10.7).

These findings reveal two interesting trends. First, it is clear that the learners who improved most (30–40%) are overwhelmingly Xhosa-speaking and from the newly added schools. Five of the six learners who improved this much fall into this category. Second, half (11) are from the newly added schools and the remaining eleven from the 2004 grade 6 catch-up class. This means that half of the learners (11 out of 22) who were selected from the newly added schools improved considerably. In comparison, eleven out of thirty-eight learners from the 2004 Catch-up class (29%) did considerably better. But of course the average baseline performance of these two groups was significantly different: the mean score of the 2004 Catch-up learners on the baseline test was 58.8% and that of the learners from the newly added schools only 39.8%. What our analysis shows is that the initial gap between these two groups of learners has now closed considerably, and this is perhaps the best indication of the value of the Catch-up classes.

SAILI Educators

Just as success among learners in schools is highly dependent on teachers' knowledge transfer skills in schools, success among learners

Table 10.7 Profile of 22 learners who improved substantially from baseline to progress tests

Teacher	Learner	Gender	Language	% Improvement	Improvement
M	A	Male	Xhosa	40	49% or less to 80–100%
B	B	Male	Xhosa	30	49% or less to 70–79%
B	C	Male	Afrikaans	30	50–59% to 80–100%
M	D	Female	Xhosa	30	50–59% to 80–100%
M	E	Male	Xhosa	30	50–59% to 80–100%
B	F	Female	Xhosa	30	49% or less to 70–79%
B	G	Female	Afrikaans	20	50–59% to 70–79%
B	H	Female	Afrikaans	20	60–69% to 80–100%
B	I	Female	Xhosa	20	49% or less to 60–69%
B	J	Female	Xhosa	20	50–59% to 70–79%
B	K	Female	Xhosa	20	49% or less to 60–69%
M	L	Female	Xhosa	20	49% or less to 60–69%
B	M	Female	Xhosa	20	60–69% to 80–100%
M	N	Male	Afrikaans	20	49% or less to 60–69%
M	O	Male	Afrikaans	20	50–59% to 70–79%)
B	P	Male	Afrikaans	20	50–59% to 70–79%
M	Q	Female	English	20	60–69% to 80–100%
M	R	Female	English	20	60–69% to 80–100%
M	S	Female	Afrikaans	20	50–59% to 70–79%
B	T	Male	Afrikaans	20	50–59% to 70–79%
M	U	Female	Xhosa	20	50–59% to 70–79%
B	V	Female	Xhosa	20	50–59% to 70–79%

participating in this program is dependent on the knowledge transfer skills of SAILI educators. This then needed to be examined, as well as educators' sensitivity to learners' knowledge and skill levels. In order to do this, a research assistant under the supervision of the authors attended two Catch-up sessions in June.

Her observation reports indicated that both facilitators displayed the necessary content knowledge needed for the session. More importantly, educators exhibited a keen understanding of learners' needs throughout the sessions, as the following excerpts from the reports indicate:

- 'The educator exhibited a positive attitude that was conducive to learning. He encouraged learners to work through their tasks. He presented his lessons with much enthusiasm and treated all the students with respect. He used language that the children could understand.'
- 'The educator facilitated the learners in a way that did not allow for much time wasting but rather maximized the amount of time that the

learners spent on a particular task. The learners were busy with their tasks when required to do so.'
- 'When the learners showed signs of fatigue the educators involved them in a short but lively physical activity.'
- 'The educator noted or asked questions to find out whether the learners had understood the work (e.g., "Is this answer correct? Who is having a problem with number 13? What answer do you have? Do you know how to find the square root?"). She would then explain how to find the answer using the chalkboard.'

The observer was also able to develop a list of recommendations for the educators in relation to the learners' needs as they were observed in the sessions in relation to the educators' skill sets. Some of these were:

- Include more examples with answers to act as a learning guide.
- Display visual aids that reinforce key aspects of the various topics at hand (e.g. what is meant by a factor and a product, and include examples).
- Arrange items from simple to more difficult and include smaller sequential steps.
- Retain the combination of the test items but make the first fifteen items far easier than the rest (i.e., differentiation). This may provide interesting information because the learners should obtain more than 60% or 80% in this section. It may also provide encouragement to 'struggling' learners to know that they could cope with the first part of the test.
- If something has just been explained, ask different learners to express their understanding on a regular basis (e.g. 'What did Anne just say?' '*Why* is it important?' '*Why* did she make that statement/ give that answer?' 'Do you agree with her explanation? Why?' 'Write down in your own words what Peter has just said,' 'Read your statement back to me.').

An Assessment of the Catch-Up Classes

We return in this section to a preliminary assessment of the Catch-up classes. Our reference point is the 'conditions of success' framework above (Table 10.1). We discuss each of the conditions briefly.

Condition 1: Catch-up sessions are based on actual learner needs. Our results from one year's evaluation indicated that the catch-up sessions were meeting learner needs, as the overall performance of the majority of learners improved. This was also evidenced by the fact that twenty-two out of the sixty learners have improved substantially beyond their baseline performance (20%+).

Condition 2: There are sufficient workshops to allow for a positive impact on learners' knowledge and skills. It was not possible to come to an unequivocal judgment on whether the workshops are sufficient after one year's assessment. There were still a significant – although small – number of learners who failed the tests, which would suggest that they need additional support. On the other hand, we have seen that there is a clear correlation between workshop attendance and performance. More to the point, those learners who attended all six workshops on average performed best.

Condition 3: Attendance levels at workshops are high. The majority of learners attended all or most of the workshops. By the middle of the year it would seem that less than 10% of learners had dropped out or were not attending all workshops.

Condition 4: Facilitators are able to transfer necessary knowledge and skills to learners. Observations show that the educators are generally sensitive to learners' needs and thus should be able to transfer critical knowledge and skills needed for the grade 7 year.

Condition 5: Assessment of learners' knowledge and skills occurs on an ongoing basis and is used for teaching purposes. Table 10.4 shows the results of four progress tests that were administered between the beginning of May and the end of June. In addition to these standardized tests, learners were given homework assignments on a regular basis. Table 10.8 provides information on the dates and topic of the homework assignments of learners and the distribution of learners in Group B who passed or failed. The same information for learners in Group M is summarized in Table 10.9.

Condition 7: Selection processes (Catch-up) carried out by SAILI result in appropriate learners to feed the learner placement program (LPP). Our discussion of the selection processes above has pointed to some possible difficulties and challenges for the future. At this point our assessment is that we need to reflect more on whether this condition is being addressed correctly or whether it requires adjustment. The end-of-year results might shed further light on this matter.

Table 10.8 Performance on Homework Assignments, Group B (% Pass/Fail)

Code	Date	Pass		Fail		Total	
		Count	%	Count	%	Count	%
B1	23 April	23	79.3%	6	20.7%	29	100.0%
B2	23 April	23	79.3%	6	20.7%	29	100.0%
B3	23 April	25	86.2%	4	13.8%	29	100.0%
B4	7 May	28	96.6%	1	3.4%	29	100.0%
B5	7 May	9	30.0%	21	70.0%	30	100.0%
B6	7 May	17	56.7%	13	43.3%	30	100.0%
B7	7 May	22	75.9%	7	24.1%	29	100.0%
B8	21 May	25	86.2%	4	13.8%	29	100.0%
B9	21 May	13	46.4%	15	53.6%	28	100.0%
B10	4 June	24	82.8%	5	17.2%	29	100.0%
B11	4 June	24	82.8%	5	17.2%	29	100.0%
B12	11 June	20	74.1%	7	25.9%	27	100.0%
B13	11 June	22	81.5%	5	18.5%	27	100.0%

Conclusion

The aims of this chapter were twofold: first, to highlight the very adverse conditions under which primary school interventions in South Africa are typically implemented; and second, how evaluations of such interventions have to be adapted to these circumstances in order to be useful to the program staff. We comment, in conclusion, on these two issues.

The very poor performance of South African learners, especially those from disadvantaged backgrounds, in mathematics and science remains a major concern for educational authorities in the country. Our discussion of one intervention that was aimed at redressing this situation through the mode of Catch-up classes has highlighted the huge constraints under which such programs are implemented. The learners in these programs are typically disadvantaged. They are often in schools that are both poorly resourced in physical terms (overpopulated classrooms, inadequate physical facilities and laboratories, lack of sufficient textbooks) and – more importantly – they are 'taught' by teachers who themselves are poorly trained and often do not have sufficient knowledge of mathematics and science. The Catch-up program discussed in this chapter is one attempt to deal with all of these con-

Table 10.9 Performance on Homework Assignments, Group M (% Pass/Fail)

Code	Date	Pass		Fail		Total	
		Count	%	Count	%	Count	%
M1	9 April	28	100.0%	0	0.0%	28	100.0%
M2	9 April	28	100.0%	0	0.0%	28	100.0%
M3	9 April	27	96.4%	1	3.6%	28	100.0%
M4	9 April	25	89.3%	3	10.7%	28	100.0%
M5	23 April	26	89.7%	3	10.3%	29	100.0%
M6	23 April	26	86.7%	4	13.3%	30	100.0%
M7	23 April	28	93.3%	2	6.7%	30	100.0%
M8	7 May	26	89.7%	3	10.3%	29	100.0%
M9	7 May	22	75.9%	7	24.1%	29	100.0%
M10	21 May	25	86.2%	4	13.8%	29	100.0%
M11	21 May	16	61.5%	10	38.5%	26	100.0%
M12	4 June	16	57.1%	12	42.9%	28	100.0%
M13	4 June	15	51.7%	14	48.3%	29	100.0%
M14	11 June	19	63.3%	11	36.7%	30	100.0%
M15	11 June	24	80.0%	6	20.0%	30	100.0%
M16	11 June	17	56.7%	13	43.3%	30	100.0%

straining conditions through a direct intervention aimed at a select group of black and coloured learners.

Traditional evaluation designs aimed at assessing school interventions assume either strict experimental conditions (random assignment, pre- and post-test testing, and control groups) or sufficiently large numbers of participants to enable the application of robust statistical tests. Neither of these options was available to us. The evaluation design and studies conducted were distinctive in three ways:

- the commitment to a theory-driven evaluation approach;
- the integration of statistical and qualitative data in the final assessment of the program; and
- the focus on individual-level results in order to provide formative feedback to program staff.

We engaged with the SAILI program staff from the outset around the development and clarification of the underlying program theory. This does not apply to the Catch-up program only, but also to the overarching program. The final program theory (as presented in Figure 10.1) was developed by the program staff themselves. We then 'translated' this into the analytical framework where we identified the individual conditions of success (Table 10.1) that guided our subsequent data collection and analysis. The obvious advantage of this approach is that it made it much easier for program staff to understand and appropriate our final evaluation results and recommendations that followed this framework.

With a relatively small but intensive program such as this, we have previously found that any statistical information needs to be augmented by various kinds of qualitative information. In this case, we have questionnaire data on learners (including open-ended responses), learner profile information, as well as observations of training sessions. By combining this information with the learner performance results, we were again able to build a more balanced composite picture of the intervention.

Finally, our focus on individual-level performance and the progression of individual learners (those who regressed and those who performed quite brilliantly) was necessitated by various concerns. Most importantly, however, the overriding concern was to provide formative results to the program staff. They needed to know which learners were doing well and which were doing poorly, and whether this was related more to matters of attendance or prior selection or socio-economic background or a combination of these factors. It is not commonplace for program evaluations to focus on this level of detail, but the nature of the program and the demands of the program staff dictated such an approach.

Interventions that are aimed at the most disadvantaged in our society often require non-standard and innovative approaches to teaching and learning. Similarly, evaluations of such interventions have to leave textbook models of program evaluations aside and focus on designing and conducting evaluations that are sensitive to the context of the learners (in this case) and the program staff.

Notes

This chapter is based on various evaluation studies conducted during the period 2002–2005 for SAILI. The authors wish to acknowledge the substantial input to all of these reports of Nelius Boshoff and other research assistants. We also wish to extend our appreciation to the staff of SAILI and the director,

Robbie Gow-Kleinschmidt, for their cooperation in all of the evaluation activities.

1   Non-governmental organizations are organizations that are not part of government and include a wide group of organizations from large charitable NGOs like Child Welfare to small community organizations like sports or civics clubs.
2   As our involvement with SAILI ended in 2006 and SAILI's intervention model has since changed, this paper discusses SAILI and its programs in the past tense. However, SAILI continues with its programs in the schools.
3   The racial category of 'coloured' refers to South African individuals of mixed-race origins. The term is socially constructed and is important in understanding the continuing legacy of apartheid (Shefer, Strebel, & Foster, 2000; Swartz, Gibson, & Gelman, 2002).

References

Department of Education. (2004) *National strategy for mathematics, science and technology education.* Pretoria: Department of Education.

Department of Science and Technology. (2002). *South Africa's national research and development strategy.* Pretoria: Department of Science and Technology.

ERA (2004). SAILI Final Evaluation Report. Cape Town: ERA.

Gilligan, R. (2000). Adversity, resilience and young people: The protective value of positive school and spare time experiences. *Children & Society, 14,* 37–47.

Johnson, M.K., Crosnoe, R., & Elder, G.H. (2001). Student's attachment and academic engagement: The role of race and ethnicity. *Sociology of Education, 74(4),* 318–40.

Kahn, M.J. (2004). For whom the school bell tolls: Disparities in performance in senior certificate mathematics and physical science. *Perspectives in Education, 22(1),* 149–56.

Kahn, M.J. (2006). Matric matters. In V. Reddy (Ed.), *Marking matric* (pp. 127–38). Cape Town: HSRC Press.

Kramer, R.C. (2000). Poverty, inequality and youth violence. *The Annals of the American Academy of Political and Social Science, 567,* 123–39.

Krovetz, M.L. 1999. Resiliency: A key element for supporting youth at-risk. *Clearing House, 73(2),* 121–3.

Lee, N. (2001). *Childhood and society: Growing up in an age of uncertainty.* Maidenhead, Berkshire: Open University Press.

Maguin, E., & Loeber, R. (1996). Academic performance and delinquency. In M. Tonry (Ed.), *Crime and justice: A review of the research*, vol. 20 (pp. 145–264). Chicago: University of Chicago Press.

Murray Nettles, S., Mucherah, W., & Jones, D.S. 2000. Understanding resilience: The role of social resources. *Journal of Education for Students Placed at Risk*, 5(1/2), 47–60.

Reddy, V. (2006a). The state of mathematics and science education: Schools are not equal. In S. Buhlungu, J. Daniel, R. Southall, & J. Lutchman (Eds.), *State of the nation: South Africa 2005–2006* (pp. 392–416). Cape Town: HSRC Press.

Reddy, V. (2006b). *Mathematics and science achievement at South African schools in TIMSS 2003.* Pretoria: Human Sciences Research Council.

Shefer, T., Strebel, A., & Foster, D. (2000). 'So women have to submit to that': Discourses of power and violence in student's talk on heterosexual negotiation. *South African Journal of Psychology*, 30(2), 11–19.

Stober, Paul. (26 August 1994). *Weekly Mail.*

Swartz, L., Gibson, K., & Gelman, T. (Eds.). (2002). *Reflective practice: Psychodynamic ideas in the community.* Cape Town: Human Sciences Research Council.

Taylor, N., Vinjevold, P., & Muller, J. (2003) *Getting schools working.* Cape Town: Pearson Education.

11 A Sample Research Proposal for a Mixed-Methods Investigation of Resilience: The Pathways to Resilience Project

MICHAEL UNGAR

For students and researchers who are hoping to conduct research in the field of resilience, the conceptual terrain covered in this text can help guide decisions regarding methods, sampling, participation, and ethics. Still, researchers new to this field (and even seasoned pros) may wonder what a research project looks like in its entirety. In this chapter, I will demonstrate how one might design a mixed-methods study to investigate resilience that reflects the key methodological considerations discussed in the accompanying chapters. What follows is the abbreviated text of an actual funded proposal for an investigation of resilience.

The research upon which this chapter is based is now funded and ongoing. The proposal was favourably reviewed by a number of anonymous reviewers nationally. It has also had the benefit of being critiqued by the project's many community partners, which include regional and national organizations comprising academics, advocates, and practitioners.

First Steps

Development of a proposal such as this is not simple; nor is securing funding. The process always begins with a question. In this case, my clinical work with at-risk youth and families across numerous service delivery systems led me to suspect that resilience was more than an individual trait. I speculated, based on earlier research, that it was a condition that reflected how well service providers made available and accessible the resources young people need to thrive (Ungar, 2005). Specifically, I was curious about how the service use patterns of young people influenced their resilience.

With that question in mind, I began to investigate the best way to design a study. As often happens in such cases, serendipity brought opportunity. I was contracted to do some consulting and training with a regional organization that has a mandate to coordinate services for young people. Most relevant to this research, the organization was seeking ways to understand how they could intervene better. They already had a network of alliances formed with senior administrators in four key service areas: child welfare, mental health, corrections, and education. While the research I detail in this chapter is not a program evaluation, the data could help to inform policy and practice. With my question firmly in mind, and a window of opportunity present to carry out the research, I could advance to step two, creating partnerships and gaining access to participants.

Third, I needed to develop a methodology in collaboration with my academic and community colleagues. While methodological choices should follow from research questions, it is naive to assume that decisions regarding methods are always blind to the politics of choice. In this case, though the questions were likely best addressed by a series of case studies, qualitative interviews, and case file reviews, the project's partners valued quantitative research as well. Funding sources too, especially in the area of health, would be unlikely to fund research that was only qualitative, at least not at the level that was required to carry out such an intense and complex investigation. As I have discussed elsewhere (Ungar, 2006b), these are very real considerations, and mixed-methods solutions can often solve both methodological and funding problems. As well, as many of the partners themselves valued one method over the other, employing a mixed-methods design was a prudent way to proceed.

Through conversations with the community partners, and by bringing together researchers with complementary areas of research expertise, a team was built that could carry out the design and implementation of the research. Face-to-face meetings were held to develop the research questions further and explore appropriate methods, including developing a sampling design, choosing instruments, developing interview guides, and planning for knowledge transfer.

The final project, as presented here, is adapted for the purposes of illustration. The actual Pathways to Resilience Project (see www.resilienceresearch.org) is more complex in its multisite, cross-cultural design. The names and details of the organizations involved have been changed as well. This simplified version, though still complex as most resilience research tends to be, is meant to illustrate the nuts and bolts of research design. I highlight the key points requiring consideration and some of the team's solutions to issues of access, confidentiality, participation, ownership, sampling, analysis, and dissemination of results.

It is not perfect. It is instead the result of a coordinated effort to answer specific research questions in a particular research context. A more qualitative investigation might have included more participatory methods; a more quantitative approach might have permitted greater use of standardized measures. My experience tells me that different research teams would likely make very different methodological choices.

Sample Project Title:

Pathways to Resilience: A Mixed-Method Investigation of the Negotiations for Health Resources among At-Risk Children and Their Families Who Experience Concurrent Child Welfare, Mental Health, Correctional, and Educational Services

Purpose of the Research Project:
The purpose of this research is to explore both the pathways children and youth travel through life that lead to involvement with multiple service providers and the pathways that protect them from that involvement. It will investigate differences in how youth identified as both resilient and non-resilient 'negotiate' for the social determinants of health (e.g., secure attachments to caregivers, a sense of belonging to their community, personal control, adequate housing and educational opportunities) with their families, community organizations, and service delivery systems that provide them support, treatment, and care.

For our purposes, resilience is understood ecologically. An ecological perspective implicates those mandated to help, such as social workers, educators, child and youth care workers, and psychologists, in the process of intervening to provide an opportunity structure around a child for that child to realize his or her potential. Therefore, resilience is defined as:

• The capacity of individuals to navigate their way to resources that sustain well-being

- The capacity of individuals' physical and social ecologies to provide those resources, and
- The capacity of individuals, their families, and communities to negotiate culturally meaningful ways for resources to be shared (Ungar, 2008).

Four service delivery systems that most influence access to social and psychological determinants of children's well-being (child welfare, mental health, corrections, and education) in one region have agreed to participate and provide access to youth across all four service delivery systems and community non-governmental organizations. Combined, these four systems, along with the non-mandated community agencies, are intended to help children facing multiple risks and to promote healthy development under stress. This research, then, will conduct a cross-sectional survey of young people and their caregivers, and conduct in-depth interviews and file reviews across service providers for a sub-sample of youth found to be resilient and non-resilient on standardized measures.

Comment: The initial statement of purpose outlines the focus of the research and defines the core concept of resilience. As resilience research is often applied research, intending to inform policy and practice, the emphasis here is on the potential for the application of the findings to practice. Working with community partners, this link was emphasized by them as an important reason for their willingness to participate. This was information they wanted as much or more than the research team.

Defining the Problem and the Research Plan

To date very little study has been done on resilience that looks at the systems of care mandated to service at-risk children. What work has been done either focuses on the psychological determinants of resilience or the effectiveness of single interventions (i.e., intensive home-based family interventions by corrections [Quinn, 2004], school based anti-bullying programs [Pepler & Slaby, 1994], family group conferencing in child welfare [Burford & Hudson, 2000]). Children's pathways through multiple services to health remain largely unknown, even though we have documented that our most at-risk children and youth form a disproportionately high percentage of clients of more than one mandated service. This research will therefore address these needs not only by identifying and analysing gaps in current knowledge, but also through a strategy for knowledge dissemination, ensuring that results are returned to children, families, service providers, and policy makers.

In order to understand how children and families 'navigate' (a term used during piloting of this research design) their way through human services delivery systems and non-formal and formal community services, marshalling together the resources they need to sustain well-being and support healthy pro-social development, we have developed partnerships with an umbrella organization that has a well-established relationship with multiple service providers and community agencies. This umbrella organization fulfils case planning, program design, research, and system management roles in the region. In addition, because the research will involve a large number of youth from Aboriginal populations who are residents in the region, leaders from their community are particularly interested in the results of the research. Therefore, the research is being conducted in partnership with their community services department as well.

Comment: The problem is defined in more detail in this section. Findings from any prior work that informs the study are outlined. The emphasis is clearly on the participation of key partners. In particular, it is emphasized that through these collaborations, access to participants and their service records, a contentious part of the design, is to be made possible. As well, the cultural diversity of the sample is assured through the partnership with a regional Aboriginal community social service organization. This partnership recognizes the need to acknowledge early in the research process who might most benefit from the research, and whose participation needs to be ensured. In this particular organization's case, a move towards self-government and the federal government's divestment of social services back to Aboriginal communities have made research that looks at what services and service use patterns are most helpful to youth at-risk a timely endeavour.

Research Questions and Hypotheses

In order to understand the pathways children and youth travel through life that lead to involvement with correctional services, as well as the pathways that protect them from that involvement, six primary questions guide this research:

1 What are at-risk children's patterns of service utilization?
2 Which patterns of service utilization are most predictive of involvement with primary, secondary, and tertiary levels of care and service?
3 How does service utilization and the provision of services affect children's abilities to overcome adversity and socially determine well-being?
4 According to children and their caregivers, what combination of intervention strategies is most effective in their support and treatment?
5 How do at-risk children construct for themselves identities as healthy and resilient as they negotiate for health resources with families, communities, and service providers?
6 What collaborative role can family and health care professionals play in the provision of primary, secondary, and tertiary levels of child welfare, mental health, correctional and educational services?

This study will help agencies better understand the service needs of at-risk children and youth, contributing to recommendations regarding effective use of limited resources to promote the social determinants of health in at-risk child populations.

Specifically, the research team hypothesizes:

1 Resilience is dependent upon integrated services being offered to at-risk children and their families in ways tailored to their culture and context.
2 Children who are provided access to integrated social welfare, educational, correctional, and recreational services will score higher on measures of resilience.
3 Youth who construct an identity as resilient will perceive themselves as having exercised personal agency over how

services were accessed and their level of participation in each.
4 Families and communities play an important role in sustaining resilience in at-risk children even when children are in out-of-home placement (i.e., in custody) or receiving specialized care or support.

Comment: Answering these questions requires both qualitative and quantitative methods. Searching for how children 'construct for themselves identities' is evidently best done qualitatively. Understanding 'which patterns of service utilization are most predictive of involvement with primary, secondary, and tertiary levels of care and service' is a question best answered using quantitative methods. The fluidity between questions mirrors the intent to conduct a mixed-methods study. The questions and hypotheses reflect both the researchers' and community members' needs. Using mixed methods will help to reassure community members the data will be both generalizable (and therefore seen as useful by funders) and contextually relevant enough for front-line practitioners to see the results as meaningful.

Literature Review

Though coordinated systems of care are mandated to respond to children's adversity, we know little about the vagaries of children's developmental trajectories through these systems (Henry et al., 1999; Jackson & Martin, 1998). This study focuses on understanding resilience as a comprehensive theory that encompasses a broad ecology of health, exploring the interface between social and individual health determinants. Some of the best-known efforts in this area are by Epstein and his colleagues at the University of South Florida (Epstein et al., 2001; Epstein & Sharma, 1998) and others who have designed instruments to examine health-related phenomena in children (see Goodman, 1997). Such positive advances aside, there remain consistent calls for better research on systems of care. Specifically, McCubbin et al. (1998) write: 'Although the use of both qualitative and quantitative data-gathering techniques may be desirable, it seems that an interdisci-plinary, multi-method approach may generate the most exciting data' (p. 44). A number of respected researchers are calling for mixed designs sensitive to temporal issues similar to that to be employed in this study, but unburdened by the demands of multiyear longitudinal approaches (Garland et al., 2001; Swenson & Kolko, 2000).

There has been a tendency to dismiss the potential contribution from qualitative methods among risk and resilience researchers (Morgan, 1998; Morse, Swanson & Kuzel, 2001; Ungar, 2002b). The present study seeks to show that methodologically a combination of quantitative methods, qualitative interviews, and the coordinated reviews of clients' records across multiple services can provide good-quality integrated data. To the team's knowledge, this has never been done as extensively as is proposed here. One notable exception is a study of 6,449 males and 6,268 females born in Stockholm in 1953 (Kratzer & Hodgins, 1997). Though methodologically weak, having relied heavily on self-reports, that study did combine teacher ratings of the children in grades 6 and 9, along with the cursory reviews of school, mental health, corrections, and child welfare files to track individuals' service histories. Research that employs more rigorous and thorough onsite file reviews has been shown to be effective in documenting the experiences of children with severe emotional disorders and their use of special education and child welfare services (Malmgren & Meisel, 2002).

Our design takes up the call for the comprehensive study of the four service delivery systems that are the focus of this research (see Pazaratz et al., 1999). Though disjointed, it is important to note that studies to date have linked youth participation in multiple service delivery systems. The youth most in trouble with the law are often found to be in the greatest need of mental health services and responsive foster care providers (Conger & Armstrong, 2002; Murphy, 2002). Similarly, homeless youth and children in care require intensive case management and mental health supports (Cauce et al., 1998; Litrownik et al., 1999). Juvenile justice programs require stronger connections with public schools to achieve effective reintegration when discharging youth to their communities (Hellriegel & Yates, 1999). Child welfare clients are often shown to be in need of mental health care and have higher rates of service utilization (Arcelus, Bellberby, & Vostanis, 1999; Haapasalo, 2000; Kroll et al., 2002; Webb & Harden, 2003) as well as needing access to a myriad of other support services such as special schools and responsive court systems (Dohrn, 2002; Sagatun-Edwards & Saylor, 2000; Saathoff & Stoffel, 1999; Wilson & Melton, 2002). In understanding these pathways through systems, the family's role must also be considered (Cook-Morales, 2002). To date, families' experiences of negotiating with systems for the care of their children have been largely unstudied (Christian & Gilvarry, 1999; Rose, 2002; Ungar, 2002a, 2004; Walter & Petr, 2000; Whittaker, 2000).

Comment: The literature review often has to accomplish several goals. It must inform the reader of the substantive area of study. It must convince them that the study of resilience is a worthwhile endeavour, complementary to the more conventionally funded research dealing with disorder. It must also set the stage for why the methodology chosen fits with this particular study. Thus, it is justified in discussing the use of qualitative and mixed-methods approaches in order to inform funders of the benefits of these approaches, especially if one expects reviewers to be more familiar with quantitative methods. The literature review may also be used to identify gaps in knowledge along with what are the dominant research questions troubling the field. Funders, of course, want to see continuity between this research proposal and previous scientific advances. While innovation is appreciated, methodologies that are too divergent in a field of study like resilience, which is already seen as unconventional, may result in reviewers being asked to stretch too far and result in negative reviews.

Study Design and Research Methodology

The Pathways to Resilience research project has three phases: (1) negotiating entry, building cultural sensitivity, and establishing the methodological design; (2) study implementation and data collection; and (3) dissemination and building community capacity.

Phase 1: Negotiating entry, building cultural sensitivity, and establishing methodological design

The Pathways to Resilience Project seeks to create a collaborative management structure. Figure 11.1 shows the relationships between co-applicants, advisory committee (members to be drawn from community organizations, parent groups and, when appropriate, youth themselves), site researchers, service providers, and the community participants.

Figure 11.1: Pathways to Resilience Management Structure

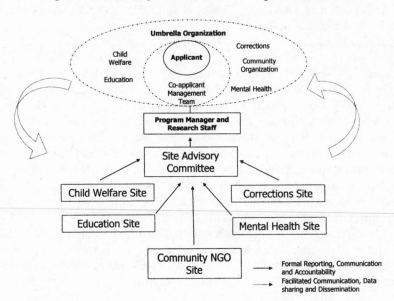

Sites and entry: The umbrella organization, the Regional Youth Services Group (RYSG), is a youth assessment and treatment program that has successfully operated for over five years coordinating services among providers through regional service committees. It brings to the sample rural/urban and cultural (Aboriginal and non-Aboriginal) diversity through the population of young people served by the member organizations. A separate affiliation is also included with a group representing a coalition of regional First Nations communities (the CRFN).

The umbrella organization has committed to facilitating access to the four individual service providers, child welfare, mental health, corrections, and education, in each site. These will be termed mandated services. In order to understand pathways to resilience among at-risk youth not under service mandates (a non-clinical sample), one community non-governmental organization in each research site will be included (these may be a provider of supports to street youth, Alateen group, or recreation centres where at-risk youth participate in non-mandated programming). These will be termed non-mandated services. When necessary, all documents will be translated into the language of participants.

Community consultation: With the assistance of the community advisory committee and a locally hired site researcher, the applicant, co-investigators, and a project research manager hired to manage the project will negotiate with each of the four mandated agencies and one non-mandated service provider in each site concerning final conditions of entry.

Comment: Striving for a congruency between process and content, the design seeks to establish the conditions where the research itself builds the capacity of the organizations involved. There are many reasons to promote this approach. Not only do the data promise to better reflect the conceptual understanding of resilience by those involved, but early negotiation and participation by community members ensure that results inform policy and practice. In this way, there is a focus on helping youth become resilient, along with their communities.

Methodological Design

The methodology discussed here was successfully piloted in two previous studies (Ungar, 2008; Ungar, Karabanow, & MacDonald, 2002). The second took place in both correctional and child welfare settings (Ungar, Teram, & Picketts, 2001). In both those studies two to eight youths were successfully engaged in file reviews and interviews were conducted with the youth and their caregivers. Though exploratory and therefore qualitative only, both studies successfully navigated through the many ethical and procedural problems in engaging at-risk youth in research across multiple service settings, accessing service records, and conducting mixed-methods research. Figure 11.2 shows the sequence of methods to be used, integrating both the qualitative and quantitative research phases of the research.

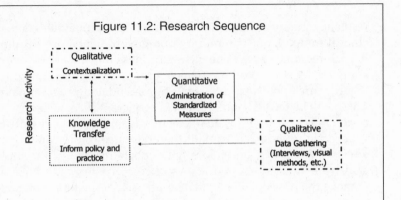

Figure 11.2: Research Sequence

Contextualizing the Research Instruments,
Interview Guides, and Protocols

The advisory committees, assisted by others locally with an interest in this research, will be asked to discuss the best way to integrate the research into their communities, including how to select participants and where and how to engage with them. A meeting of all team members, both academics and community members, will be used to finalize decisions regarding study guides, measures, and protocols.

Comment: Reviewers will need a brief explanation of how the methods will be integrated and of the role of the advisory committee. Both aspects of the research ensure the research will produce both an authentic representation of the experiences of youth and generalizable results. In this way, researchers may strike a balance between generating substantive theory qualitatively, theory that details this particular group of individuals' experiences, and data that support the generalizability of some aspects of the theory generated.

Research Tools

Quantitative Instruments

The Youth Measures
The Child and Youth Resilience Measure (CYRM) is a twenty-eight-item instrument that has been validated with a purposeful sample

of 1,451 youth growing up facing diverse types of adversity in eleven countries (Canada, US, Colombia, China, India, Russia, Palestine, Israel, Tanzania, the Gambia, South Africa) (Ungar, Lee, et al., 2005; Ungar & Liebenberg, 2005).

Youth Resiliency: Assessing Developmental Strengths Questionnaire (YR:ADS) is a thirty-one-domain, 145-item questionnaire that has been successfully used with population-based school populations across Canada in Aboriginal and non-Aboriginal youth. The measure is meant to generate a profile of either individual strengths or population strengths when results are pooled. An abbreviated version will be used.

Life Events Checklist adapted from the Life Experiences Survey by Johnson and McCutcheon (1980) was one of the first checklists specifically designed for children and adolescents. The Life Events Checklist (LEC) consists of forty-six events (with spaces to identify additional events that have had an impact on the child or adolescent's life), identification of the event as either good or bad, and a rating of the impact or effect the event had on the child/adolescent's life.

Youth Services Survey (Hernandez et al., 2001; Hernandez, Gomez, & Worthington, 2002) assesses a youth's satisfaction with services as a whole over a specified time period. This measure will be used to assess the services the youth report as being the most helpful and the service that was the least.

The Person Most Knowledgeable (PMK) Measures:
The Resilient Child Caregiver Report is a fifty-six-question adaptation of the CYRM, designed for use by primary caregivers of at-risk youth (Ungar, 2006a). The instrument triangulates the data on the CYRM by asking caregivers who know the child well for their perspectives on the child's resilience (or vulnerability).

Multi-Sector Service Contacts: This assesses the types of amounts of services children and families receive across different service settings as well as the caregiver's perceptions about whether services met the child's and family's needs.

Youth Services Survey for Families: As with the measure for youth, PMKs will be asked to rate the two services identified by the youth. They will not be told which was classified as the youth's most and least helpful service provider.

Cultural Competence and Service Provision Questionnaire: As cultural and contextual factors are an important component of this research, we will use the CCSP to assess the impact of a family's racial/ethnic customs, practices, and traditions to determine whether services were delivered in a culturally competent manner.

Final selection of items will come from these measures with consultations ongoing with community partners. The final questionnaire will be designed for administration in under fifty minutes for both children and adults and be appropriately worded for children of this age. Questionnaires administered to the adult key informants nominated by the youth will be administered without the youth present and the information gathered kept confidential one from the other.

Qualitative Methods

A number of youth from each service in each site will be invited to participate in the qualitative aspects of the study (see below for sample selection criteria). Beyond interviews, which will be taped and transcribed, summary file reviews for the child across each system in which the child was a client/patient/student/resident will also be carried out. In this way a detailed case history will be accurately constructed for a subsample of forty youth.

Qualitative interviews and other data collection methods will focus on the youth's experience of their families and service providers, the multiple risk factors they identify in their lives, their definitions of successful outcomes, their understanding of mental health, and their proposals for effective service delivery. Whenever possible, researchers are to be of the same culture as participants, or trained by the applicant and collaborators in culturally sensitive research methods.

Where appropriate, transcripts of the interviews with each youth (or detailed notes made by the researcher) will be sent back to the youth (or shared with them verbally where literacy is an issue) for comment and clarification.

A series of focus groups will be conducted at the end of the project to solicit comments on findings. Participants will be drawn from across the population of stakeholders (youth, service providers, community service clubs, etc.).

Comment: The methods are described in detail. The actual proposal upon which this chapter is based has lengthier descriptions of the tools and procedures than is detailed here. In general, reviewers want to see enough detail, within the page limits of the proposal, to convince them that the choice of measures and procedures will answer the research questions. It is not uncommon for reviewers to be unfamiliar with resilience measures, or qualitative techniques. The onus is on the research team to provide sufficient information to convince the reviewers that despite the relative newness of the field, the methods are sound and the mixing of quantitative and qualitative approaches is justified.

Phase 2: Study Implementation, Subject Recruitment, and Data Collection

Quantitative phase
Front-line workers with each service will be asked to nominate youth to the study who meet the following selection criteria: (1) youth participants must be between the ages of fourteen and twenty-one; (2) the youth must have the potential to have a person most knowledgeable (PMK), or guardian, take part in the study; and (3) the youth must have been associated with at least one other service delivery system (child welfare, mental health, corrections, oreducation) in addition to the system nominating the youth to the study. In the case of participant nominations by the education system, the youth must have had a service provided to them beyond the classroom teacher; for example, they must have received some special intervention, education plan, or counselling.

Quantitative phase participants and sample selection
A sample of forty youth ages fourteen to seventeen (twenty boys and twenty girls) from each of the four mandated services (CW, MH, C, E) and non-mandated service (NS) will be invited to participate, along with one of their caregivers (PMK nominated by the youth).

Qualitative phase participants and sample selection
For the qualitative part of the research we will select youth based on both their CYRM and LEC scores. As qualitative methods are

more concerned with youth perceptions than those of adults, only the youth scores will be used for the purposes of sampling. A purposeful stratified sample will be created by splitting all youth into two groups: those who score at or above the median on the LEC for their particular service cohort and those who score below. These two groups may be thought of as being at high and low risk. From each risk group, youth will be selected, based on their gender and score on the CYRM. For example, among the boys to be sampled from child welfare, four boys scoring highest on the LEC (a measure of the risks they face) will be selected, distinguished by their high or low scores on the CYRM (a measure of their resilience). Youth with the two highest and two lowest CYRM scores will be invited to participate in the qualitative data collection phase. Should a youth decline, the youth with the next highest or lowest score will be selected, and so on (see Tables 11.2 and 11.3).

Table 11.2: Quantitative Sample (*N* = 200)

	Sites				
	CW	MH	C	E	NS
Quantitative Sample	40	40	40	40	40

Table 11.3: Qualitative Sample (*N* = 40)

	Sites				
	CW	MH	C	E	NS
Quantitative Sample	40	40	40	40	40
High LEC/High CYRM					
• Boys	2	2	2	2	2
• Girls	2	2	2	2	2
High LEC/Low CYRM					
• Boys	2	2	2	2	2
• Girls	2	2	2	2	2
Total Qualitative	8	8	8	8	8

Names and contact information will be sent by workers to an administrative liaison at their agency or organization who will then contact the youth and the youth's legal guardian to ask if they are willing to be approached directly by a member of the research team to find out more about the study. It will be explained to the youth and caregivers that the worker who nominated them to the study will not know whether they are participating in the first quantitative phase of the research. Based on this selection, potential participants will be sent a letter, phoned, or met with directly by the agency liaison to explain the study and invite the youth to participate. The youth will also be asked to name an adult key informant or PMK (Person Most Knowledgeable) to participate with them in the research. There is no requirement that this be the legal guardian, though the person named must be knowledgeable about the youth and his or her service history.

In some cases, the consent of a legal guardian may not be available due to the lifestyles of the participants (homelessness, etc.). In such cases, a youth aged fourteen and older may consent to participate, though it is incumbent on the researchers to note the reason on the signed consent for why no guardian's signature is present and thus the youth's status as an emancipated minor. The young person's consent will also be witnessed by a third party.

Those participants in the qualitative phase of the research will also be asked to consent to have their files reviewed in different organizations that are partner to the research. Files will first be examined by the administrative contact in the agency itself. A list of documents required is to be requested and photocopies made of these specific documents. Third-party identifying information is to be expunged from the file documents that are shared with the researchers. These copies will not be taken from the agency premises.

Specifically, we require from each file only information about which services were provided, their duration and nature, and details as to the decision-making process regarding service provision.

Comment: Ensuring ethical selection of vulnerable individuals in a study of resilience is always challenging. In the above description of methods (abbreviated from the original) great efforts are made to ensure that youth under the age of eighteen are able to participate with or without their guardians' consent. These efforts are made to ensure that youth voices are heard and well represented. Most vulnerable youth, and their unique adaptations to life circumstances, can be inadvertently excluded from research when undue restrictions are placed upon their participation. As well, the methodology seeks to protect the confidentiality of participants even when referred by professionals to the study. These elaborate techniques for referral are meant to avoid coercion. Finally, file reviews are necessarily done in a way that preserves the confidentiality of third parties. Studies of resilience, in my experience, that detail the lives of youth and children at risk require complicated protocols for engagement. Ethics committees diverge in their expectations, but once sensitized to the need for youth to have a voice in the research, often find compromises that allow the research to proceed. The methods detailed here have been passed by a university ethics committee on two different occasions.

Data Analysis

Analyses will include regressions of all four domains from both the CYRM as a function of the LEC and different dimensions of service and behaviour based on the other measures employed. Our analyses will seek to understand what conditions of service (number of placements, length of service, degree of child-centred practice, impact of service, cultural sensitivity, degree of service integration, changes in caregivers, level of family involvement, etc.) predict children's resilience across all four domains, as well as differences in results between caregivers' perceptions of the dependent variable (resilience) and those of the children. A second set of analyses will investigate differences between caregivers' scores and children's in order to identify which domains are most likely to record the largest mean differences.

   With the qualitative data, we will describe the pathways that children travel with respect to resilience through several steps. First, we will undertake a step-by-step analysis of the data starting with the qualitative investigation of patterns in the transitions children make through services. Data analysis of all interview data and file reviews will be guided by Glaser and Strauss's (1967; Strauss and Corbin, 1990) constant comparative method. A process of dialogical reciprocity (theory generation is shared between researchers and participants) built into the design ensures construct validity as a grounded theory (a substantive explanation of the phenomena observed) emerges through multiple member checks and the hermeneutic process of feedback to participants. These procedures allow us to meet Guba and Lincoln's (1989; Lincoln & Guba, 1985) criteria for reliability and validity in qualitative research that parallel the standards of internal validity, external validity, reliability, and objectivity.

In order to mix methods, data analysis will follow Thiessen and Looker's (2003) work on life-course transitions as pathways. Participants will be coded as belonging to one of an anticipated five to ten pathways (number is determined by variability in the data). Using up to five indicator variables and five predictor variables that most capture the defining attributes of each pathway, based on the qualitative analysis, children will be grouped by pathway. Each pathway will then become a discrete variable that can be included independently in the regression analyses to explore the differential effects of each pathway (transition pattern) on the outcome variables (measures of resilience, perceptions of children's health by caregivers).

Ethical Considerations

Information gathered from all participants will remain confidential and anonymous to those outside the research team by changing identifying information, placing no identifying information on transcripts or audio records, and keeping these records in a locked secure place. All audio tapes will, however, be destroyed within six months following their transcription and possible review by research team members. Participation is voluntary and both staff and clients will be assured that refusal to participate will in no way affect service and that workers will not know if they are participating. All clients/residents/patients/students will be offered contact information for a mental health professional should involvement in the research cause them distress. Should a youth wish to review his or her files, a contact person at each agency will be available to explain the young person's rights. In the event that during the course of the research information becomes known that a youth is at risk, or another child or adult is in danger, the researchers will be obligated to report the matter to the proper authorities.

Comment: Data analysis will vary by project, but must demonstrate a plan to answer the research questions. It must also, in a mixed-methods study, demonstrate a way of comparing or integrating results from one methodology with the other. Ethical considerations, such as those outlined here, are relatively standard when working with vulnerable populations. Local ethics committees should be consulted for more detail on issues to consider in the study design.

Phase 3: Dissemination and Building Community Capacity

Potential benefits
The project intends the exchange, synthesis, and application of research to benefit communities. We will work through the advisory committees and the umbrella organizations to help nurture their capacity to influence policy and practice more fully. Reports back to funders and community agencies will serve as an opportunity to evaluate the effectiveness of the knowledge dissemination activities. It is also the intent of the research team to develop the capacity of each service system and the community to conduct a quality system of care research by hiring local research assistants and using this research as a forum to provide training to researchers and students.

Research team
The research team is purposefully composed of well-known researchers with familiarity with one or more of the four mandated service delivery systems in order to ensure sufficient credibility with each service and to facilitate smooth entry and data collection in each service context [a list of team members and their qualifications should be included here].

Potential risks posed to the subjects
There are no anticipated physical, social, or economic risks posed to the participants involved in the Pathways to Resilience research study, and few expected emotional risks. Participants will be asked to recall stressful situations, which may trigger uncomfortable memories. Participants will be provided with options for counselling in their community, should they wish someone to talk to.

Potential conflicts of interest
There are no foreseeable conflicts of interest.

Budget
A budget is appended.

Comment: The emphasis in this section (abbreviated) is on demon-strating that the results will be returned to the community in ways that make them of potential benefit to both professionals and fami-lies. The reciprocity is built in to each phase of the design (Rodwell, 1998), with consultations, focus groups, and the mixed methods ensuring that there is a sense of ownership of the research by those who participate and other stakeholders. A series of appendices that include all information letters, consent forms, measures, interview guides, and other relevant documentation should be included at the proposal phase when such documents are available and requested. A tentative budget is of course required and should reflect the level of in-kind contributions from both the research team and community partners.

Conclusion: A Complete, Not a Perfect, Proposal

The proposal presented above is only a model of what a research project can look like when many of the ideas found in this volume are used to inform research. In summary, the proposal stresses:

- Participation by both youth and their community
- Case studies and cross-sectional data, combined into a mixed-methods study that is intended to meet the needs of community practitioners, policy makers, and funders for a variety of different kinds of data and results
- Reciprocity in design, ensuring the ethical inclusion of youth voices and channels for reporting results back to them and other stakeholders to make the research applicable to programming and policy decisions.

There are a myriad of other ways the research could have been de-signed, varying the methods and measures. The population's age and sources of data could have been changed. The data could have been gathered longitudinally. The size of the sample could have been adjusted to reflect the resources available from the funder or community. This study, however, was meant to answer specific questions. The elaborate engagement strategies and ways in which confidentiality is maintained are expected to ensure access to information about pathways to resilience seldom gathered across systems.

A good proposal is one that is consistent in its intent and methods. In this case, the study of resilience is attempted with an eye to conducting the research in a way that will explore cultural variability in how the construct is understood, as well as foster among participants and communities a sense of competence. Resilience research, as illustrated here, reflects the very best of what research in the social sciences can become. Though far from a perfect study, this proposal demonstrates the many parts to a complete proposal that strives to integrate what is known about best practices in research that seeks to understand the positive aspects of coping and adaptation among vulnerable child and youth populations. As with any proposal, feedback is always encouraged.

Note

The author gratefully acknowledges the contributions of Victor Thiessen, John LeBlanc, and Mary Armstrong to the design of the original research proposal upon which this chapter is based. Funding for the development of the proposal was provided in part by The RURAL Center, a Canadian Institutes of Health Research–funded project, at Dalhousie University.

References

Arcelus, J., Bellerby, T., & Vostanis, P. (1999). A mental health service for young people in the care of the local authority. *Clinical Child Psychology and Psychiatry, 4*(2), 233–45.

Burford, G., & Hudson, J. (Eds.). (2000). *Family group conferencing: New directions in community-centered child and family practice.* New York: Aldine de Gruyter.

Cauce, A.M., Paradise, M., Embry, L., Morgan, C.J., Lohr, Y., Theofelis, J., Heger, J., & Wagner, J. (1998). Homeless youth in Seattle: Youth characteristics, mental health needs and intensive case management. In M.H. Epstein, K. Kutash, & A. Duchnowski (Eds.), *Outcomes for children and youth with emotional and behavioral disorders and their families: Programs and evaluation best practices* (pp. 611–32). Austin: Pro-Ed Inc.

Christian, J., & Gilvarry, E. (1999). Specialist services: The need for multi-agency partnership. *Drug and Alcohol Dependence, 55*, 265–74.

Conger, R., & Armstrong, M. (2002). Bridging child welfare and juvenile justice: Preventing unnecessary detention of foster children. *Child Welfare, 81*(3), 471 – 94.

Cook-Morales, V.J. (2002). The home-school-agency triangle. In D.T. Marsh & M.A. Fristad (Eds.), *Handbook of serious emotional disturbance in children and adolescents* (pp. 392–411). New York: John Wiley & Sons.

Dohrn, B. (2002). The School, the child and the court. In M.K. Rosenheim, F.E. Zimring, D.S. Tanenhaus, & B. Dohrn (Eds.), *A century of juvenile justice* (pp. 267–309). Chicago: University of Chicago Press.

Epstein, M.H., Dakan, E., Oswald, D.P., & Yoe, J.T. (2001). Using strengths-based data to evaluate children's mental health programs. In M. Hernandex & S. Hodges (Eds.), *Developing outcome strategies in children's mental health* (pp. 153–66). Toronto: Paul H. Brookes.

Epstein, M.H., & Sharma, J.M. (1998). *Behavioral and emotional rating scale (BERS)*. Austin: PRO-ED.

Garland, A.F., Hough, R.L., Landsverk, J.A., & Brown, S.A. (2001). Multi-sector complexity of systems of care for youth with mental health needs. *Children's Services: Social Policy, Research and Practice, 4*(3), 123–40.

Goodman, R. (1997). The strengths and difficulties questionnaire: A research note. *Journal of Child Psychology and Psychiatry, 38*, 581–6.

Glaser, B.G., & Strauss, A.L. (1967). *The discovery of grounded theory: Strategies for qualitative research.* New York: Aldine de Gruyter.

Guba, E.G., & Lincoln, Y.S. (1989). *Fourth generation evaluation.* Newbury Park, CA: Sage.

Haapasalo, J. (2000). Young offenders' experiences of child protection services. *Journal of Youth and Adolescence, 29*(3), 355–71.

Hellriegel, K.L., & Yates, J.R. (1999). Collaboration between correctional and public school systems serving juvenile offenders: A case study. *Education and Treatment of Children, 22*(1), 55–83.

Henry, B., Caspi, A., Moffitt, T.E., Harrington, H., & Silva, P. (1999). Staying in school protects boys with poor self-regulation in childhood from later crime: A longitudinal study. *International Journal of Behavioral Development, 23*(4), 1049–73.

Hernandez, M., Gomez, A., Lipien, L., Greenbaum, P.E., Armstrong, K., & Gonzalez, P. (2001). Use of the system-of-care practice review in the national evaluation: Evaluating the fidelity of practice to system-of-care principles. *Journal of Emotional and Behavioral Disorders, 9*, 43–52.

Hernandez, M., Gomez, A., & Worthington, J. (2002). *Manual for the use of the system of care practice review: Evaluating practice fidelity to system of care principles.* Tampa, FL: University of South Florida.

Jackson, S., & Martin, P.Y. (1998). Surviving the care system: Education and resilience. *Journal of Adolescence, 21*, 569–83.

Johnson, J.H., & McCutcheon, S. (1980). Assessing life stress in older children and adolescents: Preliminary findings with the Life Events Checklist. In I.G. Sarason & C.D. Spielberger (Eds.), *Stress and Anxiety,* Vol. 7 (pp. 111–25). Washington, DC: Hemisphere.

Kratzer, L., & Hodgins, S. (1997). Adult outcomes of child conduct problems: A cohort study. *Journal of Abnormal Child Psychology, 25*(1), 65–81.

Kroll, L., Rothwell, J., Bradley, D., Shah, P., Bailey, S., & Harrington, R.C. (2002). Mental health needs of boys in secure care for serious or persistent offending: A prospective, longitudinal study. *The Lancet, 359*, 1975–79.

Lincoln, Y.S., & Guba, E.G. (1985). *Naturalistic inquiry.* Newbury Park, CA: Sage.

Litrownik, A.J., Taussig, H.N., Landsverk, J.A., & Garland, A.F. (1999). Youth entering an emergency shelter care facility: Prior involvement in juvenile justice and mental health systems. *Journal of Social Service Research, 25*(3), 5–19.

Malmgren, K.W., & Meisel, S.M. (2002). Characteristics and service trajectories of youth with serious emotional disturbance in multiple service systems. *Journal of Child and Family Studies, 11*(2), 217–29.

McCubbin, H.I., Fleming, W.M., Thompson, A.I., Neitman, P., Elver, K.M., & Savas, S.A. (1998). Resiliency and coping in 'at risk' African-American youth and their families. In H.I. McCubbin, E.A. Thompson, A.I. Thompson, & J.A. Futrell (Eds.), *Resiliency in African-American families* (pp. 287–328). Thousand Oaks, CA: Sage.

Morgan, D.L. (1998). Practical strategies for combining qualitative and quantitative methods: Applications to health research. *Qualitative Health Research* (online), *8*(3), 362–76. Available at http://proquest.umi.com/.

Morse, J.M., Swanson, J.M., & Kuzel, A.J. (Eds.). (2001). *The nature of qualitative evidence.* Thousand Oaks, CA: Sage.

Murphy, R.A. (2002). Mental health, juvenile justice, and law enforcement responses to youth psychopathology. In D.T. Marsh & M.A. Fristad (Eds.), *Handbook of serious emotional disturbance in children and adolescents* (pp. 351–74). New York: John Wiley & Sons.

Pazaratz, D., Randall, D., Spekkens, J.F., Lazor, A., & Morton, W. (1999). The four phase system: A multi-agency coordinated service for very disturbed adolescents. *Residential Treatment for Children and Youth, 17*(1), 31–48.

Pepler, J., & Slaby, R. (1994). Theoretical and developmental perspectives on youth and violence. In L.D. Eron, J.H. Gentry, & P. Schlegel (Eds.), *Reason to hope: A Psychological perspective on violence and youth* (2nd ed., pp. 27–58). Washington, DC: American Psychological Association.

Quinn, W. (2004). *Family solutions for youth at risk: Applications to juvenile delinquency, truancy, and behavior problems.* Hove, East Sussex, UK: Brunner-Routledge.

Rodwell, M.K. (1998). *Social work constructivist research.* New York: Garland.

Rose, W. (2002). Two steps forward one step back: Issues for policy and practice. In H. Ward & W. Rose (Eds.), *Approaches to needs assessment in children's services* (pp. 309–19). Philadelphia: Jessica Kingsley.

Saathoff, A.J., & Stoffel, E.A., (1999). Community based domestic violence services. *Domestic Violence and Children, 9*(3), 97–110.

Sagatun-Edwards, I., & Saylor, C. (2000). A coordinated approach to improving outcomes for substance-abusing families in juvenile dependency court. *Juvenile and Family Court Journal,* Fall, 1–16.

Strauss, A., & Corbin, J. (1990). *Basics of qualitative research: Grounded theory procedures and techniques.* Newbury Park, CA: Sage.

Swenson, C.C., & Kolko, D.J. (2000). Long-term management of the developmental consequences of child physical abuse. In R.M. Reece (Ed.), *Treatment of child abuse* (pp. 135–54). Baltimore: Johns Hopkins University Press.

Thiessen, V., & Looker, D. (2003). *Effects of life course position on the development of numeric and non-numeric information technology skills among Canadian youth.* Presentation to the conference on the knowledge-based economy and regional economic development, St. John's, NL.

Ungar, M. (2002a). *Playing at being bad: The resilience of troubled teens.* Pottersfield.

Ungar, M. (2002b). Qualitative contributions to resilience research. *Qualitative Social Work, 2*(1), 85–102.

Ungar, M. (2004). *Nurturing hidden resilience in troubled youth.* Toronto: University of Toronto Press.

Ungar, M. (2005). Pathways to resilience among children in child welfare, corrections, mental health and educational settings: Navigation and Negotiation. *Child and Youth Care Forum, 34*(6), 423–44.

Ungar, M. (2006a). *Strengths-based counseling with at-risk youth.* Thousand Oaks, CA: Corwin.

Ungar, M. (2006b). 'Too ambitious': What happens when funders misunderstand the strengths of qualitative research design. *Qualitative Social Work,* 5(2), 261–77.

Ungar, M. (2008). Resilience across cultures. *British Journal of Social Work, 38,* 218–35.

Ungar, M., Karabanow, J., & MacDonald, N. (2002). Pathways to resilience: A study of high-risk youth and their involvement with human service providers. Grant submission to Dalhousie University, Faculty of Health Professions.

Ungar, M., Lee, A.W., Callaghan, T., & Boothroyd, R. (2005). An international collaboration to study resilience in adolescents across cultures. *Journal of Social Work Research and Evaluation, 6*(1), 5–24.

Ungar, M., & Liebenberg, L. (2005). The International Resilience Project: A mixed-methods approach to the study of resilience across cultures. In M. Ungar (Ed.), *Handbook for working with children and youth: Pathways to resilience across cultures and contexts* (pp. 211–26). Thousand Oaks, CA: Sage.

Ungar, M., Teram, E., & Picketts, J. (2001). Young offenders and their communities: Reframing the institution as an extension of the community. *Canadian Journal of Community Mental Health, 20*(2), 29–42.

Walter, U.M., & Petr, C.G. (2000). A template for family centered interagency collaboration. *Families in Society: The Journal of Contemporary Human Services, 81*(5), 494–503.

Webb, M.B., & Harden, B.J. (2003). Beyond child protection: Promoting mental health for children and families in the child welfare system. *Journal of Emotional and Behavioral Disorders, 11*(1), 45–54.

Whittaker, J.K. (2000). What works in residential child care and treatment: Partnerships with families. In M.P. Kluger, G. Alexander, & P.A. Curtis (Eds.), *What works in child welfare* (pp. 177–86). Washington, DC: CWLA Press.

Wilson, K.K., & Melton, G.B. (2002). Exemplary neighborhood-based programs for child protection. In G.B. Melton, R.A. Thompson, & M.A. Small (Eds.), *Towards a child-centered, neighborhood-based child protection system: A report of the Consortium on Children, Families and the Law* (pp. 197–213). Westport, CT: Praeger.

12 Youth Resilience Research and the Transformative Paradigm

DONNA M. MERTENS

Youth represent a powerful reference group in terms of both their current dynamics and the promise of their impact on society. Research about youth addresses their current experiences and their future promise through an examination of the challenges and protective factors that are located in personal as well as contextual spaces. A shift in research focus to strengths and modifications of contextual factors has emerged under a variety of names, such as positive psychology (Seligman et al., 2005) and resilience (Boykin, 2000; Luthar, Cicchetti, & Becker, 2000). Tensions between current conditions and future promises, challenges and protective factors, and personal and contextual variables make this shift in research focus particularly important when studying youth.

A resilience lens can be applied within several paradigmatic frameworks. Contributors to this volume place their work within three of the dominant research paradigms: post-positivism, constructivism, and pragmatism (see Table 12.1 for a brief summary of the basic beliefs of each paradigm). In particular, several of the contributors situate their work in the pragmatic paradigm because of its association with mixed-methods research. In the *Handbook of Mixed Methods in Social and Behavioral Research*, two paradigms are discussed as providing a potential philosophical base for mixed-methods research: the pragmatic and transformative paradigms (Mertens, 2003; Teddlie & Tashakkori, 2003).

In this chapter, I argue that resilience-related research with youth is inherently linked to the goal of furthering social justice and human rights. I will show that such research can produce even greater benefits when youth resilience research is situated within the transformative paradigm (Mertens, 2005; 2007; 2009). A close parallel exists

Table 12.1. Post-positivist, Constructivist, Pragmatic, and Transformative Paradigms: Basic Beliefs and Examples

Basic Beliefs			
Post-positivist	Constructivist	Pragmatic	Transformative
Axiology			
Adherence to prevailing ethical regulations; protection of human subjects	Ethical regulations with emphasis on human relations	Authority's approval of research strategies as being ethical	Meet regulations & codes; work for social justice & human rights
Ontological Assumptions			
Reality is knowable within a specified probability level	Reality is socially constructed	Reality is determined by what is useful to increase clarity of understanding	Reality is defined by individuals with varying degrees of power; discrimination & oppression must be recognized
Epistemology			
Researcher needs to be at a distance from subjects to ensure objectivity	Researcher needs to be involved with the community to engage participants	Researcher should adopt a stance that best fits the needs of the study	Trusting relationships must be developed; cultural competence is critical
Methodology			
Most likely to use quantitative methods	Most likely to use qualitative methods	Methods should fit the question; mixed methods have benefits	Quantitative, qualitative, or mixed; dialogic relationship is critical

between the basic tenets of the transformative paradigm and the key concepts that are integral to youth resilience research. The focus of both is on the process that youth exposed to significant threat or severe adversity use to achieve positive adaptations (Luthar, Cicchetti, & Becker, 2000). Este, Sitter, and MacLaurin (in this volume) also acknowledge that transformative research is guided by a strengths perspective, and therefore is compatible with the underlying objectives of resilience research.

Given the compatibility of resilience youth research with a social justice agenda, this chapter presents the underlying philosophical assumptions of the transformative paradigm as a mechanism to critically examine studies of youth resilience. Ethical concerns are discussed first, as they provide the frame for subsequent decisions in the research process. Construction of meanings in resilience research is examined with an emphasis on dimensions of diversity, power, and privilege that influence those constructions. The role of the researcher is described in terms of a trusted partnership with the community. The complexities associated with such an arrangement are also discussed. Finally, mixed-methods research is approached as a cyclical process with community involvement and is shown to be one avenue for addressing the challenges associated with youth resilience research.

Paradigms and Basic Beliefs

Researchers need to be cognizant of the research paradigm that guides their work and its associated philosophical assumptions. Significantly, research, especially research on the resilience of youth, has the potential to speak to social change. Paradigms are not equated with theories or particular methods of data collection. Rather, research paradigms are sets of integrated philosophical assumptions that represent the basic beliefs of the researcher. Guba and Lincoln (2005) identified four types of philosophical assumptions associated with the identification of a research paradigm:

- *Axiological* assumptions concern the nature of ethics. How do I determine that my research practices are indeed ethical within the context of the community in which I conduct the research? What goals for the research represent an ethical stance given the need for societal change to address injustice?
- The *ontological* assumption is concerned with the nature of reality. How do we know something is real? For example, how do we know that youth are resilient? Literate? Abused? What type of evidence will we accept as true?
- The *epistemological* assumption is concerned with the relationship between the researcher and the participants in the study. How

involved should the researcher be with the participants and the community in which they reside? Should researchers be distant from the community to attain 'objectivity' or involved with the community so they can demonstrate cultural competence in the research setting? What is the potential for a stance that reflects cultural competency and a respectful relationship to lead to increased validity in research?

- *Methodological* assumptions lead to decisions about the best methods by which to investigate the reality of human experience – they are not limited to quantitative, qualitative, or mixed methods. Methodological choices centre on what is the best way to capture the reality of the participants in the study.

Transformative Paradigm

The transformative paradigm provides an overarching philosophical framework for examining assumptions that underlie research, with explicit directives to examine issues of power, social justice, and cultural complexity throughout the research process. The role of the researcher is to recognize inequalities in society, strive to challenge the status quo, and possess a sense of shared responsibility. Contrasts between the transformative paradigm and the post-positivist, constructivist, and pragmatic paradigms are reflected in the nature of the assumptions for each.

Axiological Assumption

Transformative researchers base their practice on rights-based and social justice theories of ethics. According to Simons (2007), rights-based theories hold that individuals must be treated with dignity and respect and that researchers must avoid harm as a primary principle. Social justice theories build on rights-based theories, taking them to a group or societal level (House, 1993). Social justice theories of ethics emphasize the need to 'redress inequalities by giving precedence, or at least equal weight, to the voices of the least advantaged groups in society. The implicit goal is the inclusion of those who may not have sufficient power for accurate representation of their viewpoints but also to empower the less advantaged in terms of being able to take an active agent role in social change' (Mertens, 2007, p. 11).

Boothroyd, Stiles, and Best (in this volume) provide an excellent overview of codes and regulations that govern ethical issues in research with youth. All too often researchers believe that, if they have taken into account the issues raised by the Belmont Report, the Helsinki Agreement, or other internationally recognized codes or regulations, and that they have satisfied their institutional ethics review board, they have met all ethical standards applicable to their work. The axiological assumption of the transformative paradigm encourages researchers to take a broader view of ethics. As such, it includes influences from feminism, critical race theory, disability rights, and indigenous peoples' ethical issues, as well as bringing to the surface necessary changes in research methods and the growth of collaborative research partnerships.

Transformative ethics are addressed in terms of the influence of personal characteristics of the researcher in the formulation of research questions, choice of research methods, effectiveness of data collection and analysis, and interpretation and use of results. In addition, ethical issues arise in the development of community partnerships, and the contributions and needs of community members within a context of cultural complexity. Philosophical, theoretical, and practical bases that inform ethical conduct of research raise the following challenging questions:

1 How do the age, gender, ethnicity, disability status, and other personal characteristics of the researcher and participants influence ethical decision making and research outcomes?
2 How can diverse members of a research team develop ethical partnerships?
3 What do the voices of persons who are pushed to the margins, such as indigenous communities, bring to the discussion of research ethics?

Multiple aspects of the researcher's self have long been recognized by anthropology as an essential consideration in planning and carrying out ethnographic studies (Ginsberg, Mertens, & Brydon-Miller, 2007). By identifying one's preconceptions and expectations, anthropologists held, one would be able to think critically about one's observations, consider alternative interpretations of the data, and provide a basis for critical thinking by those who had access to one's research reports.

Without identification of preconceptions and biases, on the other hand, a researcher was considered likely to collect data that simply reinforced his/her preconceptions or to misinterpret neutral data so as to do so. To present such research would be unethical in so far as it provides a misleading picture of the peoples/issues being examined. Trained principally as researchers of disease and disorder, researchers who attempt to study resilience-related phenomena will be challenged to avoid such preconceptions and misinterpretations of healthy adaptations in different contexts.

Increasingly, however, theorists and researchers of many social science disciplines (those interested in culture, ethnicity, and members of disadvantaged groups including, but not limited to, immigrants, the elderly, prisoners, linguistic and cultural minorities, those with disabling conditions, indigenous or aboriginal peoples, the poor, and entire post-colonial nations) have come to recognize the importance of pre-existing characteristics of the researcher. They have realized that examination of one's pre-existing biases after a research problem has been selected is not enough. Indeed, it has become clear that selection of research questions, methods of conducting research, research outcomes, and actions based upon research knowledge are all influenced by the identity and preconceptions of the researcher her/himself. Moreover, the effects are likely to be reciprocal. That is, while characteristics of the researcher influence aspects of the research that are under his or her control, they also have an influence on aspects of the research that are outside the researcher's control. This is so because the researcher's physical appearance, gender, and interpersonal style (in addition to and outside of the research protocol itself) all have the power to influence participants. Thus feminist, critical race, disability rights, and post-colonial theories dare researchers to question not just their own biases, expectations, and preconceptions, but those of the social milieu in which they work.

Symonette (2004) emphasizes the importance of researchers examining themselves (unilateral self-awareness) and posits that how they are perceived by members of the community with whom the research is conducted (multilateral self-awareness) is even more essential:

> Even more important for the viability, vitality, productivity and trust-building capacity of a transaction and relationship cultivation is multilateral self-awareness: self in context and self as pivotal instrument. Who do those that one is seeking to commu-

nicate with and engage perceive the (researcher)/evaluator as being? ... Regardless of the truth value of such perceptions, they still rule until authentically engaged in ways that speak into the listening. (p. 100)

The development of community partnerships provides fertile ground for the examination of ethical issues in research. A critical examination of the dynamics of power and privilege has been increasingly associated with those who seek social justice through research with communities. For example, Symonette (2004) reminds us that researchers 'need enhanced understandings of related systemic processes of asymmetric power relations and privilege, not simply awareness and knowledge of difference and diversity ... How and to what extent is sociocultural diversity associated with patterned differences in access, resource opportunities, and life chances?' (p. 108).

Liebenberg (in this volume) raises issues that illuminate the implications of transformative axiological assumptions in her discussion of the marginalization of youth and barriers related to power, trust, and communication that must be overcome if meaningful research relationships are to be established. Researchers who come from contexts that differ from that of the study participants in terms of age and other significant social addresses have an ethical obligation to address the disparities in power and access to information that affect the outcomes of the research. Liebenberg explores strategies that lead to an increased sense of agency on the part of research participants, as well as methods to engage persons of power in the development of changes in policies or interventions in order to better align resources with the needs of community members. While researchers cannot guarantee that social change will occur, planning for the inclusion of appropriate parties enhances the potential for change by engaging youth in a true partnership whereby they are able to communicate the results of their study with decision makers.

What if research ethics were grounded in the ethical codes of indigenous peoples and post-colonial sites, rather than in the Western perspectives that dominate Boothroyd, Stiles, and Best's chapter in this volume? Those authors include specific guidelines developed by aboriginal and Torres Strait Islander communities in Australia (*Guidelines for Ethical Conduct in Aboriginal and Torres Strait Islander Health Research* [National Health and Medical Research Council, 1999]), and the policy statement of the Canadian Institutes of Health Research, Natural Sciences and Engineering Research Council of Canada, and Social Sciences and Humanities Research Council of Canada regarding ethical conduct for research involving humans, which includes sections specific to research involving aboriginal peoples (Canadian Tri-Council, 2005). Boothroyd et al. conclude that international research with children needs to adhere to protocols that are sensitive and flexible enough to be responsive to the culture and values of targeted groups, whatever their national or tribal affiliations.

Researcher guidelines available from indigenous communities provide insights into ethical grounding of research (Mertens, 2009). For example, Cram (2001, cited in Smith, 2005, p. 98) provided guidelines for researchers from the Maori people of New Zealand. Examples of these guidelines include:

- Show respect for people, meaning people are allowed to define their own space and meet on their own terms;
- Meet people face-to-face: Introduce yourself and the idea for the research before beginning the research or sending complicated letters or other materials;
- Look and listen: Begin by looking and listening and understanding in order to find a place from which to speak;
- Share, host, be generous: This forms the basis of a relationship in which researchers acknowledge their role as learners with a responsibility to give back to the community;
- Be cautious: Harm can come from a lack of political astuteness and cultural sensitivity, whether the researcher is an insider or an outsider;
- Do not trample on the dignity of a person: Inform people without being patronizing or impatient. Be wary of Western ways of expression such as wit, sarcasm, and irony;
- Avoid arrogant flaunting of knowledge: Find ways to be generous with sharing your knowledge in a way that empowers the community.

Another example of guidelines for researchers with the deaf community and/or the sign language community is also available (Harris, Holmes, & Mertens, 2009). A complex cultural and linguistic minority such as the sign language community includes layers such as levels and type of hearing loss, parental hearing status, access to and ability to benefit from auditory enhancing technologies, language usage

based on signs and /or voice, and use of visually accessible sign languages. Their ethical guidelines, Sign Language Communities Terms
of Reference, are commensurate with the transformative paradigm.
Some of their guidelines are similar to the Maori guidelines above;
however, the guidelines of particular significance to the sign language
communities include:

- Decentrize 'hearingness' from research so sign language and deaf
  culture are given back to deaf people;
- Recognizing that research involving the sign language community
  has to be done 'by Deaf, for Deaf and with Deaf';
- Accepting and encouraging bilingual publications including sign
  language and the majority language;
- Instead of using spoken language and providing interpreters for
  deaf members, mandating sign language as the primary language
  of research teams and providing interpreters for hearing people
  who do not know sign language;
- Ensuring increased efforts regarding confidentiality, because the
  compactness of the sign language community and the visual
  nature of sign language both require documentation through video
  (as opposed to audiotapes or transcribed interviews), making it
  difficult to preserve anonymity.

By way of illustration of exemplary transformative research, Williamson
(2007) reviewed yearbooks from residential high schools for the deaf
and noticed that very few of them had pictures of African Americans in
the graduating classes. She conducted a study of resilience factors associated with successful completion of high school and college by deaf
African Americans in order to identify the resources and strategies available to these successful youth. She centred her work on the life experiences of the deaf African Americans, interviewing them and observing
them in their current life spaces. Williamson worked in the deaf community for many years before conducting her research and is competent
in American Sign Language, so she was able to have direct communication with the participants. As the number of people who fit the criteria
was small, she had to be very careful to disguise their identities, as the
participants provided details of barriers that existed in the schools they
attended and how they overcame those barriers.

As research on the resilience of youth grows in importance,
researchers encounter complex ethical issues, well beyond the imme-

diate protection of human subjects as treated by the Belmont Report and the routine work of ethics review boards (National Commission for the Protection of Human Subjects of Biomedical and Behavioral Research, 1978). These come to the attention of the research community from a multiplicity of sources, including the theory that guides the research, methodological choices, technological innovations (e.g., online surveys), involvement of culturally complex communities, the legal system (e.g., Greenwood, Brydon-Miller, & Shafer, 2006), and the daily experience of researchers in the field. Sieber's (1992) text provides a firm foundation for planning ethical research. No recent guide to research design neglects this topic. The *Journal of Empirical Research on Human Research Ethics* (JERHRE) is a valuable resource in this regard. Professional codes of ethics, although helpful, are not sufficient to resolve many of these ethical dilemmas (Ginsberg, Mertens, & Brydon-Miller, 2007; Mertens, 2005; Mertens & Ginsberg, 2009).

The axiological assumption of the transformative paradigm explicitly recognizes the role of power and privilege. This assumption has implications for the definition of what is real, the interactions between the researcher and the community, and the choice of methods for data collection.

Ontological Assumption

The transformative ontological assumption holds that perceptions of reality are socially constructed, however, it rejects cultural relativism. It holds that reality is constructed such that certain individuals with power have a greater probability of having their version of reality given privilege. Examples of ontological questions that arise in the transformative paradigm include:

> How is reality defined? By whom? Whose reality is given privilege? What are the social justice implications of accepting reality that has not been subjected to a critical analysis on the basis of power differentials? (Mertens, 2007, p. 5)

Cameron (in this volume) describes a process by which a culturally sensitive definition of reality was constructed of well-being, adversity, and intervention mechanisms related to the concept of sexual intimacy with African or Mexican American youth (Milbrath, Ohlson, & Eyre, 2007). They used more than one method to construct meaning as well as to understand causality. The Vernacular Term Interview is a data collection instrument that is based on expressions that have particular meaning in a cultural group, rather than imposing researcher-created terms on the youth. After conducting interviews, the researchers quantified the data to reveal specific differences in the conceptualization of sexually related practices between the two groups.

The use of the youth's own perspectives on sexual intimacy is commensurate with the ontological assumption of the transformative paradigm. However, researchers should be concerned with furthering their understanding of the concepts in terms of the inclusion and exclusion of appropriate participants in the process of constructing meaning, and employment of appropriate accommodations to support inclusion of a diversity of participants from the cultural groups. Inclusion and exclusion decisions may reflect the myth of homogeneity: that the primary characteristic that defines a person's view of sexual intimacy is their identified racial or ethnic group. Considerable research has been conducted that reveals differences in concepts of sexual intimacy on the basis of gender, disability, home language, and communication mode, among others (Mertens, Wilson, & Mounty, 2007). Chilisa (2006) provides an excellent example of cultural underpinnings of the concept in African cultures and includes the importance of power differences in boys/men and girls/women as part of the constructed meaning. Questions that arise from the transformative ontological perspective include:

- How were decisions made about inclusion or exclusion of participants?
- Were members of traditionally marginalized groups included or excluded (e.g., people with disabilities)?
- How were issues of gender handled in the data collection?
- If the participants spoke a language other than English, how were their needs accommodated?
- If deaf people were included, how were their communication needs accommodated?
- For people with limited resources, what types of supports were provided to ensure that they were able to participate?
- What differences in construction of meaning present in the subgroups are of relevance in the two sampled populations?
- In circumstances with potential threats of violence against research participants, how were the youth protected?

Mouton and Wildschut (in this volume) present an example of strategies that highlight diversity in terms of lived experience used in a math
improvement project in South Africa. The community members and
researchers were aware of the diversity in the community and
attempted to get representation from both the black Xhosa-speaking
students and the coloured Afrikaans-speaking students. However, the
original black school population did not have sufficient English skills to
succeed on the selection test. Hence, their poor performance on this
pre-test resulted in a higher percentage of coloured Afrikaans-speaking
students being accepted into the program. Therefore, the researchers
sought out Xhosa-speaking black students who also had sufficient
English skills to benefit from the instruction. Mouton and Wildschut
report subgroup analyses that indicate differences based on teachers'
level of math knowledge and students' home language and attendance
in classes. By being attentive to diversity within the community, these
researchers were able to demonstrate conditions necessary for improvement in math for these learners. However, their study reveals a tension
related to social justice, as the intervention means that black students
with the greatest potential for success in an English-based program
would receive services but those who were not schooled in the colonial
language would not receive such services. A transformative interpretation of their results suggests that interventions of a different nature are
needed for Xhosa-speaking students who are not sufficiently skilled in
English.

Epistemological Assumption

As noted earlier, the epistemological assumption illuminates the
nature of the relationship between the researcher and study participants. In the transformative paradigm, issues of understanding the
complexity of the cultural context and establishment of trust in the
community are very important. This suggests an adjustment in the traditional role for researchers that includes self-examination to understand how they are perceived in the community, as well as building
trust with community members through appropriate channels and
modes of communication. Building trust implies that researchers
develop a relationship with community members that recognizes and
addresses power differences as well as cultural traditions.

As Liebenberg (in this volume) notes, a lack of trust is not uncommon between adults and youth. She argues that a need exists to build

trust in order to gather valid data. She proposes the use of visual methods to convey a sense of open communication based on a respectful relationship with youth. The youth's comments can be used to illuminate power relations and self-representation, as well as to identify inferences from the data that are grounded in the youth's lived experiences. Liebenberg asserts that development of such a relationship between the researcher and youth is not without problems; however, it brings with it the potential to reduce cultural misunderstandings. Thus, the concept of cultural competence enters the conversation through the transformative portal.

Cultural competency is a critical disposition that is related to the researcher's ability to accurately represent reality in culturally complex communities. Symonette (2004) makes explicit the implication that cultural competence in research is not a static state. It is a journey in which the researcher develops increased understanding of differential access to power and privilege through self-reflection and interaction with members of the community (Sue & Sue, 2003; Symonette, 2004). Cultural competence in research can be broadly defined as a systematic, responsive mode of inquiry that is actively cognizant, understanding, and appreciative of the cultural context in which the research takes place; that frames and articulates the epistemology of the research endeavour; that employs culturally and contextually appropriate methodology; and that uses stakeholder-generated, interpretive means to arrive at the results and further use of the findings (SenGupta, Hopson, & Thompson-Robinson, 2004). The benefits of cultural competency and culturally responsive evaluation approaches include, but are not limited to, the ability to transform interventions so that they are perceived as legitimate by the community (Guzman, 2003). In this process, the researcher serves as an agent of prosocial change to combat racism, prejudice, bias, and oppression in all their forms (American Psychological Assocation, 2000, 2002). To this end, the culturally competent researcher is able to build rapport across differences, gain the trust of community members, and self-reflect and recognize his or her own biases (Edno, Joh, & Yu, 2003).

Methodological Assumption

The transformative methodological assumption supports the use of quantitative and/or qualitative methods. However, a dialogic relationship based on qualitative inquiry principles is needed between the researcher and the study participants to ensure that the community's reality is accurately represented. Hence, a mixed-methods model is well suited to transformative research on youth resilience. The relationship that is part of the transformative epistemological assumption leads to the inclusion of community members in decisions about the focus of the research and the collection, analysis, and use of data. Community members can be involved in a variety of ways; however, their input is crucial in identifying modifications needed to collect valid data from diverse members of their community in order to tie the data collected to social action.

Mixed methods applied in a cyclical model provide a useful way to address the connections between communities, research, and social change in a culturally competent manner (Mertens, 2007, 2009; Silka, 2005). As discussed previously, community participation is needed throughout the research process. The goal to have research that contributes to sustainable change in a community requires that the research focus be established in consultation with the community, the results of the study be shared with the community, and the community be involved in using the results for social change and/or additional research. This cyclical model can be difficult to implement because of funding issues. But researchers who have grants that are short lived can still make recommendations for future studies or for policy changes that will provide the potential for systemic change based on the community's needs.

When a single method of quantitative data collection is used, one wonders what information is lost because of the strict criteria for inclusion of statistically analysed data. For example, Smith-Osborne (in this volume) conducted a meta-analysis on studies of youth with a psychiatric disorder to overcome and their resilience in terms of increased post-secondary educational achievement. She sought studies of resilience that employed quantitative measurement and reached conclusions about the participants' resilience based on statistical significance. Because of the data requirements associated with meta-analysis, she focused on only nine studies that met her criteria. Her study concludes that people with less severe disabilities who made use of productive leave/re-entry strategies experienced significantly higher educational attainment. What information is lost when a small sample of studies is used to examine resilience for youth with psychiatric disorders and their subsequent post-secondary educational attainment? As promoted by this volume, it is dialogue between methods that is most fruitful in youth resilience research. One could ask, what would be gained by combining a strict meta-analysis with a review of literature that examined this type of resilience from a qualitative or mixed-methods perspective?

Participatory action research (PAR) scholars provide numerous examples of ways to involve community members in research (Reason & Bradbury, 2006). While PAR is potentially commensurate with the principles of the transformative paradigm, its methods do not in and of themselves lead to transformative research. Whitmore (1998) noted that participatory inquiries can be framed in either a practical or a transformative way. Practical participatory research is characterized by the involvement of decision makers and those with power in the study. Transformative participatory research requires that the researcher recognize the power differences that result in marginalization of potential stakeholders from the decisions made about the research process and the use of the findings.

Cameron (in this volume) describes a cyclical mixed-methods model of research that illustrates the basic methodological beliefs associated with the transformative paradigm. Researchers of a violence-prevention initiative in Canada used a community-based, participant-action-oriented mixed-methods approach (Cameron, 2004; Cameron & Team, 2002). Research questions included those generated by community members who wanted to prevent violence, researchers with a gendered theoretical framework, and the funder's concern for protection of the girl-child. The researchers used quantitative questionnaires to determine participants' experience with violence and their desire to see change. They also used interviews that yielded qualitative data. During the intervention, participants engaged in focused discussions that led to some of the youth becoming change agents. The researchers noted that the intervention model could be replicated in other settings, and that some of the participants (quite possibly those who perhaps needed a stronger intervention) might have been negatively affected by the intervention. Based on their findings, they developed and implemented another round of research designed to examine youth reaction to stress and yet another study of an intervention to address boys' coping strategies.

Cameron and her colleagues' work is an example of a cyclical mixed-methods study that is commensurate with the transformative paradigm. Community members were involved at several critical stages of the research in terms of question generation, data analysis, data interpretation, and use of findings. The results of the initial studies were used as a basis to explore the dimensions of violence prevention in youth more thoroughly.

Congruent with these same premises, the International Resilience Project (IRP) was initiated to study youth resilience in international settings (Ungar & Liebenberg, 2005). The IRP is based on a participant action philosophy and is committed to a mixed-methods approach to data collection. It has yielded important insights into youth resilience as well as methods to study this phenomenon. However, as Cameron (in this volume) notes, the quantitative and qualitative strands of the IRP's research are not yet fully realized, a problem common to many mixed-methods studies. The next section explores some of the challenges and benefits of using mixed methods with specific reference to a transformative perspective in resilience research.

Mixed Methods: Challenges and Benefits

Ungar and Liebenberg (2005) support a mixed-methods approach to youth resilience research because they believe that it can achieve a better balance between the quality and quantity of research findings. Este, Sitter, and MacLaurin (in this volume) identify the potential benefits of combining qualitative and quantitative methods in youth resilience studies because of the complexity of the variables involved and the need to include contextual variables that surround youth. The benefits of using mixed methods are also identified by Teddlie and Tashakkori (2003), who add that mixed methods can answer questions that single methods cannot, support stronger inferences because of their ability to provide greater depth and breadth, and give an opportunity for representation of divergent views. Teddlie and Tashakkori explain that valid inferences in mixed methods are dependent on adhering to the appropriate criteria for validity and credibility in the collection of data for whatever method is used. It is not surprising, then, that the use of mixed methods comes with its own challenges as well.

Differences in meaning of research terminology present challenges in mixed-methods research. For example, theoretical validity in qualitative research refers to the fit between the data and the theoretical explanation that emerges from it. In quantitative terms, theoretical validity means the degree to which the findings are consistent with known theory in the field.

In the IRP, Cameron notes additional challenges that surface when using mixed methods: expertise of the researcher, attitudes of the researchers, and crossing over when quantitative and qualitative data are collected by separate teams. Bryman's (2006) analysis of mixed-methods studies supports the narrow range of implementation of such approaches in social research. The majority of the research studies he reviewed used quantitative surveys and qualitative interviews. He found little evidence that researchers were conscientiously applying a diversity of quantitative and qualitative methods in order to capitalize on the strengths of mixed-methods approaches. Bryman suggests that part of the problem in the use of clear mixed-methods designs stems from the lack of guidelines related to the conduct of mixed-methods research.

Elsewhere, I have suggested that researchers adhere to the quantitative and qualitative criteria for each segment of their work as appropriate (Mertens, 2005; 2009). I add several questions that are specific to the bridging of the two methods:

- What are the multiple purposes and questions that justify the use of a mixed-method design?
- How well has the researcher matched the purposes and questions to the appropriate methods?
- How has the researcher addressed the tensions between potentially conflicting demands of methodological approaches and paradigms in the design and implementation of the study?
- Has the researcher appropriately acknowledged limitations associated with data that were collected, especially if one form of data collection was used to supplement the other?
- How has the researcher integrated the results from the mixed methods? If necessary, how has the researcher explained conflicting findings that resulted from different methods?
- What evidence is there that the researcher developed the design to be responsive to the practical and cultural needs of specific subgroups on the basis of such dimensions as disability, culture, language, reading levels, age, gender, class, religion, and race/ethnicity? (adapted from Mertens, 2005, p. 302)

Milbrath, Ohlson, and Eyre's (2007) study of risky sexual behaviours provides a good example of a clear mixed-methods design with a rationale for each type of data and provides bridges between the two types of data at critical junctures in the research process. Beginning to understand concepts within the language and culture of a community leads to accurate depictions of mental models of constructs, such as sexual intimacy, and allows the diversity between cultural groups to be maintained. Using Glaser's (1998) well-recognized constant comparison method of qualitative data analysis with the interview data, the researchers created models that served as a basis for linguistic quantitative analysis.

Milbrath et al. (2007) document culturally specific differences in intimacy models and recommend using these as a basis for culturally relevant intervention strategies. In a cyclical model of transformative research, the interventions could be developed in conjunction with community members for maximum responsiveness to the specific community's needs. Quantitative and qualitative methods could be used to examine the implementation and effectiveness of the interventions.

As the examples provided throughout this chapter demonstrate, researchers of youth resilience are at an important crossroad. They may continue to use standard single-method studies and conduct their research in a non-transformative paradigm. Alternatively, they may make use of mixed methods (when appropriate) and design and implement research that is transformative for individuals and communities. Moving the field forwards will require a critical self-examination of the cultures that surround the planning, conduct, and use of resilience research. Within the research community, cultural diversity is manifest in many ways; however, the principles of social justice, building trusting relationships, and engagement of diverse perspectives in respectful ways provide an avenue to make the most of this time of challenge and promise.

References

American Psychological Association. (2000). *Guidelines for research in ethnic minority communities.* Council of National Psychological Associations for the Advancement of Ethnic Minority Interests. Washington, DC: American Psychological Association.

American Psychological Association. (2002). *Guidelines on multicultural education, training, research, practice, and organizational change for psychologists.* Washington, DC: American Psychological Association.

Boykin, A.W. (2000). The talent development model of schooling: Placing students at promise for academic success. *Journal of Education for Students Placed at Risk, 5*(1&2), 3–25.

Bryman, A. (2006). Integrating quantitative and qualitative research: How is it done? *Qualitative research, 6*(1), 97–113.

Cameron, C.A. (2004). Schools are not enough: It takes a whole community. In M.L. Stirling, C.A. Cameron, N. Nason-Clark, & B. Mediema (Eds.), *Understanding abuse: Partnering for change* (pp. 269–94). Toronto: University of Toronto Press.

Cameron, C.A., & Team (2002). *Worlds apart ... coming together: Part 1, 'She said, he said'; Part 2, Together we can.* Evaluation research findings leading to community facilitator training video (32 minutes) and accompanying handbook (16 pages). Fredericton, NB: Muriel McQueen Fergusson Centre for Family Violence Research.

Canadian Tri-Council Working Group. (2005). *Code of conduct for research involving humans.* Ottawa: Canadian Institutes of Health Research, Natural Sciences and Engineering Research Council of Canada, & Social Sciences and Humanities Research Council of Canada.

Chilisa, B. (2006). 'Sex' education: Subjugated discourses and adolescents' voices. In C. Skelton, B. Francis, & L. Smulyan (Eds.), *The handbook of gender and education* (pp. 249–61). London: Wise Publications.

Cram, F. (2001). Rangahau Maori: *Tona tika, tona pono* – The validity and integrity of Maori research. In M. Tolich (Ed.), *Research ethics in Aotearoa New Zealand* (pp. 35–52). Auckland, NZ: Pearson Education.

Edno, T., Joh, T., & Yu, H.C. (2003). *Voices from the field: Health and evaluation leaders on multicultural evaluation.* Oakland, CA: Social Policy Research Associates.

Ginsberg, P., Mertens, D.M., & Brydon-Miller, M. (2007). Beyond the IRB: Case based research ethics. Presentation at the American Educational Research Association annual meeting, April 2007, Chicago.

Glaser, B.G. (1998). *Doing grounded theory: Issues and discussions.* Mill Valley, CA: Sociology Press.

Greenwood, D.J., Brydon-Miller, M., & Shafer, C. (2006). *Action research.* Thousand Oaks, CA: Sage.

Guba, E.G., & Lincoln, Y.S. (2005). Paradigmatic controversies, contradictions, and emerging confluences. In N.K. Denzin & Y.S. Lincoln (Eds.), *The Sage handbook of qualitative research* (3rd ed., pp. 191–216). Thousand Oaks, CA: Sage.

Guzman, B.L. (2003). Examining the role of cultural competency in program evaluation: Visions for new millennium evaluators. In S.I. Donaldson & M.

Scriven (Eds.), *Evaluating social programs and problems: Visions for the new millennium* (pp. 167–82). Mahwah, NJ: Lawrence Erlbaum Associates.

Harris, R., Holmes, H., & Mertens, D.M. (2009). Ethical research in sign language communities. *Sign Language Studies, 9*(2), 104–31.

House, E.R. (1993). *Professional evaluation: Social impact and political consequences.* Newbury Park, CA: Sage.

Luthar, S.S., Cicchetti, D., & Becker, B. (2000). The construct of resilience: A critical evaluation and guidelines for future work. *Child Development, 71*(3), 543–62.

Mertens, D.M. (2003). Mixed methods and the politics of human research: The transformative-emancipatory perspective. In A. Tashakkori & C. Teddlie (Eds.), *Handbook of mixed methods in social and behavioral research* (pp. 135–64). Thousand Oaks, CA: Sage.

Mertens, D.M. (2005). *Research and evaluation in education and psychology: Integrating diversity with quantitative, qualitative, and mixed methods* (2nd ed.). Thousand Oaks, CA: Sage.

Mertens, D.M. (2009). *Transformative research and evaluation.* New York: Guilford.

Mertens, D.M. (2007). Transformative paradigm: Mixed methods and social justice. *Journal of Mixed Methods Research, 1*(3), 1–14.

Mertens, D.M. & Ginsberg, P. (Eds.) (2009). *Handbook of Social Research Ethics.* Thousand Oaks, CA: Sage.

Mertens, D.M., Wilson, A., & Mounty, J. (2007). Achieving gender equity for populations with disabilities. In S. Klein (Ed.), *Handbook for achieving gender equity through education.* Mahwah, NJ: Lawrence Erlbaum.

Milbrath, C., Ohlson, B., & Eyre, S.L. (2007). Romantic relationship trajectories of African American Gay/Bisexual Adolescents. *Journal of Adolescent Research, 22*(2), 107–13.

National Commission for the Protection of Human Subjects of Biomedical and Behavioral Research. (1978). *Ethical principles and guidelines for the protection of human subject research* (Belmont Report). Washington, DC: Government Printing Office.

National Health and Medical Research Council. (1999). *Values and ethics: Guidelines for ethical conduct in Aboriginal and Torres Strait Islander health research.* Rev. ed. Canberra: National Health and Medical Research Council. http://www.nhmrc.gov.au/PUBLICATIONS/synopses/e52syn.htm Accessed 29 December 2008.

Reason, P., & Bradbury, H. (2006). Introduction: Inquiry and participation in search of a world worthy of human aspiration. In P. Reason & H. Bradbury (Eds.), *Handbook of action research* (concise paperback edition) (pp. 1–14). London: Sage.

Seligman, M.E., Steen, T.A., Park, N., & Peterson, C. (2005). Positive psychology progress. *American Psychologist, 60*(5), 410–21.

SenGupta, S., Hopson, R., & Thompson-Robinson, M. (2004). Cultural com-
petence in evaluation: An overview. In M. Thompson-Robinson, R.
Hopson, & S. SenGupta (Eds.), *In search of cultural competence in evaluation*
(New Directions for Evaluation, no. 102) (pp. 5–19). San Francisco, CA:
Jossey-Bass.

Sieber, J. (1992). *Planning ethically responsible research.* Newbury Park, CA:
Sage.

Silka, L. (2005). Building culturally competent research partnerships. Presentation at the American Psychological Association annual meeting, August
2005, Washington, DC.

Simons, H. (2007). Ethics in evaluation. In I. Shaw, J. Greene, & M. Mark
(Eds.), *The Sage handbook of evaluation* (pp. 243–65). London: Sage.

Smith, L.T. (2005). On tricky ground: Researching the native in the age of
uncertainty. In N. Denzin & Y. Lincoln (Eds.), *The Sage handbook of qualitative research* (3rd ed., pp. 85–108). Thousand Oaks, CA: Sage.

Sue, D.W., & Sue, D. (2003). *Counseling the culturally diverse: Theory and practice* (4th ed.). New York: John Wiley & Sons.

Symonette, H. (2004). Walking pathways toward becoming a culturally competent evaluator: Boundaries, borderlands, and border crossings. In M.
Thompson-Robinson, R. Hopson, & S. SenGupta (Eds.), *In search of cultural
competence in evaluation* (New Directions for Evaluation, no. 102) (pp.
95–110). San Francisco: Jossey-Bass.

Teddlie, C., & Tashakkori, A. (2003). Major issues and controversies in the use
of mixed methods in the social and behavioral sciences. In A. Tashakkori &
C. Teddlie (Eds.), *Handbook of mixed methods in social and behavioral research*
(pp. 3–50). Thousand Oaks, CA: Sage.

Ungar, M., & Liebenberg, L. (2005). The International Resilience Project: A
mixed methods approach to the study of resilience across cultures. In M.
Ungar (Ed.), *Handbook for working with children and youth: Pathways to
resilience across cultures and contexts* (pp. 211–26). Thousand Oaks, CA: Sage.

Whitmore, E. (1998). *Understanding and practicing participatory evaluation* (New
Directions for Evaluation, no. 80). San Francisco: Jossey-Bass.

Williamson, C. (2007). *Black deaf students: A model for educational success.* Washington, DC: Gallaudet.